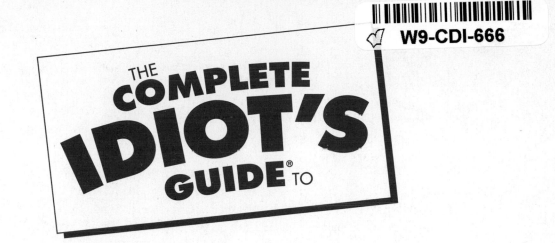

THE COMPLETE IDIOT'S GUIDE® TO

A Successful Family Business

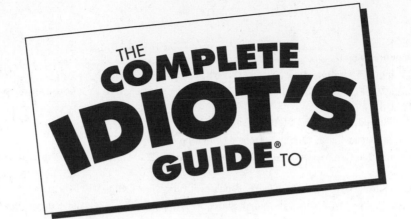

THE COMPLETE IDIOT'S GUIDE® TO

A Successful Family Business

By Neil Raphel and Janis Raye
in collaboration with The Family Firm Institute, Inc.

ALPHA

A member of Penguin Group (USA) Inc.

To Ben and Adrienne,
Our next generation.

ALPHA BOOKS

Published by the Penguin Group

Penguin Group (USA) Inc., 375 Hudson Street, New York, New York 10014, USA

Penguin Group (Canada), 90 Eglinton Avenue East, Suite 700, Toronto, Ontario M4P 2Y3, Canada (a division of Pearson Penguin Canada Inc.)

Penguin Books Ltd., 80 Strand, London WC2R 0RL, England

Penguin Ireland, 25 St. Stephen's Green, Dublin 2, Ireland (a division of Penguin Books Ltd.)

Penguin Group (Australia), 250 Camberwell Road, Camberwell, Victoria 3124, Australia (a division of Pearson Australia Group Pty. Ltd.)

Penguin Books India Pvt. Ltd., 11 Community Centre, Panchsheel Park, New Delhi—110 017, India

Penguin Group (NZ), 67 Apollo Drive, Rosedale, North Shore, Auckland 1311, New Zealand (a division of Pearson New Zealand Ltd.)

Penguin Books (South Africa) (Pty.) Ltd., 24 Sturdee Avenue, Rosebank, Johannesburg 2196, South Africa

Penguin Books Ltd., Registered Offices: 80 Strand, London WC2R 0RL, England

Publisher: *Marie Butler-Knight*
Editorial Director: *Mike Sanders*
Senior Managing Editor: *Billy Fields*
Senior Acquisitions Editor: *Paul Dinas*
Development Editor: *Nancy D. Lewis*
Senior Production Editor: *Janette Lynn*
Copy Editor: *Megan Wade*

Cartoonist: *Steve Barr*
Cover Designer: *Bill Thomas*
Book Designer: *Irina Wurst*
Indexer: *Angie Bess*
Layout: *Brian Massey*
Proofreader: *John Etchison*

Contents at a Glance

Contents

Introduction

Dr. Joyce Brothers once said, "When you look at your life, the greatest happinesses are family happinesses."

This book is about the happiness that comes from running a successful family business. Sure, there are a host of problems to be solved if you want to have a successful family business, but the family businesses that do succeed are sources of wealth and opportunity for generations of other family businesses.

In addition to a strong business plan, successful family businesses bring morals and traditions to work every day. Successful family businesses are started by entrepreneurs—the men and women who bring a sense of purpose with them to work every day. They are driven to succeed, and they want and need to bring their family members into the business with them.

Especially at the start, the family provides the employees and the brains for the family business. The family also often provides the finances to get the business running in the first place. And when the family business grows and succeeds, the family business gives back with jobs and income for future family members.

One of the biggest issues faced by every successful family business is who should take over as the new leader of the family business. Which of the children—or cousins—is the best one to run the business? Should the family look for the best possible CEO, regardless of whether that person is a family member? This book will help your family answer these important questions.

Sometimes family businesses, like families themselves, face some tough problems. This book will help you see the possible pitfalls of a family business and how you can avoid them—or solve them if you're already there.

As the family business prospers, it can be a source of true happiness to many people. We hope this book will enable your family to share in all the riches of doing business as a family.

What You'll Find in This Book

Family businesses are the backbone of American society. Family businesses are started by entrepreneurs with ideas and energy. They enlist family members to help them make their business dreams come true. This book shows you all the excitement and challenges of running a family business.

We've divided the book into several parts that reflect the main elements of running a successful family business.

In **Part 1, "Understanding the Family Business,"** you'll find that family businesses differ from other businesses in many important ways. Typically, a family business is started by an entrepreneur who sees a business opportunity and grabs it. The entrepreneur is supported by other family members who help out by taking ownership and management positions in the new company. Family businesses can provide more benefits, income, and security for family members, but family businesses might achieve lower growth because they are more risk-averse and less willing to accept outside debt. If you're in the early years of your family business, you'll learn the basics of running your family business here.

In **Part 2, "Running a Family Business,"** you'll learn that as a family business grows, ownership and management decisions move out of the family living room. Many successful family businesses have a board of directors with several outside directors to give an independent perspective to the family's business decisions. A strategic plan will help the family plot business growth into the future. Growing family businesses have to address personnel decisions and must decide how to compensate all employees fairly. The family business must decide whether it will run on nepotism and preference for family members or put the business needs above family considerations. If you have a family business that is growing, this part will help you bring more professionalism to your company.

In **Part 3, "Unique Challenges of the Family Business,"** you'll discover that unlike other businesses, the family business brings its own set of issues. The relationship among family members who also work together can be the cause of great stress if family tensions are left unresolved. Most people in family businesses try hard to keep their work lives from invading their home lives, but it can be hard to separate the two worlds. As new generations of the family come into the business, opportunities must be made to help them learn and develop as the business expands. And don't forget your nonfamily employees—they are critical to the success of most family businesses, but they need to know there is a place for them in the business, too. This part will give you a heads-up on the issues family business face that you might not have considered!

Part 4, "Outside Advice," discusses how consultants can help a family business preserve its wealth through difficult times. Financial advisers can help founders manage succession while still keeping a financial cushion. Lawyers can help the family business handle internal and external complaints. Insurance protects the family business assets against unforeseen contingencies and can place umbrella protection around the family's personal assets. Family business consultants give advice on difficult problems such as succession, and mediators are helpful when an internal dispute threatens the business. Every family business will run into problems from time to time, and this part will give you the help you'll need to solve them.

After a family business is established and running smoothly, the owners must think about the future. This is where **Part 5, "Taking the Family Business into the Future,"** comes into play. Plans for a smooth transition to the next generation of ownership and management are of utmost importance. Transferring the business to the next generation requires a well-thought-out succession plan. Selling a family business to an outsider can sometimes be the best way to secure a family financially. The future of the company requires capable leadership, and there might not be enough family members with the necessary skills. By the third and later generations, family businesses begin to resemble other successful businesses, with the best-qualified managers as leaders. If your family business is getting ready for new leadership, this part will help you understand how to put your best plan in place to keep your company successful through the transition.

Extras

We've included suggestions, statistics, and definitions to make your reading experience more enjoyable and easier. Look for these special highlights for more information you can use:

Family Stats
These are facts and figures of interest about family businesses in the United States and around the world.

Suggestion Box

These are some good ideas for what to do in various situations that will come up in your family business.

Told You So!

Here are the don'ts for your family business—what to watch out for and guard against doing. We want you to avoid these minefields.

def•i•ni•tion

We've explained some terms you'll hear used in connection with family business that you might not know. Some are business concepts we've specifically identified as relevant for family businesses. The glossary in the back of the book lists them all.

Acknowledgments

Many people have helped us with the ideas and the writing of this book.

We'd like to thank Neil's parents, Murray and Ruth Raphel, for their advice and encouragement. We learned much of what we know about family businesses from admiring their many years of successfully working together. And thanks to Janis's dad, Irvin Raye, for teaching us about the value of old-fashioned hard work.

We'd like to specially thank Judy Green, executive director of the Family Firm Institute (FFI), Inc., for her assistance in reviewing this book and introducing us to much of the research and many of the resources available in the family business arena. Background research of the FFI's various publications provided valuable resource material for this book.

We also thank *Family Business Magazine* for being a principal source for stories about actual family businesses that appear in the book.

Paul Dinas, our acquisitions editor, has played an important role in helping us focus the book in the right direction. Our development editor, Nancy Lewis, has been instrumental in molding our copy into a final edited version. Thanks also to our agent, Marilyn Allen, for recommending us and for working with us on its development.

Hannah Smith and Bennett Raphel did some great research for us on the book. Thanks to both of them for all their hard work.

Special Thanks to the Technical Reviewer

The Complete Idiot's Guide to a Successful Family Business was reviewed by an expert in the field of family business. Special thanks are extended to Judy Green, the executive director of the Family Firm Institute, Inc., Boston, Massachusetts.

Special Thanks to the Family Firm Institute, Inc.

The Family Firm Institute (FFI), Inc., is an international professional membership organization dedicated to providing interdisciplinary education and networking opportunities for family business and family wealth advisors, consultants, educators, and researchers. FFI also is committed to increasing public awareness about trends and developments in the family business and family wealth fields.

FFI members advise and consult with family businesses at all stages of development and growth. To access the FFI Directory of Consultants & Speakers, visit the website at www.ffi.org.

Special Thanks to *Family Business Magazine*

Family Business Magazine is written and edited for family company owners, shareholders, and senior employees, and serves the unique information needs of multigenerational family businesses. Each issue contains case studies, profiles, and in-depth studies of key issues such as wealth management, succession planning, shareholder relations, conflict resolution, financial management and compensation, as well as our regular Directory of Advisers—a listing of key family business service providers.

Family Business Magazine also offers a series of targeted handbooks for family businesses, an online searchable library of more than 700 articles, and a twice-monthly eNewsletter.

Subscribers to the magazine receive five print editions per year, as well as free access to the magazine's articles library. For more information, please visit the magazine's website at: www.familybusinessmagazine.com.

Special subscription offer for readers of *The Complete Idiot's Guide to a Successful Family Business*: e-mail Barbara Wenger at bwenger@familybusinessmagazine.com and mention that you're reading this guide. You'll earn a special $20 discount on a subscription to the magazine.

Trademarks

All terms mentioned in this book that are known to be or are suspected of being trademarks or service marks have been appropriately capitalized. Alpha Books and Penguin Group (USA) Inc. cannot attest to the accuracy of this information. Use of a term in this book should not be regarded as affecting the validity of any trademark or service mark.

Part 1

Understanding the Family Business

The majority of businesses in the United States today are family businesses. Their founders are usually entrepreneurs with a desire to create something the family can own and be proud of.

The opening chapters of this book describe the strengths and weaknesses of a family business and how a family business gets started. The beginning years of a family business are often filled with struggle, but there are tremendous rewards for family businesses that survive the beginning stages.

Family Business Basics

In This Chapter

- ◆ Definition of a family business
- ◆ How family businesses start
- ◆ Challenges of family businesses
- ◆ Strengths and weaknesses of family businesses

Justin was working in the family business founded by Don, his father. Justin was a young man in his twenties. When Justin wanted to take a few days off work to travel with a friend, he asked his department manager, who told him it was a busy time at work and he couldn't spare him. But Justin left anyway and had a great time. When he returned to work a few days later, he was called into Don's office. "Justin," said Don, "I wear two hats. I'm your father, but I'm also the owner of the company. And as the owner, I have to fire you. We needed you here at work and you left us in the lurch."

Justin, in shock, went back to his department to collect his things. A few minutes later he got a phone call. "Justin?" the voice on the phone said. "It's Dad. I heard you just got fired. Is there anything I can do?"

A family business is a "business," but it also is a "family." Sometimes, those two worlds collide. Other times, the family and the business are a cohesive team.

The term *family business* means different things to different people. The mom-and-pop dry cleaner down the street is a prime example of a family business. So is the 100-employee law firm started 75 years ago that now features the son, granddaughter, and nephew of the original founder on the letterhead. But the list of family businesses also includes such giant corporations as Ford Motor Company, Viacom, and Gap.

What do these companies have in common? It's all in the family. The family owns all or part of the company, and family members are active in the ownership and/or the management. Whether large or small, every family business has to face issues based on the fact that family members are part of the business.

> **Family Stats**
>
> One-third of all Fortune 500 companies are family businesses. Two-thirds of all the companies traded on the New York Stock Exchange are family businesses.

In this chapter, we describe the various combinations of family involvement that make a business a "family business." The company may consist of husband and wife, or it could be a large, family-controlled corporation. But whatever the size, family businesses all share certain characteristics that nonfamily businesses don't.

What Is a Family Business?

Generally, a family business has at least two members of the same family who participate in the business. Although the degree of ownership by the family can vary from none to 100 percent, the family has some influence on the strategic direction of the business. This very broad interpretation of the term *family business* encompasses as many as 90 percent of all the businesses in the United States today.

Family Businesses in the United States

Not only are family businesses in the United States numerous, they also encompass virtually every category of industry. The industries represented include food, clothing, automobiles, retailers, construction, media, telecommunications, medical products, toys, aerospace, finance, and many more.

Most of the oldest family businesses in the United States that are still in existence today started out as farms. When you consider what the possibilities for business were in the early stages of the country's development, this makes sense. Most of these centuries-old farms are still thriving agricultural enterprises today. But the oldest family business currently headquartered in the United States—Avedis Zildjian Co.—wasn't founded in this country. The company began as a manufacturer of cymbals in Constantinople in the early seventeenth century and moved to the United States in 1929. It's still led by members of the founding family, who all happen to be women.

Top 10 Largest U.S. Family Businesses

	Company	Family	Industry	Revenues (billions)
1.	Wal-Mart Stores	Walton	Retail	$378.79
2.	Ford Motor Co.	Ford	Automotive	$172.45
3.	Koch Industries	Koch	Oil/Gas/ Agriculture	$98
4.	Cargill	Cargill/MacMillan	Commodities	$88.26
5.	Carlson	Carlson	Travel/Hotels/ Restaurants	$37.1
6.	News Corp.	Murdoch	Media conglomerate	$32
7.	Comcast	Roberts	Cable provider	$30.895
8.	General Dynamics	Crown	Defense contractor	$27.24
9.	Bechtel Group	Bechtel	Engineering/ Construction	$27
10.	(tie) HCA	Frist	Hospital operator	$26.9
10.	(tie) Tyson Foods	Tyson	Food Processor	$26.9

(Source: Family Business Magazine, *Winter 2009)*

The 10 Oldest Family Businesses Founded in the United States

Company	Founded	Business	State
Tuttle Farm	1635/38	Agriculture	New Hampshire
Shirley Plantation	1638	Historic site	Virginia
Barker Farm	1642	Agriculture	Massachusetts
Seaside Inn	1667	Hospitality	Maine
Saunderskill Farms	1680	Agriculture	New York

continues

The 10 Oldest Family Businesses Founded in the United States (continued)

Company	Founded	Business	State
Allandale Farm	c. 1700	Agriculture	Massachusetts
Orchards of Concklin	1712	Agriculture	New York
Smiling Hill Farm/ Hillside Lumber	c. 1720	Agriculture Lumber	Maine
Nourse Family Farm	1722	Agriculture	Massachusetts
Clark Farm	1728	Agriculture	Massachusetts

(Source: Family Business Magazine, *Summer 2008)*

Family Business Today

Let's look at the current picture of family businesses in the United States. Most have a similar trajectory: they started from humble beginnings and built into successful firms. Because the majority of family businesses don't survive past the first generation, those that do are worth examining to figure out how they did it.

Almost all family businesses begin life as the effort of an entrepreneur. Sometimes a family business is started by more than one entrepreneur; for example, a husband and wife might start a business together, or sisters might decide to go into a new business as partners. Most of the time, entrepreneurs aren't specifically thinking about building a family business—they're just trying to start a successful company. As time goes along, however, other family members may join the business. If finances and control remain in the hands of the family, the budding company will take on the qualities of a family business.

> **Family Stats**
>
> Around 30 percent of all family firms survive to the second generation; 10 percent make it to the third generation.

This was certainly the path of many businesses in the United States during the country's periods of great economic growth. Publix Super Markets was founded in 1930 by George Jenkins in Winter Haven, Florida, as a single grocery store. Over time, the company grew and George's son Howard joined the business. He became CEO in the 1980s. In 2001, Howard's cousin Charlie Jenkins Jr. took over as CEO and is currently chairman of the board. From a Great Depression-era food store to one of the most successful and admired supermarket chains, Publix has retained its tradition of family values, including in its mission statement the importance of being involved citizens in the company's market areas and its commitment to its employees.

"Familiness"

What is it about a family business that makes it special? Many researchers in the field of family business have agreed on a term they call *familiness*. It's that intangible quality that the family itself brings to the family business. It usually involves a bundle of resources held by a family business as a result of its unique systems, interaction among the family, individual members, and the business itself that helps to establish a strategic advantage for that business.

Familiness is a distinguishing factor of any family business. But it is only a positive factor if it helps the business succeed. Familiness is a useful characteristic in day-to-day strategic business activities such as setting goals, identifying potential customers, and evaluating the competition. Because they tend to be more interested in the long-term success of the business, the family members in a family business can be better suited to perform those kinds of activities than employees in a nonfamily business. The unique familiness of a family business often leads to a strong orientation toward the needs of the customer. Such market orientation is often a road to business success.

def•i•ni•tion

Familiness is the essence of any family business that helps to make the business successful based on the unique qualities of that family.

Source: *Family Business Review*, March 2007

But the familiness of a family business can be harmful in considering major strategy decisions such as acquiring a new company or selling part of the business. These kinds of decisions might go against the concept of maintaining family control over the family business.

Unique Challenges of Family Businesses

Combining business with family can be a recipe for disaster in many families. Problems with the business can spill over into family life. Family harmony can be split because of disagreements in the business, and brother can become pitted against brother, and cousin against cousin. One of the first priorities of any family business has to be setting up the business in the way that minimizes personal disputes.

Family Business Structure

In a family business, some family members are involved in the ownership, management, or work of the company. Some do all three.

In the past, the corporate structure has often mirrored a stereotypical structure of the family. Patriarch Granddad, the Chairman of the Board, heads the family, with patient, wise Grandma quietly at his side. Son and daughter are busily raising their separate branches of the family. They represent the separate business units in the business. Grandkids abound, growing up, having teenage crises, and enlivening all the family gatherings. Think of them as the entrepreneurial spirit of the firm that will carry it into the future.

But when the family members actually fill the positions at the family business, the analogy gets too close. Everyone can be playing two roles, one in the business and one at home.

A healthy family operates with a very different set of rules than a healthy business. Families strive for the good of each member of the family. Businesses operate with the goal of perpetuating the business as a whole. All family members are welcomed and accepted automatically for who they are; in a business, employees remain only if they are qualified and can do the job. In general, businesses put the business first and families put family members first because they believe that's how the family will survive.

Family Dynamics

The relationships that exist among family members can seep into their business relationships. Can Daughter tell Dad that his new product ideas don't take into account the latest technology? How can Younger Brother give Older Brother a performance review? Imagine the arguments that can fly across the dinner table when the family business is discussed.

Daughter complains, "You never liked my choice in friends. No wonder you won't accept my new hiree."

Son argues, "I need more money to buy the new house we're bidding on. Just give me a bonus this year."

This kind of family dynamic can destroy a family business. When the roles of family member and business colleague are kept separate, the family business will be in a better position to deal with conflicts when they arise.

Strengths of Family Businesses

How can family businesses be stronger than nonfamily businesses? What makes the family business a beneficial way to organize a company?

More Independence and Flexibility

In general, a family business can operate more independently than a nonfamily business. When the majority of shareholders are family members, the major business decisions can be made within the family. Outsiders need not be privy to decision-making, and market influences can be minimal.

Family businesses seem to require fewer outside networks for their survival. They collaborate less often with other firms, use fewer subcontractors, and show less reliance on outside companies.

Many family businesses are characterized by a lack of formal bureaucracy. At its best, this less rigid structure allows for quicker decision-making and more innovation.

Long-Term Business Goals

Family businesses tend to have a longer business horizon than nonfamily businesses. Whereas managers of nonfamily corporations might have to satisfy shareholders every quarter, the owners of a family business can have a more comprehensive view. Because they can invest in projects that don't have to immediately turn a profit, they can look toward the future of the company.

Often, one of the goals of a family business is to be able to pass the business on to future generations. Such a goal is unique to family businesses. A nonfamily business might have a long-term perspective, but it won't be because Mom wants to leave the company to her son.

Ready Pool of Employees

In a family business, the business supports the family. So when personnel are needed, family members can usually be found to fill the jobs. This principle holds whether the family business is a small neighborhood coffee shop or a large, multinational furniture manufacturer. Both types of businesses require people to work there and manage the operations. It's natural to bring the kids in when they are old enough to help with the work and to have them learn the business from the ground up. They contribute to the whole family's well-being and usually adhere to the family's standard of how the family business works.

Whether specific family members are right for the job available can be debated. But the family does offer a steady supply of employees who are likely to be predisposed to working for the business. And these employees will probably fit in with the business culture because that business culture usually coincides with the family culture.

Family employees have some other pluses, too. As team members, people in the same family can be very effective. Often a high level of trust exists among family members that facilitates their working together. And family members are working toward a common goal—not their individual egos or opportunities, but for the whole family. This can be a powerful motivator for maintaining and building a family business.

Higher Wages

Studies have shown that family businesses tend to pay higher than the prevailing wage to employees, whether the employees are family members or not.

The reason behind this fact is unclear, but it might stem from the parent-child model of the employer-employee relationship of the family business. A concern to take care of the employee in the way a parent cares for a child might encourage family businesses to set wage rates higher than the competition requires.

Strong Organizational Culture

Family businesses tend to develop a strong identification with the business that extends to everyone who works in the business, family members or not. Often, the business is located in one community and at one place for many years. This kind of close relationship among employees helps everyone in the business understand the core values and what is important to the business. Decisions made in the firm will likely be more readily accepted by all the employees, giving the company a greater chance for success.

Employee and Customer Satisfaction

Family businesses have been shown to care more about employee satisfaction than nonfamily firms. The family business apparently wants to maintain a contented workplace—akin to the "happy home" goal of the family.

Family businesses also tend to be more concerned with customer satisfaction and maintaining a customer-focused market orientation. And customers often have good feelings about a family enterprise, especially in industries in which trust is an important factor.

Lessons of a 1,400-Year-Old Family Business

The world's oldest family business—until its closing in 2006—was Kongo Gumi, a Japanese company founded in 578 as a builder of Buddhist temples. The incredible longevity of the firm was due to some of the unique strengths it had as a family business. Although the family business was absorbed as a subsidiary of another larger construction company, family members continued to work there as carpenters.

In choosing successors to lead the company, the company looked to the family member who was best suited to run it. At different times, the leader was a son, a son-in-law, or a daughter. Even sons-in-law were required to change their names to the Kongo family name, which kept the company under the same family name despite the successor.

This insistence on maintaining the family business, combined with the flexibility to select the best leader in the family, served to keep Kongo Gumi in business for more than 14 centuries.

Weaknesses of Family Businesses

The flip side of the family business coin is that the very characteristics that help make family businesses successful can also weaken them. The family bonds and relationships that keep the organization independent, flexible, and caring can have some negative consequences for the business as well.

Economic Needs of the Family Compete with the Business

In a family business, there can be competing family needs for capital. When this occurs, the business can suffer in favor of taking care of the family. Although this could be an admirable family trait, it is not usually good business practice.

Told You So!

Often the second or third generations of a successful family business start to milk the cash cow. The business is generating lots of money, owners and managers get complacent, and they take their profits without reinvesting in the business. Before you know it, the business is dying while the family is living it up.

More Risk-Averse

Family businesses are often led by an owner who is an organizer and a generalist. This type of person might feel that innovation is too risky and therefore shy away from new ventures that require accepting risk.

In studies of family businesses where the management is interviewed, creativity and innovation are seen as less important to the family business than to the nonfamily business. When risk is taken on, it can seem to counteract the family-centered idea of holding the business for the long run to pass it down to future generations. Because a risky move could wipe out the business if it doesn't succeed, many family businesses are reluctant to try something new.

Slower Growth Rate

Risk-aversion leads to less growth in family businesses compared to nonfamily businesses. For a family business, the value of the business is more than its stock price. The value of the company also includes its traditions, creating jobs for family members, and maintaining familial power in the business for many years. This leads to a family business's financial considerations being somewhat different from those of a nonfamily business.

Family businesses are less likely to take on additional debt or other financing. They show preference for self-funding their growth. Again, these decisions can be explained by considering the family focus of the business and the desire to maintain business control at all costs. Family businesses often have difficulty making decisions to acquire or divest business units because those decisions can compete with an overarching need for complete familial control.

Employees Don't Participate in Decisions

Though concerned about the general well-being of their employees, family businesses tend to be far less progressive in their personnel policies than nonfamily firms. Fewer opportunities are given to employees in the areas of decision-making, working conditions, and ownership possibilities. Less attention is paid to employees' desire for self-fulfillment and education. Employees also have fewer opportunities to participate in profit-sharing and policy-making.

Talented outsiders might feel trapped in a family business. They know that family members have the inside track for management positions and also will reap most of the financial benefits if the business does well.

The Least You Need to Know

♦ Adding the family into a business sets it apart from nonfamily businesses.

♦ Family businesses come in all sizes, ages, and industries.

♦ The corporate structure of a family business can often mirror the hierarchy of the stereotypical family.

♦ Family businesses usually have higher wages and higher employee and customer satisfaction than nonfamily businesses.

♦ Family relationships can cause financial and managerial problems in a family business if the problems are overlooked.

Chapter 2

Founding the Family Business

In This Chapter

- ◆ Founder sets the direction and culture
- ◆ When a couple starts a business together
- ◆ Starting a family businesses at any stage of life
- ◆ Determining the right legal structure

Bernabe Cabrera is the founder of a family business. At 75, he owns a successful supermarket in the Bronx and has developed and sold several other markets throughout his career. Cabrera lives a very comfortable life in a suburb outside New York City. He has earned everything he has through hard work, knowledge, and persistence. But his path to success was not easy.

Born and raised in Cuba, as a young man Cabrera opposed Castro's government and spent two years in prison, marked as a dissident. Finally released, he was forced to live five years in Spain before he could make his way to the United States. He saved his money and bought a small bodega in a Latino neighborhood. Over time, he bought a supermarket and then built another and another. His family joined him in the business, with his son and daughter helping to run the new supermarkets. A modest man, Cabrera doesn't think his experience is remarkable.

His is the story of founders of family businesses everywhere, who start with an idea against what often seem like insurmountable odds. With work, determination, and help from the family, the founder builds a lasting enterprise that other family members join.

What does the founder bring to the fledgling business to make it succeed or fail? In this chapter, we discuss the steps the founder of a family business takes when he establishes the new company. We also examine how a family business starts and the important role that is played by the founder to make the business successful for the next generation of the family.

Owner-Entrepreneur

Most family businesses start with one person—the founder. This person has an idea for a business that she thinks will be successful. Maybe it's a new product the founder created or discovered. Maybe it's a favorite hobby or activity the founder wants to turn into a business. Or maybe the founder has earned a professional skill and is ready to set up shop. In any case, this *owner-entrepreneur* wants to establish a new business.

def•i•ni•tion

An **owner-entrepreneur** is the original founder of a family business who purchases or establishes the business and controls every facet of the business in the first generation of ownership.

The owner-entrepreneur has a vision of how the product or service can be brought to the marketplace and starts a business in accordance with this vision. For someone starting what she hopes will be a family business, more considerations come into play: "Will the business sustain my family in the future?" "Will other members of the family join me in this business?" "Can this business last long enough to attract my children and perhaps their children?"

Starting a Business

When someone starts a business, there are many factors to consider. First and foremost is the selection of the type of business. In most cases, this idea comes from the founder based on interests, opportunities, or prior experience. For many founders, *what* the business will be is the easiest of all the decisions to be made. The *who*, *where*, *when*, and *how* come next and can be much more complex.

Funding the New Business

The start of a business requires seed money, or *capitalization*. No matter the type of business you choose to be in, money is needed at start-up for the many costs associated with setting up a business.

Funding for a new business can come from any number of sources, but the founder of a family business has an additional resource: the family. Often family businesses are capitalized by other family members who are willing to invest with a trusted relative in a new venture.

Many new businesspeople don't have the track record to show a bank or *venture capitalists* to prove that they are creditworthy. So they turn to Grandpa, or Aunt Sue, or Mom's retirement account as their funding source.

def•i•ni•tion

Capitalization is the money required to start a business, which might be used for outfitting a store, purchasing inventory, paying initial salaries, purchasing goods and equipment, and paying for other expenses associated with start-up.

Venture capitalists are investors, often in a group, who fund start-up businesses usually by taking an ownership share in the business.

Family businesses from the smallest to the largest have been started with family money. For many founders, the family is the first and often only source of start-up funding.

Location

Where a business is located can have a strong impact on its success, if the business is location-based. A family business is usually founded in the town or area where the founder lives, and near where other members of the family live if they are going to be part of the business. This might be the right decision for lifestyle, but not necessarily for business success.

Suggestion Box _____

If your family business is tied to a specific location (such as a car wash or dry cleaner), choose your location wisely. Customers will need to have ready access to your location. Choosing a location in your hometown may not be the best strategy if customers can't find your business easily. But if your family business sells its products or services to customers across the country, either through the Internet or a distribution system, your company's physical location will be less important.

Henry Ford chose to locate his company headquarters in Dearborn, Michigan, near his family's summer home compound. The decision helped to make Detroit the capital of the automotive world for the next century.

More than ever, people are starting family businesses based in their own homes. The many reasons for this trend include the following:

♦ Desire to remain accessible to the family

♦ Availability of Internet-based opportunities and communication

♦ Start up expenses are less—no rent for office space, and a portion of home costs can be written off taxes as office expenses

♦ Desire to lessen the environmental impact of working—that is, no commuting is necessary

♦ Desire to live and work where you choose

Can Other Family Members Help?

Members of the family can have a strong influence on the founder's business. Besides providing financial support to a new business, family members can also be influential in the direction of a new business, its location, and its organization.

For example, Gordon's Youth Shop, a clothing store started in the early 1950s in New Jersey, was started by Milton Gordon and his wife Shirley. But Shirley's father, Herman Dichter, had a great deal of influence on the new business. He was the one who recommended they start a children's clothing store, figuring correctly that following World War II a baby boom would occur. He cautioned them against renting a storefront, telling them that if they bought the entire store building, they would have an additional asset for the future. His business advice was valuable to the fledgling entrepreneurs, as were his banking contacts that helped them secure financing to open their business.

Often, when a family business starts, employees are needed who can pitch in for any job that is required. Here's one place where family members are especially useful. Because no real hierarchy is established, a founder can ask various family members for help with anything, and usually, the family will help.

Family Experience in Business

It's not unusual for the son or daughter of an entrepreneur to have the same inclination. But the offspring might not want to operate the same business as the parent. Instead, they might decide to set up their own shop and use the parent as a resource to help them develop their new business.

Marc Forgione, son of acclaimed New York chef Larry Forgione, decided to start his own restaurant in New York, Forge. Sofia Coppola has become a respected filmmaker, no longer walking in the footsteps of her famous father, director Francis Ford Coppola. And Ben Taylor, son of legendary folk-rock musicians James Taylor and Carly Simon, founded his own music label, Iris Records, learning from his parents how little musicians typically make from each CD sold.

The business experience of other family members can be helpful to the new founder. The smart entrepreneur will ask for information and advice from family members with the know-how.

First Stage of Family Business

When the owner-entrepreneur founds and operates the business, it is considered to be in its first stage. As time goes on and the business management shifts to other generations and other family members, the business moves into stages two, three, and beyond.

The founder's attitude toward the company strongly influences its organization and ultimate destiny. Is the business there to serve the family's interests? Is it to be built strictly for shareholder value? Or is the business to be sustained for future generations? These different points of view produce very different results for a business.

For the Family's Interest

In some companies, the founder views the family business as an entity that he is in total control of and that exists for the benefit of the family. The family comes first—before the business—and the business is maintained to support the family financially. Such a founder is extremely controlling of all facets of the business.

When a family member needs a job, the business finds a spot for her. If someone in the family needs money, the business makes it available. No one but the founder needs to be consulted on the decision to help the family, and no one else has the authority to do so. This type of founder is likely to limit growth and keep the company's focus more narrow so as to not risk losing the firm, and, by extension, the family's means of support.

For the Shareholders' Interests

A founder who is concerned with maximizing shareholder value makes decisions that increase investors' holdings in the firm. For such a founder, family interests are secondary to shareholders' interests.

Business strategy for this type of founder is markedly different from the family-oriented founder. This founder takes on more risk, looking for ways to grow the company. If it means selling the business to another firm to make the share value increase, the founder with an eye to shareholder value will usually sell.

For the Interest of Longevity of the Business

A founder who sees herself as a steward of the business does not identify herself as one and the same with the family business. Here the goal is to keep the business going for future generations of the family to run.

The business keeps the family together in this approach to a family business. Growth is slower and more controlled than when a business-first point of view prevails. Such a firm takes on less risk than a business that has growth as a significant goal.

> **Family Stats**
>
> Approximately 86 percent of family-controlled companies believe the family business will be controlled by the same family in five years.

This type of family business founder sees the business as something separate from herself, even if she maintains total control over the business. The founder views the business as its own entity that is worth building and maintaining over time. The business is *not* the family, and vice versa. The founder's business goal is to put the business in its best position to succeed over the long haul, which naturally means long after the founder is dead and gone.

Time and again, family businesses fail when the original founder dies because the founder was too strongly identified as the company itself. Founders of family businesses who see themselves as stewards of the business create systems of management that keep the business growing and improving, thereby creating family businesses that can last over generations.

Founder Sets Organization's Culture

The business founder has the greatest influence on the family business's *organizational culture*.

The entrepreneurial founder of a family business generally knows how she wants the organization to run. Usually, the founder has strong opinions about how to manage the business, how to make decisions, how to innovate, the importance of hierarchy, and other business functions that are critical to success. The founder communicates her opinions directly and indirectly to the others in the business. Decisions are made, problems are solved, and the organizational culture is developed over time.

> **def•i•ni•tion** _____
>
> **Organizational culture** describes the patterns of behavior used by people in a business to solve problems and deal with issues. These behaviors are strongly influenced by assumptions founders bring when the business begins.

Sometimes the founder's personality impacts the organizational culture in a negative way. Often a founder states that she wants to delegate authority, but in actual practice, she is involved in every detail of the organization, down to the buying of the pencils. In a family business, this culture can be doubly difficult if Mom or Dad is the founder and refuses to cede authority. Adult children who have been given responsibility by the founder (parent) recognize that such authority is really a sham. They might act like children and set up elaborate ways to get around dealing with the founder, or simply stop working effectively because their own authority seems to be recognized.

Copreneurs

Family businesses can also be founded by couples. These founders are being referred to as *copreneurs*.

def•i•ni•tion

Copreneurs are couples, usually married, who start a business together.

Couples have been founding businesses together for many years, but in recent years the trend has been increasing. More often, the business is professional rather than retail, and it often has a global component. More women are likely to have started the business and have their husbands join them.

Copreneurism Is Catching On

Some of the reasons couples want to work as copreneurs include ...

- Professional couples each can get tired of working for someone else and want the challenge of building a new business with a partner they trust.

- More people can work out of their homes with the proliferation of the Internet and computer technology.

- The increase in franchise opportunities allows couples with relatively little business experience to set up a business together.

- Changes in gender roles have leveled the field between men and women with respect to business opportunities.

Family Stats

Copreneur CEOs (husband-and-wife teams) of family businesses increased from 8 percent of family business in 1997 to 14 percent in 2002. Current estimates are that more than three million U.S. small businesses are couple-owned.

- Women are increasingly more college-educated than men and are moving into previously male-dominated fields such as computer science and engineering.

- Both men and women are seeking a work-family balance.

- Favorable tax implications exist for female-owned companies, which has encouraged couples to found businesses with the wife owning 51 percent.

When It Works

Couples who are business partners often say the business brings them closer together. When they are both fully invested in making the same business succeed, they have double the interest when their partner discusses the job.

They experience family business pride when they establish a business together. Copreneur couples talk about the satisfaction of building on their dreams together. Robert LePera, co-founder with his wife Deborah of Acorn Food Services, says, "I love sharing our firsts—clients, contracts."

Many couples who found new businesses together talk about the level of trust each one has in the other. A wine importing company founded by a couple who later married works because each one has the highest respect for the other's business abilities. The combination of her e-commerce marketing knowledge and his knowledge of the wine market make for a business that hit $16 million in sales within six years of its founding.

Clients of copreneurs see the partnership as a plus, too. "It's like getting two consultants for the price of one," according to a client of Moxley Carmichael, a public relations firm owned jointly by husband and wife Alan Carmichael and Cynthia Moxley.

When It Doesn't Work

The stress of being business partners can put stress on being married partners. Entwining personal and business lives is fraught with difficult situations.

If one member of the partnership is not happy with the business and wants to leave, that can be difficult when the partners are married. Rejection of the business does not need to be interpreted as rejection of the spouse, but most people have trouble separating the two.

Sometimes the couple might feel as though there is no relationship outside the business, especially when work threatens to overtake all their time together. So copreneurs might want to establish rules about how much shop talk they can share outside the office.

It can be scary to put all your eggs in the same basket, financially speaking. Money is cited as the most common source of marital stress, and when all your income comes from a joint business, many couples cannot stand the strain. Gail and Barny Foland, who own a training center for self-defense and yoga, say that the bills cause plenty of arguments in their business.

 Told You So!

When a business is owned equally by both members of a married couple, it can get complicated if the couple divorces. One partner will probably want to buy out the other partner, especially if that partner is also leaving the business.

Suggestion Box _____

If you and your spouse are planning to start a new business together, it might be prudent for one of you to keep your current job for a few months while you get the new
business underway. Having one partner bringing in a consistent income for a while
can help with cash flow for the new business and probably make applying for credit
easier. Plus, you can keep the health insurance from the spouse's job during this time to
save on an additional business expense.

Ron and Denise Provenzano started their day spa business together in 1985, and
today have built it into a $9 million business with four locations. But their lack of
experience handling finances almost destroyed the business and their marriage, as
well. In their first expansion to a second location, they were undercapitalized and
some unexpected expenses took all their cash. They had to resort to borrowing from
Ron's profit-sharing account from a previous job to make payroll.

Three Couples Are Better Than One

How about co-co-copreneurs—three married couples founding a business together?
Florence and Keith Chamberlin and Kate and Martin Bertolini founded Elements, a
restaurant in Vermont, in 2003. The Chamberlins were already partners in a graphic
design firm. Kate ran a women's clothing store, and Martin owned a construction
business. So the four were excited to start a new restaurant together. To add to the
mix, they found another married couple to join them as chefs, Ryan and Allyson
O'Malley.

How does such a complicated copreneurship work? Over time, each couple has shared
the work and found their separate niches. Every other day, each couple takes turns
being on duty at the restaurant. Florence and Kate have taken the lion's share of the
management responsibilities, allowing the husbands to maintain their other businesses (Kate no longer has the clothing store, and Florence has greatly reduced her
duties at the graphic design firm). The chefs have free rein to run the kitchen and set
the changing menu, with everyone's understanding that chefs are the experts in that
arena.

"It can be done," says Keith. "But it takes a lot of trust in each other and confidence
that everyone will do their job. We're really glad we didn't take this on ourselves,
though. The collaboration with our partners is what makes it work."

Two CEOs in the House

Sometimes the husband and wife are both in charge of a company, but it's not the same company. Two family businesses under the same roof sounds like double trouble. But it can be easier to manage two separate businesses than one joint one—at least for some couples.

Each entrepreneur can have her own success and share the good and bad times without the other being directly involved. Being married to another business owner can be helpful when one spouse needs to bounce ideas off the other. And each one certainly can understand the need for cooperation when it comes to household and child-rearing duties.

> **Told You So!**
>
> Married CEOs who run separate businesses in the same industry need to establish clear business boundaries. A highly competitive situation could be fatal for the marriage.

Changing Face of the Founder

The founder of a family is no longer the archetypical dad who starts a business to provide for the wife and kids. Today, founders come in all shapes, sizes, genders, and ages.

Second Careers

With the baby boom generation nearing traditional retirement age, the number of people who want to start a second career is increasing. The AARP might contact you at 50, but many professionals are just reaching their stride at that age.

After amassing 25 to 30 years of experience, more people are striking out on their own to start companies as a second career. These people are looking for the autonomy, flexibility, and satisfaction that owning a business provides. Sometimes the new career grows from a hobby, as in the case of Al Rapp, who started a boat-moving business at age 65. His first career was in medical sales, but when he was ready to retire from that, he wasn't ready to quit working altogether. His new business allows him to do what he loves—spend time on the water—and provides additional income, too.

Family Stats

According to a survey of 3,500 Americans aged 44 to 70 by Washington, D.C.–based D. Hart Research Associates, up to 8.4 million baby boomers are embarking on so-called "encore" careers. Those are careers that start after people have retired. Often an encore career is in a completely different field from the previous career.

Other second-time-around entrepreneurs lose interest in working for someone else and have the nest egg to start a new business based on the skills they have developed throughout their career. Don Gallegos, CEO of King Soopers Supermarkets in the Denver area for more than 30 years, has segued into a successful speaking career after retiring from King Soopers. His customer service knowledge built throughout his tenure in the supermarket industry, combined with his love of people and a natural speaking style, has provided him with a new business. Don is thrilled to be able to donate the proceeds from his new career as a speaker to a philanthropic organization he and his family have established.

Forbes.com, in a recent article on careers following retirement, noted two of the best options for the second career as "self-employment" and "franchise and business owner." Qualifications for both careers include varied experience gained through previous employment, with no specific requirement for education.

Young People

Another trend in new business founding is seen on the opposite end of the age spectrum. Young people directly out of college—or still in college—are starting their own companies with little to no business experience.

A prime example of this phenomenon is Bill Gates, founder of Microsoft. With his friend Paul Allen, he started the business to create software for home computers, leaving Harvard in his junior year. The rest, as they say, is history. In his biography, *The Road Ahead*, Gates notes the support given to him by his parents when starting the new company.

Sergey Brin and Larry Page, founders of Google, have a similar story. Both Stanford graduate students when they started the search engine company, they had a mix of initial investors to help them start their business, including family members.

Michael Dell, founder of Dell Computers, started his first company—PC's Limited—with the help of a loan from his grandparents. Like Bill Gates, he dropped out of college to run what would become an incredibly successful company.

These young entrepreneurs are among the most successful of the many young people who see entrepreneurship as their first road to business success. With little experience, but big ideas, they are building the family businesses of the future.

Explosion of Women-Owned Businesses

Today, the face of the business founder is as likely to be female as male.

Women are a major force in entrepreneurship. As mentioned earlier, tax incentives are often given to female-owned businesses, which is a strong incentive to a woman contemplating starting her own company.

Some female entrepreneurs say the reason they started their own companies was to be able to spend more time with their families. And women who run family businesses tend to hire more family members than male-run family businesses do.

> **Family Stats**
>
> Between 1997 and 2002, the number of women-owned businesses grew twice as fast as all businesses. In 2008, 40 percent of all firms were women-owned businesses, according to the Center for Women's Business Research.

Legal Organization Options for Founding

When a business is founded, there are several options for setting up the business structure.

Sole Proprietorship

A sole proprietorship is the simplest and least expensive way to set up a company. It works when only one person is the founder of the business. The drawback is that the person and the business are the same entity, and the owner is personally liable for everything that might go wrong in the business.

Partnership

The partnership form of organization is similar to sole proprietorship, except that two or more people are involved. Partnerships are typically formed by professionals: attorneys, doctors, accountants, and so on.

Told You So!

Experts caution business founders to choose their business partners wisely because their fortunes are literally tied together.

In a general partnership, all the owners have equal management rights, no matter how many ownership shares they might have in the company. All the partners are liable for all the debts of the business.

A limited liability partnership (LLP) has one or more general partners who actively manage the business, along with limited partners who do not. The general partners are liable for the debts of the partnership, however, unless they are protected with a limited liability limited partnership agreement.

Corporation and LLC

Corporations and limited liability companies (LLCs) offer personal protection from the debts incurred by the business. In C corporations, shares can be publicly traded, so this structure is appropriate for larger, public companies. S companies are more often used for smaller businesses.

An LLC is less restrictive than a corporation, not requiring a board of directors and officers. An LLC can be started with only one person—the founder. An operating agreement is needed when the business is created, which sets up provisions for who can make decisions, how owners will contribute money to the company, and how company income will be shared.

Suggestion Box

Filing as an LLC is usually the best choice for the new family business, unless the owners plan to take the business public in the near future. Naturally, the decision of which business structure to use should be made with the advice of an attorney.

Taxation is handled differently for corporations and LLCs. With a corporation, the income of the company is taxed. Under the LLC organization, the company does not pay tax on its profits, but rather, the profits flow through to the owners who pay the taxes.

More discussion of the legal considerations for a family business is in Chapter 14.

Keeping the Family First

In the founder-owner stage of a family business, the business often takes over all aspects of family life. The founder might spend most of her time working at the business. The children might be required to work summers and weekends to pitch in, and the discussion at the dinner table might be all about the business. The family usually excuses the business intrusion, even if it isn't welcomed, because everyone knows that a new business takes a lot of effort to be successful and the founder is doing the lion's share of the work.

But this focus on the business as all-important creates the feeling that you can't be close to your family unless you are involved in the business. That can cause family stress as the business develops in the future, when some family members might not want to be part of the business.

Knowing When to Let Go

The biggest issue facing founding entrepreneurs of a family business is knowing when to exit the business. Most founders of businesses are self-confident, charismatic people who truly enjoy running the businesses they have created. They aren't usually thinking about leaving the business—since they are completely involved in the day-to-day management and feel they are essential to the business success. But for the health of the family business, it is critical for the business founder to consider how and when to leave during his tenure as the founder-owner.

If the founder deals with this issue while at the helm of the business, it signals to everyone else in the company that he expects the firm to live on past the founding stage. This offers future opportunities to others in management and helps to set the business apart from the family and the founder, as its own entity.

We return to the succession question in greater detail in Chapter 17.

The Least You Need to Know

- ◆ The founder of a family business influences almost everything about the company, driving the culture of the firm well into the future.

- ◆ Couples founding businesses together have twice the brainpower, but sometimes twice the stress.

- ◆ Family members and family considerations are brought in at the start of many businesses.

- ◆ The founder of a family business has to think about when and how to leave the business, for the sake of the business's success.

Part  2

Running a Family Business

Many family businesses start out with enthusiasm and promise. There are many challenges, but it is an exciting time with plenty of potential.

A growing business must develop a strategic plan to guide its future growth. Financial decisions are critical as a business grows, and the family must decide whether it wants to take on debt or give up some control to grow.

In this part, you learn ways to ensure that your family business is a professional organization with the tools it needs to grow and succeed.

Chapter 3

Family Business Structure

In This Chapter

- ◆ What structure does for a family business
- ◆ Levels of formality in a business structure
- ◆ Elements of the family business structure
- ◆ Minority shareholders' influence on the family business

A business is like a building—it needs a structure to keep it strong. A family business is complicated by a family structure that shares many of the same members, but not necessarily the same roles, as the business. When the head of the family is not the head of the business, who is really in charge? When family members own the business but not all of them work in the business every day, who makes the key business decisions?

A clear family business structure can help everyone understand their roles better and perform better in the business. In this chapter, we describe which kind of business structure is useful at various phases of a family business lifecycle.

Overlap of Family, Business, and Ownership Concerns

Every family business has three major groups of people involved in the success of the business: the family, the managers and employees of the business, and the owners.

These three groups overlap in various ways. Some members of the family, but not all, are active workers in the business. Some family members might be partial owners of the family business but not have any day-to-day working or management role.

When a typical family business is starting, those three groups all have the same central figure—the owner-entrepreneur. At first, there is often no other owner. A few family members might work in the business during the early stages, and perhaps a few outsiders might work there, too. At the beginning of a family business, the overlaps among the three groups are great.

The Three Circle Model of Family Business shows the interaction between the family, the business, and the business owners.

(Source: Renato Tagiuri and John Davis, 1982)

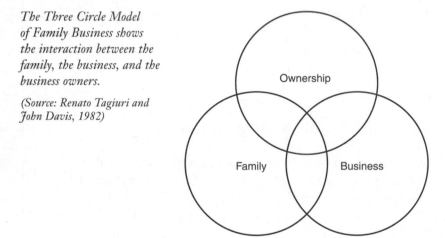

As the family business progresses and more people enter each of the three groups, the overlaps naturally lessen. More people entering the picture, whether they are workers, owners, or family, complicates the running of the family business. Structure needs to be put in place to ensure that the business is run as effectively as possible.

Does a family business need structure more than a nonfamily business does? At least as much, and probably more. The three groups just described have emotional ties to each other that you don't see in a nonfamily business. Let's say that Uncle Billy is in charge of the books and one day, some money is missing. Who has to be the one to ask dear old Uncle where it went? No one wants to draw the short straw for that duty. If an organizational structure was in place that ensured regular oversight of the accounts, Uncle Billy might not have had such a free hand with the business funds.

Even if the amount of money involved is small, the problem is huge for a family business. It's stressful to confront any employee about possible financial irregularities—imagine if the employee you're confronting is your dad's older brother. Accountability measures put into place early on can keep this from occurring, or at least make the investigation process easier and more straightforward.

Constituencies of the family business such as banks, lenders, suppliers, and wholesalers, want to see that the CEO of a family business can make the best decisions for the good of the business. If the CEO is burdened with pleasing family members or takes on all the decisions without conferring with anyone, those outside constituencies might have less confidence in the CEO and the business.

Structure Can Be Formal or Informal

What's most important about your family business structure is that it works. There isn't a one-size-fits-all recipe for every family business.

During the first phase of a family business, when the founder owns and operates the business alone or with her spouse, most major business decisions are made around the kitchen table, not the board table. Other people are not accountable for deciding how to spend money, or which new clients should be added, or how to create a market for the goods.

After the business has had some success, the founder or founders usually look to someone else for advice and counsel. It's human nature to want to have someone else to bounce ideas off or to seek a validating opinion. At this point, a small advisory group can be established—either formally or informally. This group often consists of a few people whose opinions are considered by the founder to be useful. Perhaps it's an old family friend who has been successful in business and has experienced some of the issues the family business is now going through. It could be someone who has retired from your current line of work, whose experience in the same field could be invaluable. Often an attorney or accountant is part of this informal board of "trusted" advisors.

As a family business grows, the CEO has to become more accountable to all the groups—the family, the owners, and the management. Information about the family business has to be shared with these groups, who will make their evaluations of whether the business is being run properly. At this point, more formal business structures will have to be put into place.

Elements of the Business Structure

Although not every family business needs them at all times, several groups can help a business ensure its success. In general, they are part of what is known as family business *governance*.

def•i•ni•tion

Governance is the method or system of sharing the rights and responsibilities of a family business with its various participants, including owners, managers, and family.

Through effective governance, a family business sets its direction, has policies that all the members of the business agree to work by, and enforces the values that are part of the business.

Besides the specific processes, customs, and policies that affect the family business, governance also includes the relationships among the parties involved in the business. These parties can be diverse: shareholders, management, board of directors, employees, suppliers, customers, banks and other lenders, regulators, the government, and the community. With effective governance of a family business, the framework of rules and practices put in place ensures accountability, fairness, and transparency in the firm's relationship with all these parties.

Top Management

The highest level of management in a family business is usually the first organizational structure put into place. The entrepreneur, the copreneurs, or the initial organizing group of the family business comprises the top management ranks at the beginning stage.

As the company grows, more complex management roles are needed—for example, director of sales and marketing, vice president for new product development, and controller. Management positions usually develop according to the needs of the business. In a family business, family members who are in management try to divide responsibilities according to each member's strengths and talents.

Suggestion Box

Family members need to be as qualified for the positions they hold as nonfamily members—maybe more, to be sure the family members are really right for the job.

Senior management members speak for the company's employees. The function of senior management is to run the business on a day-to-day basis as well as set strategies for the business.

Board of Advisors

Few entrepreneurs really act alone in starting a family business. They talk about their business ideas with their spouses, parents, children, friends, bankers, attorneys, accountants …. Eventually, the new business concept develops and the entrepreneur sets up shop. All these people who acted as a business sounding board might be part of the fledgling business's advisory board.

The board of advisors is not the same as a board of directors. It is an informal group with which the founder of the family business consults to assist with decisions. Sometimes a founder never actually convenes the board of advisors as a group, but instead, consults each person separately as needed. Other founders set up occasional meetings with their advisors as a group, bringing their expertise together.

> **Family Stats**
>
> A survey of U.S. family businesses found that having a board of advisors was one of the most significant factors affecting the company's success.

At the start of a family business, the founder is often reluctant to seek other opinions. Advisors chosen by the founder are often family and friends who may be there just to second the founder's decisions.

But who belongs in a board of advisors for a family business? Probably not family members. They will often give advice without asking. A volunteer board of advisors should include people whose business judgment is trusted and respected by the founder. People in a related business, or a person who has gone through similar business challenges can be useful advisors. Lawyers and accountants can help find a few people who might be willing to offer advice on an informal basis.

 Told You So! _____

Don't be afraid that your advisors will find out more about your business than you want them to know. You'll get worthwhile advice only if you take the risk to give them the information they need to understand the issues affecting your business. Family businesses are usually overly concerned about privacy and try to keep information a little too close to the vest.

Board of Directors

A board of directors is a more formal advisory mechanism for a family business. It can serve the same function as the board of advisors, but as a formal board, it has legal responsibilities and duties.

In most family businesses, a true board of directors is not organized until required by law or by the expansion of the business. When the founder is willing to relinquish some control to a board of directors, then it can be a helpful part of the business governance.

Family members who are part owners of the family business are frequently members of the board of directors. This is appropriate if those family members want to take an active role in major decision-making for the company. But the most effective boards of directors are largely independent of the family and the business. This type of board can provide an objective viewpoint for the CEO of a family business. Generally, smaller boards of directors with fewer family members work better together. A key factor in the effectiveness of a board of directors is the members' interest in the good of the company, as opposed to the good of any specific family member or family faction.

The board of directors holds the management team accountable for what it does in its running of the company. The board of directors also speaks for the owners of the company. It is responsible for ensuring that the business strategy mapped out by the owners and top management is followed as closely as possible. This includes assessing the financial practices of the business.

The board should assess the company's strategic business plan annually. It is responsible for evaluating the management activities of the CEO and setting her compensation, as well as hiring a new CEO when necessary. Besides monitoring the accounting practices and financial reporting, the board of directors is also responsible for the company's business practices and is the monitor of both ethics and legal requirements.

This sounds like a mouthful! Who would want to take on a board directorship in a family business, except for a family member with a vested interest? Luckily, plenty of businesspeople are willing and excited to be members of a board of directors. When your family business is ready to avail itself of the services a board of directors can offer, business people will be there to join your board. If you have an informal board of advisors, those people are the logical choice for your first official board of directors. Again, your lawyer and accountant will have business contacts in the community who might serve on your board. Members of a company board of directors are often paid for their services.

At the start of the Italian importing business Vietri, the founders understood the need for a board of directors to offer expertise in areas they felt they lacked. Two sisters, Susan and Frances Gravely, began the firm to import ceramic dinnerware they discovered on a trip to Italy with their mother, Lee. With Lee's financial backing, the sisters set about starting the business. They carefully selected people for their board of directors who had business acumen in areas they wanted to tap. Within the first year, they had five directors on board. They chose friends and business associates who had a variety of experiences, both successes and failures. A number of their directors since the company's founding in 1983 have been entrepreneurs in their own family businesses.

Suggestion Box

To maintain links between the board of directors, management, and family, most family business consultants recommend that the CEO and another family member serve on the board. It's best for the board to be chaired by a family member, if one is available who is fully qualified.

Family Council

When the ownership of a family business is spread across several generations and branches of the family, it's time for a family council. At this stage of the family business's life, a number of family members likely have some ownership stake in the business but don't participate in the management or daily workings of the firm. These people need a voice in the governance structure of the family business, and it's best for it to be formalized.

Even if a family member is not part of the business, he is likely to feel part of it in some way. Every family member feels the effects of what goes on in the family business. The family council is a way for all family members to learn about the company firsthand.

The family council's main responsibility is to be the family's voice to the company's board of directors. The council must reach consensus on the issues that concern the family and then communicate their recommendations to the board. This helps the board of directors represent the family's interest in the family business.

The family council is a formalized structure that maintains the founder's values and ensures that they continue to be respected in the family business, no matter how many generations have passed. As discussed in Chapter 2, the founder's goals and values set the tone for the corporate culture of the entire family business. If the family wants to keep the essence of the original founder in the business, its voice must be clear. Creating a family council that meets regularly and discusses family issues that affect the business is the way to do this as the business grows and passes to succeeding generations.

What kinds of issues does a family council deal with? Here are some examples many family councils have confronted:

- The hiring of family members
- Developing long-term goals for the business
- Determining philanthropic goals for family business earnings
- Maintaining the founder's long-term vision
- Creating redemption policies for family-owned stock
- Developing general policies on stock ownership
- Educating family members about the business itself

Told You So!

Don't wait too long to start a family council. Experts caution that as soon as the second generation is old enough to start working in the family business, a family council should be created to keep the family lines of communication open.

Often, a family council is started because some family members feel left out of the loop of the family business communication. As an example, the family business Smart Parts, an auto and truck recycling business, had eight family members in the business. Three of them were the owners and served on the board of directors. The other five—spouses and children—felt they were not privy to information about the business. As the older generation began planning for retirement, many questions about the family's role in the business emerged. A family retreat with all eight working family members was their first step toward discussing sensitive issues.

One of the jobs of the family council is to communicate the family values that guide the business to the board of directors. In the case of the Thorp Seed Company, some of those values conflicted with the business goals of the firm. The Thorp family council agreed that its family's core values included frugality, responsibility, and compassion in its business dealings. The emphasis on frugality tied the board of directors' hands when they wanted to borrow to invest in new equipment. The concern for compassionate business practices meant that the company was keeping some family members as employees who were poor performers, leading to low morale among nonfamily staff. Eventually, the family council and the board of directors agreed that the two groups should agree on business values that would be useful practices for company policy. They agreed on a slow growth policy and career counseling for family members whose performance was substandard. These policies were derived from the family's values but helped to keep the company on firmer footing for business success.

Shareholders

The *shareholders* are the owners of a business. A business can have only one shareholder, or it can have millions. Many family businesses that begin with an owner-entrepreneur have a single shareholder—the founder—who owns all the stock in the firm. As the business grows, the founder might take on a partner and give or sell stock to that partner. The business might need capital for growth, and shares of stock might be sold to others, both inside and out of the family. Over time, shares of stock in the family business are spread among many people who have varied interests in the business.

def•i•ni•tion

A **shareholder** is an individual or a company that legally owns one or more shares of stock in a corporation.

Shareholder rights and responsibilities are mandated by law in a corporate structure. Most companies have an annual shareholders' meeting, at which members of the board of directors are elected by the shareholders.

In many family businesses, a great deal of overlap occurs between the shareholders and the family. Often, ownership of a family business remains largely or entirely in the hands of family members. The founder gives her stock to her children, who do the same for their children. Many family businesses make stock available to people outside the family only when the company has a major need for capital.

Minority Shareholders in the Family Business

Multiple generations of a family in a family business usually create multiple shareholders. Not every shareholder has an equal stake. Some will be *minority shareholders*.

The Inadvertent Creation of Minority Shareholders

It's easy to create minority shareholders in a family business. Say the two founders of XYZ Family Company originally hold all the stock as equal partners. When they die, their ownership of the company passes equally to their children—but Founder Jim has three children and Founder Sally has two. Founder Jim's kids each has one-third of 50 percent of the stock, or 16.67 percent. Founder Sally's kids each has one-half of her stake, or 25 percent apiece. Now each owner of the company has a minority ownership stake that has no relationship to whether the kids participate in company management.

def•i•ni•tion

A **minority shareholder** is an individual or a company that owns stock in a firm but holds less than a controlling interest.

There are many stories of family businesses that have created a number of minority shareholders by trying to be fair to the next generation. A machine tool company in the Midwest ran across this problem. The husband-and-wife founders wanted their three children to share ownership of the company and gifted stock to each. One of their children was much more involved in the management of the firm and became the head of the company. But his decisions were second-guessed by his siblings, who owned enough stock that together they could keep him from making any important decisions. The distribution of stock by the parents made effective management of the company nearly impossible.

Suggestion Box

Don't bequeath family business stock to family members who have no interest in the business. Be fair to them by bequeathing other valuable assets, such as real estate. At a minimum, consider giving nonvoting shares to family members who aren't in the business.

Don't let this happen to your family business. You can be fair to all your children without compromising the success of the business you have worked so hard to build. If you keep the number of people who own stock in the company, and who are part of senior management, to a minimum, you will concentrate the power in the hands of the family members who are responsible for the business. Remember, "fair" is not necessarily "equal."

Role in Management

In general, a minority shareholder acting alone has little influence in the decisions of a business. But in a family business, the situation is different. A minority shareholder who happens to be the older brother of the majority shareholder might not be reluctant to question why his sibling is taking so many trips at the company's expense or why the dividend of the stock isn't greater. He can make a lot of trouble for the majority shareholder, even if he has little voting power, especially if he involves other family members who are shareholders.

Minority shareholders have a right to expect that the family business will be run profitably and create economic return for all the owners. This doesn't mean they should expect big dividends all the time. But owners of a family business, even small owners, should expect their investments to pay off. Because selling shares in a small family business is difficult, a minority shareholder has a keen interest in ensuring that those shares retain and increase their value.

As family members, minority shareholders are also part of the group that should expect that the family business behave in accordance with family values. If the business strays away from a fundamental value of the family on which the business was founded, they should speak up—in the family council or the shareholder's meeting—to ensure that the family has a voice.

If a minority shareholder is a member of the board of directors, it is critical that he care about the success of the firm. Sometimes, influential family members insist that they be put on the board, even though they have little interest in the company. This kind of family member director can be a thorn in the side of management, questioning and criticizing without understanding the issues.

Keeping the Stock in the Family

Unless your family business is large enough to warrant being a public company, most experts agree that the best practice for most family businesses is to keep most of the stock in the hands of family members to help ensure that the family maintains control of the company.

Family members who are part of the top management of the family business should have the majority of the business's stock, so squabbles among family shareholders with less knowledge of the company don't enter into strategic business decisions.

The Least You Need to Know

♦ Business structures are key to ensuring a family business answers to all the groups that are part of the business.

♦ Advisors outside the family can provide an important perspective to the family business leader.

♦ Senior management is the voice of the employees; the board of directors is the voice of the owners; the family council is the voice of the family.

♦ Transfer of stock across generations can impact family business decisions.

Chapter 4

Family Dynamics

In This Chapter

- ◆ Family businesses mirror family relationships
- ◆ Whether to employ family members in your business
- ◆ The importance of trust
- ◆ Business focus versus family focus

The relationships between parents and children, siblings, cousins, spouses, in-laws, and the myriad other family connections that are all part of a family business make for a challenging and complex working environment. In this chapter, we examine ways to help your family tread carefully around the family dynamics land mines of the family business terrain.

All families have some healthy and some unhealthy dynamics. The relationships between people that are developed in the family throughout the years are strong. They are different from a business relationship, which is built on the day-to-day experiences of working with each other or the expected roles of boss/employee. Family dynamics are far more complex and deep-seated, with behavior patterns that develop and grow throughout a lifetime.

If left unexamined, family dynamics issues can bring down a family business. They can be far more instrumental in a family business's failure than traditional business factors such as the market, the economy, technology changes, and so on. Many family businesses have either folded or were sold to outside investors because members of the family couldn't separate their family relationships from their business interactions.

Here's a story that could only occur in a family business—but it could be in almost *any* family business. Debra and Arthur are brother and sister, each president of one of the two corporations in the family business. Dad is semiretired but stays involved. Mom likes to be part of everything they do. Arthur enjoys joking with his sister in front of the employees, but Debra interprets the humor as put-downs. Debra thinks the employees hate Arthur for the way he treats them and her, but she doesn't know how to stop him. She's ready to quit and let Arthur run the whole business, but her new husband Stan doesn't want to see her taken advantage of. Can this family be helped?

def•i•ni•tion

> **Family dynamics** are the patterns of relationships or interactions between family members. The dynamics of every family are unique to that family, but similarities are seen in common situations.

While all businesses have their back-room politics, members of a family business bring another set of relationships to work with them every day. The relationships between parent and child, among siblings and cousins, with those who marry into the family—the overall *family dynamics*—cannot be denied in the family business. And these family dynamics cause family businesses to make decisions and develop business strategies in different ways from nonfamily businesses.

Business Focus vs. Family Focus

Family businesses fall into two basic camps in their overall approach to decision-making: they are either business focused or family focused.

A business-focused family business makes decisions primarily on the basis of what is best for the business. Hiring decisions, financing decisions, growth decisions, and so on are all made according to the goals and needs of the business. Family wishes are not a consideration.

A family-focused family business makes its decisions primarily based on family needs. Employees are hired, retained, and promoted because they are family members. New financing opportunities are found within the family, such as stock offered to family members who want to increase their shares in the business. Growth opportunities are evaluated by how they will affect family members—for example, when Brother Ted decides to move to a new state, the family business decides to open new stores in that location for Ted to manage.

Most family business experts agree that business-focused family firms are more successful and, interestingly, have fewer family problems. When a family business can set aside its unproductive family dynamics and run the business without regard to individual family members' wishes, the business will be on more secure footing. And if the business is more secure, the family often is, too.

You might think that a family focus makes sense for a family business. After all, isn't that why Granddad went into business 80 years ago—to provide for the welfare of the family? But when providing for the family includes hiring Cousin Lauren's husband who spends more time on the golf course than making sales calls, or making Uncle Dan a director of the company so he can collect the $30,000 fee and snooze through the meetings, you might be harming the company more than you realize.

Although we discuss succession planning more fully in Chapter 17, a cautionary word is appropriate here. When a family business maintains a business focus, planning for the future of the business can be handled more professionally. The continuation of the business is the key issue when it is time to plan for a new CEO for the company. Family leadership does not have to be in the same hands as business leadership.

Suggestion Box

When possible, let two people act as the head of the family and head of the family business. It's a big burden for one person to have to handle both roles, and other family members are likely to resent the person who succeeds as head of the business and wants to take charge of the family as well.

Benefits of the Family in a Family Business

The family unit can be both a positive and a negative influence on a family business. Let's look at how the family itself can act as a strong business advantage.

Trust Factor

If you can't trust your family, whom can you trust? That's a truism that is repeated in the boardrooms of family businesses around the world. As Godfather Don Corleone said, "Never let anyone outside the family know what you're thinking."

Organizations benefit from a high degree of trust among people. Trust helps employees cooperate better with each other, and it promotes strong relationships between people. When people who work together trust each other, the degree of conflict is reduced. Trust has been found to lower the cost of transactions and improve group effectiveness.

Family businesses usually have a high degree of trust among the family members, especially in the early stages of the business. The history that family members share allows them to predict how family members will behave. This kind of interpersonal trust takes a long time to establish in a nonfamily firm but is common in the family unit. Typically, nonfamily firms don't begin with a high level of interpersonal trust among employees. Family businesses have a real advantage in the early stages over nonfamily companies because this high level of trust is already established at the start, by virtue of the people in the business being family members.

Trust among family members helps start and build family firms. Family members trust the family with their money when they invest in the family business. People in family businesses report that part of the reason they want to work with family members is that they know their family won't cheat them or try to do them wrong.

Ease of Finding Employees

Another benefit of family businesses that nonfamily businesses can't share is the nearly automatic access to employees. When manpower is needed, a family business can call on the "natural" candidates for jobs—the family. When a child grows up with a family business, the expectation is often that she will move into the business, especially if the child has been involved in the business as a youth. Larger-scale family businesses often engender pride in the family name through the business, which leads to family members being drawn to work for the company.

Family members are more likely to easily fit in with the corporate culture because that culture is derived from the family's values, beliefs, and attitudes. Compatibility is particularly important if the family business is small and has few employees.

Family members know that the family business is often the chief financial support for the family, and they recognize that the whole family depends on the success of the company. This is a great motivator for family members to join the family business and give it their all. They will make a commitment to the success of the family business that can be much stronger than the one employees make to a nonfamily business.

Family businesses tend to emphasize the importance of strong relationships, both among employees and with customers. Family members who share the family values can help create and maintain the goodwill that such a family business builds with its customers.

When Being Family Doesn't Help the Family Business

There are many reasons including the family in your business is a good idea. But the relationships among family members are complex. Sometimes, family dynamics get in the way of successfully operating a family business.

Breakdown of Trust

Although many family businesses start with high interpersonal trust among members of the family, over time, that kind of trust isn't enough to sustain business success. Tightly knit family management groups who trust each other's decision-making run the risk of relying too heavily on their own small group. They can become insular and ignore warning signs from outside the family. If this happens, they can make poor business decisions that can harm the company.

As the business grows, family members need to feel trust in the competence of new additions to the staff. When a family member is hired simply because he is part of the clan, there is no way to evaluate whether that person is the best one for the job. Other employees will question the new-hire's abilities and lose confidence. Family members who have an ownership stake but not a day-to-day role in the business will likely question the capability of other family members to handle the jobs. They might trust them not to willingly do wrong because they are family, but they won't trust them to know how to run the family business.

Told You So! _____

Don't let family issues become the focus of your day at work. It's easy to get pulled into family disputes when family members are in the workplace with you. But arguments between Mom and Dad, or older and younger sisters, will distract you from getting work done and might even influence your business decisions.

Entrepreneurs are notable in their distrust of other people, including family members. They might trust their own instincts, sometimes without sufficient regard for the facts, but they often don't trust their own offspring to run the businesses they started.

They are often unwilling to relinquish control of any kind, and in being so, communicate their lack of trust to the next generation of potential leaders for the business.

When Family Members Feud

A breakdown in trust among family members can quickly lead to arguments about how to operate the family business. Patterns of behavior that develop in the family setting resurface when family members work together.

Good relationships among family members can be beneficial to a family business; poor relationships can wreck the business. The following example from an actual company (with identifying details changed) shows the kind of internal strife that dysfunctional family dynamics can inflict on a family business.

The Jones family owns a business begun by the grandfather. The son, now retired, ran the business for 20 years and now serves as chairman of the board. He wants his children to maintain control over the family business. Three of the Jones children work in the business, along with the spouses of the other two siblings. Firsthand knowledge of all the players, in this case, did not help them to work together. On the contrary, their patterns of behavior from childhood have divided the siblings into two factions. Each faction sees the other one as dangerous to the health of the business.

Suggestion Box

Take time to let family members prove themselves in their roles in the family business. It's easy to judge them according to the family's established patterns, but it's more prudent to step back and evaluate their business behavior, separate from their family behavior.

On the one side are two brothers with a high acceptance of risk. On the other side are three sisters and their husbands who want the expensive entertaining bills to end. Sister Ellen says of her two brothers, "I know Harry doesn't have the ability to run the business. And Bob lies to me about everything." Harry and Bob call Ellen a tattletale. Dad tries to mediate, but he really wants them to work out their problems without him. Instead of acting as adults, Ellen, Bob, and Harry are replaying their childhood roles and bringing down the Jones business with them.

Rivalry Among Siblings/Cousins

The Jones family example is one of millions of *sibling rivalry* issues that surface as the second or third generation of a family share management of the family business.

The concept of sibling rivalry in the family business is complicated by the idea that the brothers and sisters are usually somehow trying to win their parents' love and attention. When Mom or Dad is the head of the company, arguments among siblings don't just stay in the family—they can escalate to major business disagreements. Siblings are still in competition with each other to win their parents' approval, which, in the case of a family business, can mean promotion, raises, and power—not just a simple hug or pat on the head.

def•i•ni•tion

Sibling rivalry is emotional competition among brothers and sisters. It's usually thought of as vying to win parents' approval, love, and attention away from the other siblings.

Siblings who work together, especially while their parents are still in charge of the company, can have a hard time forging true adult relationships with each other because of this long-seated rivalry for their parents' approval.

The three ways brothers and sisters show their continued sibling rivalry in the family business are as follows:

◆ Stereotyped roles

◆ Resentfulness

◆ Dependency on parents

Stereotyping

A sibling might feel pigeonholed into a certain role in the company based on her childhood role. For example, the youngest sister might have been the pet of the family, allowed more latitude, and been given more opportunities to branch out. The oldest brother might have been expected to be the family leader, to adhere to his parents' expectations, and to succeed at all costs. In the family business, that oldest brother might be stereotyped into being the only sibling considered for leadership of the company. The youngest sister might be stereotyped by the family as flighty and not serious, and therefore not eligible for real responsibility in the family business.

It's dangerous to treat siblings this way. You'll miss opportunities for encouraging qualified people when you stereotype based on childhood behavior. People do change as they mature, and maintaining the family pecking order doesn't always translate into effective business management.

Resentment

Siblings might become resentful of each other when not treated fairly by their parents. This doesn't mean everyone getting exactly the same thing; rather, fairness means that each sibling receives equitable treatment according to his needs. Parents often continue to make the same mistakes into adulthood when they give their children equal shares of a family business without regard to the individual needs or talents of those children. Siblings might resent each other if one has equal ownership but no real interest or involvement in the business. The sibling who is working hard in the family business might resent the sibling who owns an equal share but contributes nothing toward the business's success.

Remember Tom Smothers's cry, "Mom always liked you best"? Siblings who grow up with the idea that one child in the family was favored by Mom or Dad will harbor ill will toward that sibling far into the future, even if the siblings are compatible in all other respects.

Dependency

Siblings who never learn to make decisions independent of their parents will also be in jeopardy if they become managers in the family business. Checking with Mom or Dad to resolve family conflict inhibits a collaborative approach that would be a better choice for a strong sibling management group.

Parents in a family business can help facilitate independence in decision-making by withdrawing from active management when the next generation is ready to take the reins. If the parents stick around and second-guess the children's decisions, there will be confusion throughout the company as to who is really in charge.

Individual Needs

Psychologists agree that the process of sibling rivalry as children grow up can be helpful for each sibling to develop her own individuality. The competitive nature of sibling rivalry helps a child understand what is unique about herself. But individuality is not necessarily prized in the family business. There's an all-for-one-and-one-for-all mentality in many family businesses.

For some siblings, the family business is not for them. When one sibling chooses not to work for the family business, other siblings might become angry. Breaking away from the business is viewed as breaking from the family.

Parent-Child Issues

The roles of parent and child are clear in most families. Parent takes care of child through youth and adolescence, gradually allowing the child autonomy and responsibility as the child matures. But in a family business, the move to adult autonomy is more complicated when the parent remains as the company boss.

Many parents have a hard time seeing their children as actual adults. This can have a destructive effect on the family business. Parents might reject new ideas for the business that come from their children, based on the parents' notion that their children can't know more about their business than they do. Or they summarily reject business decisions made by their children, using the same kind of logic.

Adult children in the family business remind a parent of his impending mortality. Many people don't want to be reminded of the fact that they will die, but in a business, it's critical to plan for the future leader of the company.

 Told You So!

Many families are afraid of having more than one strong adult in the family, desiring to maintain the "head of the household" formula. This is dangerous for a family with a family business because the business needs to develop competent and confident adults who are able to manage the enterprise over time.

Parental control over children can be the motivation for perpetuating a family business in the most dysfunctional situations. Parents can guide their children toward a career in the family business while they are growing up, offering them little other choices for adult employment. "It's for the good of the family" are powerful words.

These adult children often end up joining the family business, but with resentment toward their parents and the business. And if that child eventually succeeds the parent as head of the company, it can be disastrous for the business if the child felt pressured to be part of the family company.

In-Laws in the Business

How do you deal with in-laws in the family business? Are they family or not? Should they be treated as members of the family or outsiders who have joined the firm?

Most people think that the rules for hiring in-laws are the same as hiring anyone. If your company policy is that the best person is chosen for every job, that policy must apply to the in-law, too. But if your family business makes a job available for any family member who wants one, make sure the in-law is also given that opportunity.

Conversely this point of view holds that it is unfair to expect a spouse to join the family business. Like a child who is pressured by her parents to join the family firm, the in-law should join the family business willingly, not because the family requires it.

The Least You Need to Know

- ◆ Family dynamics always seep into a family business.

- ◆ Family businesses are more successful when they focus on business success, not family interests.

- ◆ Trust among family members is critical for a family business to succeed when family members are in control of the business.

- ◆ Established patterns of family behavior often control family business decisions, whether or not they are helpful to the business, and often unconsciously.

- ◆ Have clear rules on the involvement of in-laws in the family business.

Chapter 5

Strategic Planning

In This Chapter

◆ The founder's vision underlies the strategic plan

◆ CEO buy-in to the planning process is critical

◆ Steps of the strategic planning process

◆ Reviewing the strategic plan

Successful family businesses are always looking to the future. In preparing for the future, family businesses should engage in a strategic planning process. Strategic planning for a family business is a bit like going to the dentist. It takes some time and it might hurt a little, but you know that if you do it on a regular basis it's good for your business health.

In this chapter, we look at why strategic planning is critical for the family business to ensure its success. We also present some strategies you can use to start your own planning process.

A Vision for the Family Business

Strategic planning sounds like a fancy concept, but it really is about the core of a family business.

def•i•ni•tion

Strategic planning is the process of putting together a game plan to guide future family business decisions. Most strategic planning documents last from three to five years and are reviewed on an annual basis.

In a business that is just starting, the planning process is important but relatively simple. The plan is to develop the product, decide how to market it, and so on. As a business matures, issues of growth, succession, employees, compensation, benefits, diversification, and other competitive challenges become increasingly important. At that point, strategic planning becomes necessary as larger businesses have more complicated challenges. But any business, large or small, has to start out with a vision. Only after a business has settled on a vision will it be able to make the key planning decisions that will enable it to achieve success.

The vision of a business comes before strategic planning. It is the reason the original owner/entrepreneur started the company. Every family business must have a vision.

The Role of the Founder

Colonel Harland Sanders started Kentucky Fried Chicken with a "secret" recipe of herbs and spices, plus recipes for gravy and mashed potatoes. He would visit Kentucky Fried Chicken (later KFC) franchises around the country to make sure the chicken and mashed potatoes were up to his standards. He had a passion for getting the little things right every day.

Steve Jobs, the founder of Apple Computer, launched his company with a vision for a consumer-friendly personal computer. Jobs was instrumental in the growth of the business. When the company grew and brought in professional managers, Jobs left—and with him went much of the original vision for the company. Only when Jobs returned and imparted his vision on breakthrough products like Macintosh computers, iPods, and iPhones did the company really begin to prosper again.

Many family businesses start with the vision that the founder brings to the firm. Family businesses are notable for their ability to bring that vision forward in time through the passing of leadership across the generations. The best successions from one generation to another in a family business occur when the founder's vision is clear and an integral part of the business philosophy.

Basic Answers

The vision of the family business should answer some basic business questions:

- **What will you sell?** A company that tries to sell too many products to too many people might have difficulties in achieving a clear focus for its business. On the other hand, if a family business's vision is too narrow, it might not have enough customers to sustain it.

- **To whom will you sell?** Identifying a target market is a crucial step for all businesses. For example, suppose you want to start a book publishing company. You might have a lot of good ideas for books, but if you can't figure out how to distribute the books, your company can end up losing money. These days, many smaller publishers are having difficulty selling to bookstores, and many companies devise market plans based on Internet sales or direct selling by authors to distribute their books.

- **How will you beat the competition?** It's not enough to have a good product or service and also a plan to sell it. You must investigate what the competition is doing. If other companies are selling similar products or services, you must decide whether you have advantages in price or quality that will make your products or services stand out in the marketplace.

Sharing the Vision

In family businesses, it is crucial that the founder share his vision with other family members. If other family members are invested in the founder's vision, they will provide support during the tough times that are almost inevitable in a startup.

If family members do not share the founder's vision, then they might not be willing to make the financial and emotional sacrifices necessary in many young enterprises.

The Mission Statement

A chief way family businesses communicate their visions to the rest of the world is through a *mission statement*. Employees, customers, and shareholders need to understand what is at the core of the company and why people are working so hard to make it successful.

Many companies include their mission statements in their advertising or corporate reporting. It's a part of the business they want people to understand.

Family businesses vary in the kinds of issues they mention in their mission statements. Here are some examples:

◆ "… produce quality products, on time, at competitive prices, with customers who are committed to the same idea." (Falcon Plastics, South Dakota)

◆ "… provide quality building products and services to our 'Born to Build' customers with our valued team of unique people who are committed to both professional and personal growth." (McCoy's Building Supply Centers, Texas)

◆ "Respect of each other and our customers, and doing what's right." (Fran Johnson Golf and Tennis Headquarters, Massachusetts)

◆ "… committed to product excellence, business integrity, professional management, and loyalty to and from our employees, our communities, environment and family history." (Wilcox Family Farms, Washington)

◆ "Focus on People; Offer the Highest Value in Quality, Product and Services; Reach Potential through Empowerment; Tradition of Integrity; Enrich Lives by Encouraging Music Participation." (Willis Music Company, Kentucky, which has developed a mission-oriented FORTE award)

Although they are all different, mission statements like the ones quoted here generally refer to the company's products, services, and customers. Many mission statements of family businesses reference the importance of the family as well.

Developing the Strategic Plan

Establishing a vision for your business is the first step in putting together a strategic plan. In a business just starting out, a vision and mission statement might be all that is necessary. It is hard to look down the road when you are in survival mode. With a strong vision, an entrepreneur can concentrate on the business and put off serious planning for the future for a while.

However, as a family business begins to grow and add employees, planning becomes necessary. Second-generation family members want to know what their roles will be in the business's future. Banks or other creditors will want to see a strategic business plan to decide whether they should risk their money in the business. If the family business plans to grow by seeking capital from extended family members and outside investors, the family business will need to put together a strategic plan that will make investors want to buy a stake in the company.

Many family businesses never develop a strategic plan. They tend to be tied to traditional ways of doing things, so a strategic plan seems unnecessary. Family businesses are often led by a forceful head of the family who thinks that her hand on the tiller is enough to guide the business into the future. And other family members can be reluctant to push for a strategic planning process because they fear creating family conflict.

After a family business has progressed beyond the startup stage, it must take the next steps in strategic management. They include:

1. Developing a system for putting together a strategic plan—who will be involved and what areas (such as succession and future business opportunities) the strategic plan will address.

2. Creating the plan with the designated people.

3. Implementing the plan over the designated time horizon.

4. Adjusting the plan for new market conditions and changes in the family business.

> ### Family Stats
>
> According to the 2007 American Family Business Survey, slightly more than one half of family firms have a written strategic plan.

Because the strategic plan impacts the family as well as the business, family members should be part of the planning process. It is advisable to take planning members from different sectors of the firm (management, sales, production, and so on) and include a balance of family members and nonfamily members. If no one on staff is capable of leading the planning process, an outsider can be hired to facilitate it.

Suggestion Box

The role of the CEO is crucial to gaining acceptance of the strategic plan. The CEO should be fully invested in the process because top management must endorse the plan to make it work. However, the CEO should not personally write the plan alone because she might be too invested in the status quo.

The first part of a strategic plan development involves an assessment of where the family business is now. In family businesses with fewer than 50 employees, a small group of 3 or 4 might be sufficient to complete the assessment and map out the plan. A small family business is likely to have close access to customers and information it needs to develop its strategic plan. In companies with more than 50 employees, a group of from 6 to 10 employees might be necessary to assess the business and work on the plan. Customer surveys and focus groups might need to be conducted to obtain customer and market information required for the planning process.

Many companies use a tool called *SWOT analysis*—which looks at a company's strengths, weaknesses, opportunities, and threats—to assess the position of the firm.

def•i•ni•tion

SWOT analysis is a tool for strategic planning that provides a simple way to examine factors both inside the firm (strengths and weaknesses) and from the outside (opportunities and threats).

SWOT analysis can be helpful in reducing the time spent on developing a strategic plan because it is a simple and direct technique. One of the problems many companies continue to cite about the strategic planning process is the amount of time it can require. Companies can spend as much as three years or more on simply the information-gathering phase of the process, never getting around to the real planning work.

The plan then deals with formulating a direction for the company. The issue of where the firm wants to go in the future is key for the planning group to agree on. Know the time horizon for the plan—from three to five years is acceptable for many companies—and develop the objectives of the plan based on that time frame.

Finally, the plan must address how to get the company from point A to point B. What steps are needed? How much will it cost? How much time will it take? Who is responsible for which parts?

When a family business has dealt with these issues successfully, it has created a plan of action that everyone in the firm can work with to reach the company's goals.

Strategic Plan Topics

The general themes of the strategic plan are similar to the company's vision—what do we do? who are our customers? and how do we best compete? But these straight-forward questions need well-considered responses.

A family business's strategic plan should address a number of topics to guide the company's efforts toward success. Some of these can be different from subjects addressed in strategic plans developed by nonfamily firms. They include

- **Succession issues.** The strategic plan for a family business should include how a successor to the company's leadership is selected. Whether family members should be chosen or preferred is an important matter for a family business to consider.

- **Corporate governance.** A family business strategic plan should address the question of whether outsiders should be named to the board of directors.

- **Family issues.** The strategic plan, for example, can spell out the family rules concerning the hiring of family members. It might also address whether non-working family members can own stock.

- **Goals of the business.** The strategic plan can address the values of the family by dealing with the issue of family reinvestment in the business. What is the growth potential of the business? Are there new markets or new products in which the business should be investing? The strategic plan should note the major opportunities in the marketplace and how the business will conquer them.

After the members of the planning committee have considered these issues, they should put together their recommendations for the future of the family business. These recommendations should be considered by the family, and the family should formally adopt (or reject) each of the recommendations the planning committee proposes.

Strategic Plan Goals

The strategic plan should include specific goals for the family business. The plan should identify what needs to be done. It should recommend a detailed project plan for each change, including staffing requirements, time frame, and budget. The plan should also set out ways to measure the progress of each goal of the plan.

The plan's directives should be detailed and complement the existing goals of the business. A strategic plan can make recommendations, such as the following:

- Developing or improving information databases for the company to keep track of customer purchases, buying habits, likes, and dislikes

- Creating or enhancing an e-commerce site to acquire new customers and provide current customers with a new way to transact business

◆ Identifying new markets in which to sell existing products and services

◆ Determining which new products and services to introduce in the marketplace

Implementing the Plan

Putting together a strategic plan for the family business is challenging and exciting, as well as difficult and time-consuming. However, the next step in making the plan work is even tougher: implementing it. Even though a plan has been thought out, committed to writing, and agreed to by the family, putting that plan to work requires a strong commitment from top management, especially the CEO.

Making the Plan Work

There are some important considerations to make a strategic plan useful for the family business. The CEO should be involved in the process, but he should not run the strategy sessions. Top managers should be encouraged to think about the well-being of the entire company, not just their individual departments.

The strategic plan should not look at every conceivable business opportunity for the family business. It should focus on the most promising of these opportunities. The family business should look at competition and what those companies are doing. But the family business should forge its own path based on its capabilities and strengths.

The strategic plan might call for new investments. The family business can acquire other companies that fit in with its core business strategy. Or the family business can decide to expand into a new business area. In either case, the family business needs to develop a financial plan to raise the capital needed for this capitalization. The financial plan has to be incorporated into the strategic plan to give a clear blueprint to top management of the impact the strategy will have on the firm's financial well-being.

Time Frame

The time frame of a strategic plan is usually at least from three to five years and is often accompanied by annual reviews. However, the implementation of a strategic plan is necessarily dependent on changing market conditions, including the competitive atmosphere and overall economic conditions. What works in an expanding business environment might not be the best plan of action when the country falls into a recession.

Financial Information

A strategic plan cannot be implemented in a vacuum. Information about how the family business is doing in the marketplace is needed. This information should flow into the company on a daily, weekly, and monthly basis.

Every day, managers of a family business should examine the cash status of the company, orders, and inventory. Each month, the company managers should receive operating reports and cash projections, and the managers should compare budgeted figures to what is actually happening. Also, the managers should look at receivables to ensure the company is not owed too much money. On a quarterly basis, the company should take a broader view and look at indicators such as *return on investment (ROI)* and the company's profit margin on its sales.

def•i•ni•tion

> **Return on investment (ROI)** is how much money is made relative to the amount invested. This measurement helps a company determine how a project is doing compared to other possible investments. ROI is usually calculated on a yearly basis.

Examining those financial measures helps the company managers to decide whether the company is profitable enough to carry out the recommendations of the strategic plan. In addition to those financial considerations, the family business should also consider other information not directly related to sales. For example, the managers should examine returns and customer complaints, which are early indicators of customer dissatisfaction. Sales manager reports should also be closely scrutinized because they give an indication of future orders.

Looking at financial and customer reports is especially important for a family firm. The family CEO and managers must balance the needs of the family against the business needs as detailed in the strategic plan. For instance, family members might be more concerned with maximizing their income than with launching new products. Minority shareholders, including family members who don't work day-to-day in the business, might want to see the business pay out dividends before it starts any new ventures. It is because of these family pressures that many family businesses take a conservative view of new ventures and new opportunities.

The Strategic Plan and the Family

Many surveys of CEOs have found that a major family business objective has been to keep employees happy, productive, and well paid for their work. To accomplish these goals, employees have to understand the strategic plan and be behind it.

Communicating with Employees

Suppose a supermarket business with seven stores decides to open three new stores in an adjacent state. This will be a significant expansion of the company business. Employees can be confused about how the company made the decision and, most importantly, what the expansion will mean for them.

Employees should be told about the expansion before the news hits the media. Employees should also be informed about how the change will affect them personally, especially whether the opening of the new stores will give those employees opportunities for advancement. A family business can have an informal working environment, but changes in business direction should be communicated in a formal way, in a meeting in which employees can understand the business changes without relying on gossip.

Achieving Family Goals

Another goal that CEOs have is to deliver financial security and benefits to the owners of the company. That is one reason family firms have historically been more conservative than nonfamily firms in matters of risk-taking and diversification. In the same vein, family businesses have often been vehicles for personal growth and autonomy for family members. The CEO and top management have to evaluate how new business opportunities might impact the personal growth of family members.

In a family business, top management is also concerned about achieving job security for family members and other employees. If the business expansion detailed in the strategic plan entails more risk than usual, executives must balance that risk against expected gains.

Review of Strategic Plans

Although most strategic plans have a specific time horizon, they are not meant to be written in stone. Changing financial conditions in the firm and the economy can lead to significant revisions in the plan.

Strategic plans should be reviewed every year to ensure they are being followed and also to delete or rewrite portions of the plan that have to change. Strategic plans are best used as a baseline for change that is tempered by actual business conditions.

When companies have done a good job of integrating the strategic plan into the business, they establish a *feedback loop* between the business and the family.

The family sets the cultural goals and traditions of the family. The strategic plan shows the business opportunities and costs of new ventures, and the management team reconciles the needs of the family with the dictates of the strategic plan.

def•i•ni•tion _____

Feedback loop is the way in which information is fed back into a system to give new results. A strategic plan needs to be revised by new information about the family's goals and finances.

Every year, the strategic plan of the company should be checked against the original vision and mission statement of the company. If the strategic plan strays too far from the founder's original view of the company, top management should carefully consider whether the new directions contained in the strategic plan are consistent with the family business's original goals. When a discrepancy occurs, the family should be consulted to ensure it agrees with the new direction of the family business.

Reinventing the Family Business

Experts agree on the need for strategic planning in family businesses. One study of 200 family-owned Illinois manufacturing firms showed that only 13 percent survived three generations. The firms that survived and prospered were the ones that showed the most planning and the greatest ability to reinvent the business each generation.

The firms that failed often lacked a coherent vision of the family's future. Those companies also became prey to sibling rivalries and the tendency among some family members to take all available cash out of the business rather than plan for the future. The firms that prospered were willing to set aside personal rivalries and short-term gain for the long-term success of the family.

One firm that prospered began its business life selling fresh fish to restaurants from a seaport's dock. The next generation began to use coolers to store and truck fresh and frozen fish and vegetables to various retail outlets. And the third generation expanded the family business to dry good storage and transportation. Now the firm is expanding into national markets and even exploring export opportunities.

Another firm began as a stationery supplier and then added furniture and interior design services. Now the company is opening stores to sell stationery, gifts, and cards. These two examples show how strategic thinking and planning helped to keep both of these businesses fresh as business conditions shifted over time.

> **Told You So!**
>
> Most family firms do not survive beyond the third generation. Reasons for firm failure include no strategic plan, the business's unwillingness to invest capital into the business, and squabbles among family members over management and policy issues.

The Least You Need to Know

◆ Through strategic planning, a family business can develop its best business alternatives for the future.

◆ Family businesses with a strategic plan will have a greater likelihood of surviving changing circumstances.

◆ The CEO and top management team must implement the plan with an eye to family finances and other family needs.

◆ The strategic plan should be reviewed every year and modified based on changing economic conditions and family goals.

Chapter 6

Day-to-Day Management

In This Chapter

- ◆ Handling relationships between the family business and customers, employees, investors, and suppliers

- ◆ The need for reliable information

- ◆ Monitoring the management experience of the next-generation family members

- ◆ Using a crisis management plan to handle unexpected management difficulties

Imagine you are a college graduate trying to decide on your first job. You have two offers—one from a family business and one from a nonfamily business. How will you choose between the offers?

The family business seems friendlier, more informal, more caring. The family business offers a lower starting salary but better healthcare benefits than the nonfamily firm. The nonfamily business seems more of a competitive environment, but one where you can climb to the top based on your own merit. The family firm does not have as many management opportunities for outsiders.

These descriptions are stereotypical, but they ring true. In general, the day-to-day management of family businesses relies on the involvement of family members. Outsiders can join a pleasant workplace, but they might not have as many advancement possibilities as they would in a nonfamily firm.

A family business that needs to attract qualified employees outside the family structure should pay attention to how managers interact on a day-to-day basis with everyone in the firm. In this chapter, we talk about how the family business handles the management of the company, especially when most of the firm's management is part of the family. We also look at how everyday relationships between management and the company's customers, employees, suppliers, and the rest of the outside world must be considered carefully. Getting every family member in the business on the same track is important for the family business to maintain professional and profitable relationships with all its constituents.

Family Business Owners as Managers

How a family business handles daily management activities is crucial not only for the maintenance of company profits, but also for the long-term survival of the firm. Creating an environment in which all employees feel they can succeed will make the firm attractive to new employees, as well as enhance the company's long-term prospects.

One of the distinguishing characteristics of a family business is that the owners often perform the top management roles in the business. Because of the overlapping nature of the owners and managers, family businesses are often run in a more conservative manner than many other businesses, with longer-term goals in mind.

When ownership and management are not aligned, a conflict between ownership and management can occur. This is commonly called *agency loss* because managers can have a different agenda from owners.

def•i•ni•tion

> **Agency loss** is the loss a business suffers when owners are not also managers. Family businesses tend to not suffer as much agency loss as nonfamily businesses because family members often hold top management positions.

Managers can become concerned with their own advancement and compensation to the detriment of the business. Managers can also be focused on short-term results and become prone to risk-taking, especially when their compensation hinges on quarterly or annual results. In a family business, there is not as much pressure to make the largest possible quarterly profit. The owners/managers have an equity stake in the long-term success of the business. Also, these owners/managers see the business as providing opportunities for succeeding generations.

However, there are also downsides when owners are the firm managers. Family members might be given jobs they are not qualified for, simply because they are family members. Compensation might be based on family connections, not performance. And outsiders might be less likely to take positions with family firms if they think they will not have opportunities for career advancement. The attitudes of the family business managers and the procedures family businesses have in place will determine whether the family firms are able to compete successfully with nonfamily businesses.

Relationship Management in Family Businesses

Many of the day-to-day management challenges faced by family businesses are relationship based. How management deals with customers, employees, suppliers, shareholders, and family members determines how successful the company is in the marketplace.

Managing Employees

Working with employees is crucial for the management of a family business. Among the issues management has to work with are salary, job promotion, evaluations, and communication.

One of the hottest water cooler topics in any business is employee salary levels. Despite admonitions from employers to not discuss salary and benefits with co-workers, word of salary discrepancies invariably leaks out. That is why it is important for management to develop clear standards of how salaries will be calculated.

Salary calculations can be different for different kinds of employees. For example, the sales force might be compensated partially by commission on completed sales. By contrast, someone in accounting might be compensated based on merit and/or longevity. The important factor is that the basis for compensation should be explained to all employees.

 **Told You So!**

One of the biggest complaints nonfamily managers have is that their salaries are lower than family members who perform equivalent tasks. Merit-based salary decisions increase retention of nonfamily members.

A transparent salary policy is especially important for a family business. Often in a family company, family members are compensated differently than nonfamily members are. Sometimes, the salaries of family members are all made equal, so as not to cause disharmony in the family ranks. Other times, family members are paid more than nonfamily members because family members want to keep most of the business's revenues in family hands. In other businesses, family members are actually paid less than nonfamily members to preserve equity and encourage nonfamily members.

All these policies invite dissention, either among family members or nonfamily members. The best policy is to compensate family members and nonfamily members on the same criterion: job performance. If employees see that merit is the basis of compensation (and promotion), then nonfamily members will be more likely to stay with the company.

Employee Complaints

Employee complaints are always part of any business. Evaluating complaints made by nonfamily members can take some delicate handling. First, if the complaint is against a family member, the family business should take care that the complaint is handled in a way that does not give preference to the family member. This is especially true if the complaint involves any form of sexual harassment or sexual discrimination. In those cases, it is important for the family business to address the problem quickly and in a nonbiased way. It is often important to have a professional outside the family business evaluate the charge and practices of the family business.

Complaints by family members should also be taken seriously. A procedure for handling complaints should be in place, as should an appeals process, so that all employees know that their complaints will be taken seriously.

Employee Evaluation

Evaluation of employees is another crucial area for any business. An annual performance review is standard in many large businesses. However, employees should not have to wait a year before they are made aware of how they are doing. If an employee performs well, she should be complimented on the spot. If there is a problem, or if an employee needs to modify her behavior, the problem should be addressed immediately, rather than being left to fester.

Evaluations in a family business are especially crucial for nonfamily members. All employees should know what their career paths might look like. If an outsider does not have a chance of entering the senior management ranks, it is only fair to let that employee know at a fairly early stage in her career. Not every employee aspires to be CEO. Many do not want the headaches that go with having a top job in a business. But it is crucial that employees know which career paths are open to them.

Evaluations are especially crucial as part of the succession planning for a family business. Even though a CEO and the top management team have identified a successor CEO, the evaluation process makes it clear to that successor where she has to improve. If performance evaluations are low, the current CEO and management team might want to revisit the question of succession.

Family members should know how their work will be evaluated. Often in a family business it is implicitly understood that a family member will be offered the top management jobs. But all family members should understand how the process will work, and whom among the next generation will be considered for leadership roles. Often, companies advise or require family members expecting top management positions to work several years outside the family business to show they can succeed in another environment. And sometimes family members are encouraged to develop skills or obtain an additional academic degree if they want to rise to a top position in the family business.

Suggestion Box

Any manager who gives evaluations should be trained in how to handle the evaluation process. Evaluations can help under-performing employees learn how to improve their work. Successful employees can learn how much their good work is appreciated by management.

Some family businesses make the decision that nonfamily members are eligible for the CEO and other top management positions. In that case, evaluations are a necessary part of forming a plan of succession to top management jobs.

Working with Customers

Customer relationships are a crucial factor in the day-to-day management of family businesses. Customers are the lifeblood of every business. Many family businesses have deep roots in the community, so customers tend to be more loyal but also have higher expectations for a family business.

Some customers prefer dealing with a family business because they can interact directly with the owners of the company. When a customer asks an owner of the business whether a special deal can be made, the answer can be instantaneous. In a family business, family members in management must be clear on who is able to represent the business and adjust the usual policy for preferred customers.

A manager in a family business must keep track of income from customers, including sales, orders, and accounts receivable. But the manager must also take into account customers' opinions about the company. Customer complaints, suggestions, and compliments must be addressed in a timely fashion. One way to effectively gauge customer satisfaction with a family business is through *focus groups*.

In addition to evaluating and responding to feedback from customers, family businesses should have a strong marketing presence. It is important that the marketing message from the business reinforce the "family" message: the family ties to the community and the personal service that the business delivers.

def•i•ni•tion

Focus groups are periodic gatherings of customers to ascertain their reactions to a family business. Focus groups should consist of 6 to 10 customers who are encouraged to criticize business practices they do not like and to provide suggestions on how the business could improve.

A family business can reinforce the family message to its customers in several ways. Top managers of the company who are also family members should personally reply to customer complaints and suggestions. Letting customers know that the business is like a family delivers a message of friendliness, community involvement, and responsiveness to customers.

The Importance of Suppliers

Suppliers are another audience for the family business. Suppliers are critical for a number of reasons. Without timely delivery of quality merchandise, businesses suffer. Many day-to-day management decisions concern the delivery of merchandise, the quality of the goods delivered, and the payment for the goods. Family businesses have to develop trust with their suppliers to remain profitable.

Some family businesses like dealing with suppliers who are also family businesses. A mutual respect and trust often exist between such businesses, as does an informality that helps the parties work out problems that might occur.

Dealing with Investors and the Family

Family business managers must also always be mindful of investors in the business, including other family members. Managers must keep two thoughts in mind—"What's good for the business?" and "What's good for the family?" Sometimes these two cannot be reconciled and a meeting of the family is needed.

For instance, a competitor might approach the family to talk about a merger or a sale of its company. From a business perspective, the merger might make a lot of sense. But it may not be clear that the merger would bring benefits to family members. A consolidation might involve layoffs and reduce opportunities for advancement in the merged company.

In such a case, the manager might want to call a meeting. Such important managerial decisions should be reviewed by top management. If the decision involves a major business expense or has the potential to change the business, a family meeting might be necessary to decide on the possible merger.

How management handles decisions involving family members corresponds somewhat to the stage of development the family business is in. Young companies without many employees are usually dominated by the founding CEO. This manager usually feels that the business is his. The founding CEO often makes decisions—including decisions that have a large impact on the company's future—without consulting other family members. At this stage there is a strong identity between the company and a founding CEO.

As a company matures, important decisions often are made by several family managers. If a decision involves the future of the company, or if the company is preparing to go in a new direction, a family meeting might be convened.

When a family business is large, a different dynamic exists. Some, if not all, of the management team might be outsiders to the family. Often an independent board of directors must be consulted for important decisions. The family might be consulted only on decisions that involve the sale of stock or sale of the whole business.

Day-to-day management thus involves mundane matters but also can involve decisions that have an impact on the family business for years to come. A manager of a family business must have the ability to make large and small decisions and know which other family members have to be involved in the decision-making process.

The Importance of Information

To make correct managerial decisions, family business managers need information. Some of that information needs to be supplied on a daily basis, while other information can be reviewed on a quarterly or yearly basis.

What Data Managers Need

The types of information family business managers need include:

- Sales information from the company

- Margins on sales and cash flow

- Cost and availability of supplies

- Industry sales figures

- The family business strategic plan for growth

- What competitors are doing

Although some of this information will not affect the day-to-day management of the company, it is important for managers to see trends in sales, profits, industry results, and other indications of profitability of the company. By closely monitoring financial results, managers can prepare the company and the family for the future.

After sales trends, expense figures, and competitors' plans become clear, managers can start making strategic decisions for the company. Those decisions should be in line with the strategic plan the company has developed.

Information and the Strategic Plan

Managers should inform the family of any deviation from the strategic plan. Often in a family business, the strategic plan involves decisions that will impact the fortunes of family members. For example, if the company is in a growth period, dividends to family members might have to be cut or postponed to have enough internal capital to fuel the growth. If strategic assumptions or the strategic plan is changed, family members should be advised of the change. In some instances, family members should be given a voice in the decision-making process.

The involvement of family members will depend on the stage and structure of the family business. In the start-up phase, the family business acts more like a nuclear family. Children may be consulted in big family decisions, but often the parents make decisions and then inform the children. Likewise, in the beginning stages of a family business, the CEO often takes the initiative and makes important business decisions without consulting other family members.

Delegating Decision-Making

As time goes on and the family business expands, management responsibilities are divided up. When that happens, management decisions might be made on a consensus basis, as more family members have a stake in the management of the company.

However, the founding CEO might be reluctant to delegate managerial control for several reasons:

♦ CEOs might fear that delegating control to managers will threaten company success and lessen the value of their stake in the companies.

♦ Managers constitute overhead expense, which dilutes profits, especially in recessions and tough economic times. CEOs in family businesses therefore often strive to keep the number of managers low.

♦ CEOs often feel that managers' decisions are unproductive. Therefore, they might dislike giving managers too much authority.

♦ Because many CEOs have little formal management training, they might rely on "informal" management policies that make ad-hoc decisions. These CEOs can feel that a lack of formality gives them the flexibility to manage difficult circumstances. However, managers might view this informality as giving the CEOs the ability to undercut their decisions.

Separating Responsibility

Even CEOs who distrust other managers have to divide responsibilities as the business grows. For small but expanding family businesses, responsibilities might be divided by functions of the business. This makes sense when a number of members of one generation are running the family business. Using the example of a family manufacturing business, the founder had five sons, all of whom were interested in management positions in the family business. To divide responsibilities among the siblings, each was assigned a specific area. One son was in charge of sales and marketing. Another managed the transportation systems in the business, while another brother handled the firm's financial needs. Yet another brother had responsibility for the computer system. The eldest brother had overall responsibility for operations, but he would never make an important decision without consulting his brothers.

By giving each member of the family a clearly delineated area of responsibility that matched with his expertise and interests, the company was able to retain all the siblings within the family business. Many family businesses use this technique to make room for the new generation of family management.

Encouraging Entrepreneurship

When there are too many family members to handle the needs of a particular family business, which often occurs by the third generation of a family business, a new solution is necessary. Because not every cousin can rise to the top of the company, some family businesses encourage third-generation family members to take a more entrepreneurial route. The family can provide seed capital and other resources for family members to start new companies. Sometimes the family business takes a substantial stake in this new business in return for a capital contribution. This helps diversify the family business's assets and encourage other risk-takers in the family to start their own enterprises.

One of the most important functions managers can perform is to train the next generation of managers in the family business. To learn how to manage on a day-to-day basis, younger family members have to be given responsibility. Their duties can be gradually increased. Meanwhile, more experienced managers can monitor their progress and give suggestions for improving their performance.

Creating Apprenticeships

Apprenticeship is a valuable method for teaching younger managers how to perform their jobs; it also gives those family members a close view of how an experienced manager handles difficult situations. The apprenticeship also helps new managers learn about the family business culture and traditions.

Apprenticeship programs are also useful for making sure the current generation is comfortable with a new generation of managers. By having frequent contacts with the management trainees, the current generation of leadership can make more informed choices about who is qualified to lead the company in the future.

Confronting Crises in a Family Business

Crisis management is one of the most important management responsibilities for a family business. The crisis can be personal: the CEO or another important executive in the family business could die suddenly or suffer a major health problem. The crisis can be related to business trends: the economy can be in a severe downturn or the industry can be depressed. The crisis can relate to business decisions: one of the company's products can have cost overruns or sales for another product can be far below expectations.

When a crisis occurs, management's response is crucial. In a family business, several crucial decisions must be made immediately:

- **Who should be told about the crisis?** The more people who are involved, the greater the chance of word getting out. Information flow is critical to managing a crisis situation.

- **Should the family be involved?** In a family business, family members want to be informed about significant business changes. The management team has to decide whether to let all the family members know about the current situation.

- **Should a statement be given to the media?** If there is a good chance of the crisis becoming public knowledge, thought must be given to how to handle press relations. A statement to the press is often more helpful than ignoring media inquiries.

If the crisis goes to the very core of the business, customers and employees must be informed. Before issuing any press releases, a meeting of employees should be held so everybody is aware of the official company response to the crisis. A letter or an advertisement to the public might be necessary to have the company's version of events conveyed without the filter of press coverage.

In major crises, a family meeting should be convened. Family members have the most to lose when a crisis hits the family business, and their views should be solicited.

The Least You Need to Know

- A family business manager must spend each day handling problems and concerns of employees, customers, suppliers, and investors.

- To make informed decisions, managers need a constant flow of data on company operations.

- As the family business grows, the CEO will delegate some management decisions to facilitate business growth.

- Apprenticeship programs help next-generation family members learn the business under the current generation's guidance.

- Handling crisis situations in a family business often involves information meetings with family members and key employees.

Personnel Issues for Family Members

In This Chapter

- ◆ Developing the next generation of family business leaders
- ◆ Policies for hiring family members
- ◆ Careful treading in the minefield of family member compensation
- ◆ When the family business needs a personnel department

A television ad shows two young boys walking along a rural road. One says to the other, "No one ever asks me what I want to do when I grow up." The other boy responds, "Well, when your name is Smucker and you live in Orrville, Ohio, everyone just knows what you'll do."

That image of the children just naturally working in the family business is cultivated by the J. M. Smucker Company, founded in 1897 and managed today by members of the fourth generation of the Smucker family. Its brand is built on the idea of small-town family folksiness, despite the fact that the company is a multibrand, multimillion-dollar corporation that is the U.S. industry leader in the categories of jams, jellies, peanut butter, shortening and oils, ice cream toppings, and more.

What Smucker's doesn't tell you in that charming advertisement is how risky it can be to bring family members into the family business. When the young Smucker boy grows up, should a place be saved for him in the company or should he have to earn it? Should he work somewhere else first? Are the salary considerations for a family member different than for nonfamily employees? How should company stock be divided among family members who work in the business?

These and other personnel-related issues for family members in the family business are discussed in this chapter. While there are several schools of thought and many practices being used by family businesses, we offer some commonsense advice to help your family business deal with some of the trickiest issues you can face—hiring, firing, promoting, and paying family members.

Business-First Approach

Most experts who advise family businesses agree that successful family businesses need to adopt a business-first approach to management issues. We have discussed this idea throughout this book. Family business decisions are best made based on how the business will benefit.

Nowhere is this more true, or more difficult, than in the decisions that relate directly to how family members are handled as employees of the business. The kinds of management decisions that really "hit home" for the family business are in the general field of personnel. These include the subjects of:

- Hiring
- Firing
- Promotions
- Demotions or reassignments
- Job responsibilities
- Qualifications for the job
- Setting salaries
- Bonuses
- Other compensation
- Health insurance
- Noncompensation perks (such as a company car)

Naturally, these are important considerations for any company. Making bad decisions in any of these areas can be costly and can lead to a firm's failure if left unchecked. But for a family business, these personnel considerations can become personal.

Working with your loved ones is one of the benefits of being part of your family's business. But when you have to choose between doing what's best for the business and making a family member happy, the conflicts can be too intense.

Family businesses often have unwritten rules about hiring, salaries, and perks for family members, but they are usually reluctant to make them firm policies. In general, if you adopt a business-first approach to all personnel decisions, including the ones that involve family members, you'll be guided by a steady hand.

Training Family Members as They Grow Up

In most families that have family businesses—whether they plan to do it or not—the family talks about the business during family time. For example, our family spent the majority of every dinner with Mom, Dad, Aunt, and Uncle discussing every sale made that day—how they convinced a customer to buy one more item, how they finally sold that very expensive piece of merchandise they thought they'd have to put on sale, which customers were especially hard to please that day, and so on.

Many families involve their children in the family business in the same way we were involved—as soon as we were old enough, we started working after school and on weekends. One of my sisters was a born salesperson. The other was a natural at buying. I was best in the back office. But we knew the business was part of our lives and the family expected us to help out. In doing so, we all learned a lot about how businesses are run.

> **Told You So!**
>
> It's not a good idea to force a family member to work in the family business. If he doesn't enjoy the work, he will resent the business, at best, and at worst, will be a poor performer. Instead, let family members know that the family business is an option, but he should consider other options, too.

Developing Good Work Habits

What should a family business do to ready the next generation to work in the family business? When children are young, they can learn good work habits that will serve them well as they grow. Babysitting, lawn mowing, and newspaper routes are all tried-and-true methods of earning a buck and learning the value of working hard.

Jobs in the family business can accomplish the same goal, especially if the child's immediate boss is not Mom or Dad. Parents might be likely to let a poor-quality job slide "just this once." Or they might be harder on their own children than on other employees to ensure they aren't showing favoritism.

Families can foster leadership and teamwork skills by encouraging and supporting children in their sports teams, scouting, or other community-based organizations. These activities can help set a firm base for key business skills as a child develops.

Teaching Young People About the Business

If families want involvement in the family business from the next generation, they have to do more than have dinner-table conversations. At a young age, children should learn that the business premises are a serious place, not a place to play. Employees of the business are to be treated with respect at all times. When young children grow up understanding that the family business is important, they develop a respect for the business.

Teenagers working in the family business can learn about the business itself. Although they won't be given responsible positions, they can learn the business from the ground up, handling at first the simplest jobs available and moving into more complex tasks as they get older. Many family businesspeople today say that their exposure to the business as children helped them develop their eventual interest in the business.

Danger of Entitlements

Sometimes families who own family businesses can be very generous with their children—maybe to a fault. Grandparents might decide their grandchildren would love a new pool and use proceeds from the family business to build it. It's not uncommon for the family business to fund interest-free mortgages for the younger generation, with the rationale, "They need the money now—let's give it to them." The problem with this kind of thinking is often that the business really needs that money. This lack of business-first behavior can put the family business in jeopardy. Many are the family businesses that have failed for this reason—so to speak, killing the goose that laid the golden eggs.

Children raised with the experience of receiving entitlements from the family business are unlikely to grow up with the best interests of the business in mind. Rather, they will learn from their parents' and grandparents' behavior that the family business is a piggy bank to be robbed whenever we have something special we want. The family that stops investing in the business in favor of investing in the family desires is playing a dangerous game with its business and teaching its children the same bad habits.

Hiring Family Members

When it comes to hiring family members into the family business, most people wouldn't even question the idea. Naturally family members would work for the business—isn't that what makes it a family business? But in keeping with the business-first approach to personnel matters, the decision to hire family members is full of complex issues.

Most people who belong to a family with a family business feel a certain sense of entitlement to a job at that business. After all, the company needs employees, and you might have worked there in the summer as a teenager. Why wouldn't the business want you now that you're ready for full-time employment?

When Nepotism Is the Right Policy

We've talked about one of the benefits of having a family business as its ability to easily attract employees, also known as family members. They can be a ready workforce when the business needs them. *Nepotism* as a family business hiring practice can have its benefits.

Despite its negative connotations, nepotism, if applied sensibly, can be an important and positive practice in the startup and formative years of a family firm where complete trust and willingness to work hard are critical for its survival. Family members are often willing to put in long hours for little or no immediate reward. They recognize that helping to build a successful family business will bring them money down the road. Outsiders will not necessarily share that vision.

def•i•ni•tion

Nepotism is the practice of appointing relatives to positions in the family business.

Hiring family members often means a shorter learning curve for those employees. Family members have already learned a lot about the business, its culture, and the expectations of the company, just by being part of the family. They know what to expect when they enter the firm, and they are more likely to be satisfied with what they find. They tend to be loyal to the company because of their family ties.

But as a family business becomes more successful, hiring decisions are best made based on the qualifications of the job applicant. That can mean that cousin Ron, who hasn't cut his hair or beard since age 16, may not be the best choice to meet customers if the business is selling hearing aids to elderly folks. Can (or should) you employ Ron? Maybe, if Ron is willing to change his appearance or take a job without customer interface. Or if Ron has learned some specific technical skills that are necessary in the business. But most experts would advise that the family business has no obligation to hire Ron just because his grandparents founded the company.

One company that understands the value of family connections in its hiring decisions is the Thomas Publishing Company, publishers of industry product information. A family-owned and managed company in New York for more than 100 years, the firm welcomes applicants who are both Thomas family members and family members of current employees. No applicant is a shoo-in, however; they have strict employment policies and standards. And family members don't report directly to other family members, to eliminate the appearance and possibility of favoritism. Their experience has been a lower turnover rate in their staff and better job performance because family members who are hired feel they are under more scrutiny and must do an even better job to prove they weren't hired just because of their family connections.

Policies for Hiring Family Members

Family businesses take many approaches to how they handle hiring relatives. Policies vary from company to company and are often associated with the size and longevity of the family firm. Smaller family businesses often don't have a policy until a specific instance arises. Some larger companies use the formal mechanism of a family council to establish guidelines for the hiring of family members. Because this is a key issue that affects family members, the family council can be an appropriate arena for debating the company's policy on hiring relatives.

Sometimes a larger family business prefers to have no specific policy on hiring family members. Those companies don't want to send their employees a message that there will be any special treatment for family members. They authorize their personnel departments to handle employment decisions for the firm and keep the family out of the policy-making altogether.

The J. R. Simplot Company is one family-owned company that does not encourage family members to work there. The company, founded by J. R. Simplot in 1923, is a large agricultural products business. Three Simplot children sit on the firm's board of directors, but family members are given no preferential treatment for employment.

Family Stats
An informal survey taken by *Family Business Magazine* showed that family businesses tend to develop formal guidelines for hiring family members only after they have grown to a certain size, which varies based on industry. But very large family companies tend to have no special rules for employment of family members, choosing instead to have employment decisions handled the same way for family and nonfamily members alike.

As a family grows over time, policies regarding the hiring of family members can become difficult to maintain. The original founder might have set the tone for hiring family members with an unwritten rule of "We'll always have a place for you in the business if you're part of the family." But a family three or four generations removed from the business founder might have many members who want to be part of the business. If the business is small, there might not be adequate opportunities for all the brothers, sisters, nieces, nephews, and cousins who want to come aboard—not to mention their spouses. And if the firm has grown to be a large one with many employees from outside the family, those outsiders can feel resentful of family members who breeze in and take jobs that might otherwise go to deserving employees who aren't part of the family.

Working Outside the Family Business First

Many family businesses today agree that the best family employees are the ones who started their careers working at another firm. In fact, some family businesses have gone so far as to make it a condition of employment for family members.

Much can be gained when a family member in the next generation is encouraged to work outside the family business when seeking that first full-time job.

Building self-esteem. The young person has a chance to make it on her own, without being the boss's kid. Other people will accept the young person's business capabilities more readily and see his job performance as a real achievement or failure. If your child meets with success in carrying out job responsibilities, experiences unbiased performance reviews, and perhaps even gets a promotion while working for another company, he will know he can do well on his own. Naturally, the young person should find and get the job without any family member's help.

Broaden experience. Working outside the family firm, and even outside the industry, is a great way to develop new skills and gain experience that might not be available inside the family company. When a young person starts his career at a company outside the family business's industry, there is less chance the family name will have any influence. Jeff Hawk, grandson of the founder of American Trim (a metal components manufacturer based in Ohio), did just that. After receiving his MBA, Jeff worked as a financial analyst for the Ford Motor Company. He says that the financial experience and training he received at Ford was great background for the family business. Plus, the experience proved to himself and everyone in the family business that he could get a job on his own.

Learn from early mistakes. Errors made early in a career with another firm won't impact the family business negatively. And it's also easier to rebound from mistakes that can be made by an inexperienced young person who is not overseen by family. Early errors made at the family business will doubtless be remembered by family members forever.

Young people who go straight to work in the family business often have trouble feeling adult separation from their parents. As most parents know, criticism from a respected mentor, teacher, or supervisor is easily accepted, but not when it comes from Mom or Dad. Parents might be too hard or too easy on their children in the workplace. When this happens, children can't gauge when their work is good or when it truly falls short. Dad could be overly critical because he sees his child as evidence of his impending mortality.

Parents might also encourage a child who is searching for meaningful work to settle down and join the family business. While well meaning, this can be harmful to a young person who hasn't been exposed to enough choices to understand what he likes or doesn't like. There are many sad tales of people in their 50s who wish they had tried a different occupation before settling for the family business. Later in life they feel they gave up their dreams for the business and often don't think they get the appreciation they deserve from other family members for sacrificing their wishes. As you might expect, someone who leads a family business and feels this way is most likely unhappy and transfers that dissatisfaction to the rest of the company.

If the young person is needed at the family business, there is another way to achieve some of the same benefits. He can simulate the experience of working outside the family firm by developing strong contacts at other businesses and organizations. By regularly meeting with contacts at other family businesses, volunteering for civic organizations, and visiting other workplaces, a family member can learn from the world outside the family business. These activities can invigorate a young person who stays employed by the family business but wants to learn fresh ideas from sources outside the business. This kind of activity can be a great antidote to becoming insular and unaware of what is happening outside the firm, one of the downfalls of many family businesses.

Is there a danger to encouraging your children to work outside the family business first? Some family business leaders are afraid that they won't be able to "keep 'em down on the farm after they've seen Paree." But usually, after the child has gained experience elsewhere, he brings his new perspective back to the family business. Remember, you have been subtly teaching him about the benefits of the family business for years. Often, young people find that the family business is run better and more successfully than they had realized. Knowing that the option of employment in the family firm, where ownership opportunities might exist now or be possible in the future, is a great draw to the young person who has begun a career elsewhere.

Graniterock, a 108-year-old family company in California with 650 employees, has a firm rule about hiring family members. Before working at Graniterock, they must work at least five years elsewhere. Bruce Woolpert, president and CEO and grandson of the founder, insists that the family members should be sure they want to work in the family business before they do so. Working in another company gives them the opportunity to find out what really interests them. According to Woolpert, if a family member decides to stay with the outside firm, then that is the best fit for them, and they may not have been happy at the family business.

Educational Requirements

Should a family member be required to have a certain level of education before being hired in the family business? If the job requires it, yes.

Family businesses are notorious for taking on family members who need a job, rather than being necessarily qualified for the position. A policy that doesn't clearly spell out the education required for employment is a path to trouble in a family firm. Too often, the family business will hire the family member who lacks the educational background that's really needed. Although there is much to be said for on-the-job training, some skills are more readily learned in the classroom.

Sauder Woodworking Company in Ohio, a large family-owned and managed furniture manufacturing business, has 3,400 employees and annual sales of $700 million. Throughout the years, the company has developed rules for hiring family employees. It requires an undergraduate business degree if career goals are in management. It also requires family members to work outside the company after college for a time before entering the family business. Kevin Sauder, grandson of the founder, is currently president and CEO. Other members of the third generation hold senior management positions in the company. All agree that adhering to the standards of education and outside experience for family members helps Sauder maintain its strong position in the furniture industry.

Because specialized training is so necessary for many companies today, more and more family businesses require it for family members who want to work there. Whether the specialty is technical and related to the core business, or more administrative, such as marketing or finance, a family business can set a level of specialized training for family members as a condition for employment.

The beer magnate Coors Brewing Company requires family members to go back to school for training in their job specialties. For those in operations, it is likely to be an engineering degree. Family members in management are required to obtain an MBA—sometimes in addition to other degrees. The large company has made a practice of sending family members back to school for graduate degrees to ensure that those executives are fully qualified to handle the business demands. With family members from the fifth generation now employed in management positions, substantial competition exists for jobs at the top, both from family and nonfamily members.

Should Any Family Member Be Hired?

Occasionally, a family-owned company makes the decision that no other family members should be hired. Such is the case at PBT Communications, a 105-year-old, family-owned telephone company in rural South Carolina. Owned by six members of the third generation, the company employs about 100 people, none of whom are members of the family. Their reasoning is that they want to keep family and business relationships separate. The town in which the firm is headquartered is very small, and the owners feel it's best to keep spouses and other relatives out of the company. They feel in their tight-knit community, too many relatives working in the company would cause resentment among the current employees. Work disputes among family members can be brought home, and domestic problems can boil over into the workplace.

Of course, such a policy won't work in the long run if they want management to stay in the family's hands. But the issues raised by PBT are all too common for many small family firms. Many family members get along well and enjoy the special relationship of being both family and business associates, but it can be tough to separate the two when tensions arise. A family business that limits the number of family members it employs could be a healthy way to operate for all concerned.

Suggestion Box _____

If you are considering establishing rules for hiring family members in your family business, first think about whether you want to work with more family members at all. Ask yourself these questions: Do I trust other members of my family? Can my family handle disagreements comfortably? Does my family speak candidly with each other? Do family members have the skills and experience the company needs? Can I make decisions with my family, rather than making decisions for my family? If you answer "yes" to these questions, you can probably work well with family members. But if not, your family-owned business might benefit more from staff drawn from outside the family circle.

Compensation of Family Member Employees

Issues abound for family businesses when family members work there. Perhaps the most contentious is—not surprisingly—compensation. Who gets paid what and why might be the most discussed topic in any workplace. In the family business, add in the fact that workers are related to each other, and you have a very combustible situation! Let's discuss what's important for the family business in determining how to pay family members.

Equal Isn't Always Fair

A common way family businesses pay family members is to pay them all the same. They want to avoid conflict. "We have three kids and they are all working in the business, so it's fair that their salaries should be the same." "Each of our children has an equal ownership share in the business because they're our kids and it's our business. That's fair."

But equal isn't always fair. Fair is fair. And that means paying the family member the same salary anyone else would earn in the same job if her name weren't the same as yours.

Parents often think that paying their children equally will eliminate conflict among the kids. They want their children to have the benefits of their hard work. Sometimes they want to control their adult children, by offering salaries that effectively make them captive economically to the family business.

Here are two examples of the kinds of toxic situations that can arise when family members are paid equally:

- One sibling works for the company straight out of college and progresses upward. A younger sibling takes time off, goes to graduate school, and then eventually joins the family business in a specialized area. Both are paid the same, but the older sibling is resentful. "Why should we be paid the same? I've been here much longer and sacrificed my education so I could help the family business years ago."

- Three cousins with joint ownership of the family business draw equal salaries. They are equal owners of the firm. But the cousin who is seen by everyone in the company as in charge feels she should be paid more than the other two. "They can get equal distribution of profits as owners, but I should be paid more in salary, according to the job I am performing."

These situations, based on actual family businesses' experience, create a great deal of stress and turmoil within the family and the business. The family members involved will question why they are not being paid better than their relatives. Their spouses will doubtless feel resentful of the siblings or cousins and the parents who made the decision to keep their salaries the same. Often, these equal-but-not-fair compensation issues exist as long as the parents are alive and, sometimes, even after their death.

One large retail company owned and managed by a sibling group of two brothers and a sister had this very problem. While the eldest brother was the de facto head of the company, the parents had instituted a system that required all three to receive equal compensation. Even after both parents had died, the same salary structure persisted. The two younger siblings insisted that it was what their parents had wanted, and they were all three equal owners of the company. The brother, now CEO, continued to fume in silence about the issue. He felt taken for granted and angry. Only when a situation arose in the business that required the eldest brother to step in and resolve a financial crisis did he negotiate a change in compensation for himself.

Such difficulties can be addressed by a compensation policy that recognizes that equal isn't necessarily fair and fair isn't necessarily equal. A system that sets a salary range for each position based on the market rate for the position and the value to the company will make the decision on how much to pay family members simpler and fairer for everyone. Then the family business must adhere to the compensation system for everyone, including family members.

Often, the reason Mom and Dad institute an equal-for-all-siblings salary plan is to provide additional income from the business when no dividend is paid to owners. They want to avoid double taxation for dividend distributions, so they inflate salaries and pay equally to the children who have equal ownership in the business.

Suggestion Box

A compensation committee or board can help set compensation policies that will be accepted as fair to everyone in the family business. When the head of the family business shares that responsibility with others or even takes himself out of the decision-making process, there is less opportunity for family-based emotional decisions to rule.

A more equitable plan is to pay owners of the business through some mechanism that is not salaries. Bonus systems based on the profitability of the company can serve this purpose. As a company grows larger, dividend distributions might have to be put in place, as more family members have ownership shares. But salaries should be based on the job performed.

Sometimes paying a premium to family members who work in the business is not unwise. If the family member could command a higher salary working elsewhere, she should be compensated to that level. Most family businesses understand the value of having family members committed to the growth and strength of the business, and most want to continue family involvement in the business. For these reasons, it can be justified to pay a family member at a premium.

Told You So!

It's important to examine why family members are paid equally, even when they perform different jobs. There can be a reasonable rationale based on the outside job market. Sometimes when one family member starts working at the company years after the first, the actual market rate for the position has increased significantly. So the starting salary for the second sibling might be correct, even if it puts that sibling's salary as high as the one who has been there for years. Or that sibling might have earned an advanced degree that commands a higher starting salary in the market. If this is the case, there is no problem with paying the two the same, and this could help to lessen the resentment the siblings might be feeling.

It's a Salary, Not an Allowance

It's not uncommon for the head of a family business to pay family members according to their needs. "Cousin Bruce has eight kids, so he'd better get a raise this year." "Aunt Tillie just bought a new house and her mortgage payment is high, so we need to up her wages."

Sometimes family members receive salaries that are too small compared to their job responsibilities, hours, and position. This happens when the family business leader rationalizes, "They will eventually own the business anyway—they shouldn't draw a high salary now."

Studies show that most family businesses overpay their family members compared to the going rate for the job. Emotion is a strong determinant for compensation in family businesses. Perhaps it's because Mom and Dad feel guilty about working so hard to build the business that they didn't pay enough attention to the kids at home when they were small. They might want to reduce family conflict by adjusting salaries. Families often have a "that's the way we've always done things" mentality about their business practices that can keep them paying family members the same way others were paid years earlier. Or they can be reluctant to confront family members who insist they are entitled to a certain salary level.

Clearly, emotional decisions are not the best way to set compensation levels for family members. A company that pays based on what it interprets as best for the family is in for trouble. Either the employees will be unhappy or the business will suffer.

The advice we gave in the section about hiring family members is appropriate for paying them, too. Make decisions on a business-first basis, not according to what might seem right within the family structure. When possible, use the same compensation policies for all your employees. Pay family members based on their positions, their job performance, and what's appropriate in your market. Provide nonsalary *employee benefits* and *perquisites* (also called perks) on the same basis.

def•i•ni•tion

Employee benefits are compensation provided to employees in addition to their normal wages or salaries. Employee benefits can include but are not limited to group insurance (health, dental, life, and so on), retirement funding plans, sick leave, vacation, Social Security, profit sharing, employer-provided or employer-paid housing, daycare, and tuition reimbursement.

Perquisites are compensation in addition to regular pay and usual employee benefits, resulting from one's position of employment. The term perks is often used colloquially to refer to special privileges that are more discretionary. Often, perks are given to employees who are doing notably well and/or have seniority. Common perks are company cars, hotel stays, free refreshments, leisure activities on work time (like golf), stationery, and allowances for lunch.

Like it or not, there's plenty of water-cooler talk about salaries. Everyone compares salaries, even if we'd like to believe such things are kept confidential. And family members have many more opportunities to discuss their salaries with each other than nonfamily members have. Family businesses need to have a consistent rationale for how all employees, including family members, are compensated. Then everyone in the organization should understand the policy.

Establishing Compensation Policies

In the early stages of a family business, compensation decisions tend to be made using a "back-of-the-envelope" analysis. The head of the company makes the hiring decisions and sets the salaries. As more employees join the growing business, issues of equitable compensation practices arise, similar to the types we've been describing in this section. A set of pay policies that treats all employees—whether family members or not—will be necessary.

Many compensation policies are used in companies across the United States. Here is one example of a reasonable compensation policy: "All employees will be paid according to the recognized standards for their job in our industry in our area. Salary increases will be evaluated annually and will be based on job performance." Such a stated policy makes it clear to everyone in the company that salary rates for jobs are based on the going rate in the region, and raises are based on how well each person does in his job, regardless of family connections.

In a family business, it's advisable to establish a committee for compensation decisions that includes both family and nonfamily executives whenever possible. This gives a group of people decision-making power for setting salaries, which can help keep compensation decisions from being influenced by family matters. Include your employee benefits and perks in the same set of policies, so all employees understand the total compensation offered at the company.

When a fair system for determining compensation is instituted in a family business, all employees can feel comfortable with the pay scale. Start with the obvious: understand the going market rates for your company's jobs and decide where your firm wants to be on the competitive scale. Most companies choose to pay at the going rate for employees, but some pay above the rates. Others may pay more conservatively but balance the wages with generous benefits or bonuses.

Such a program necessitates knowing what all the jobs are in your firm and having (preferably written) job descriptions for each. Clear descriptions of each job's responsibilities will help you establish pay rates as well as evaluate each employee's performance in the job.

Some family businesses deliberately pay more than the market rate for jobs because, as family businesses, they know they will never offer the option of stock ownership. This is especially true in areas where the job market is tight and there is a lot of competition for skilled managers. At the Caster Companies, a real estate and self-storage development firm located in San Diego, California, the policy is to pay from 10 percent to 15 percent above market rates for managers. Brian Caster, president and CEO, recognizes the ownership limitations of his family business for upper management, so his response has been to pay better and provide more employee benefits than his competitors. Eric and Douglas Hagopian of Hoppe Tool, Inc., in Massachusetts take the same approach to attracting employees to their family business. They find out the market rate for jobs in their precision machine shop and then pay more to get the best employees. Although stock options aren't part of the compensation package, the company does offer health insurance, a pension plan, and profit sharing based on company performance.

When family member employees are involved, performance reviews are best handled by nonfamily members. Most people have a tough time telling their relatives some personal bad news, and even a glowing performance review can be suspect if it's cousin Barbara giving you the good report. Larger family businesses establish human resources departments to ensure the objective carrying out of these policies, but even small family firms can keep family out of the performance and salary review process. A mentor relationship between nonrelated employees can serve well in this purpose.

Karen Caplan, President and CEO of Frieda's (a California-based specialty produce wholesaler), changed the rather arbitrary approach to compensation her mother, founder of the company, had used. Although Frieda Caplan had been able to respond to employees' requests for raises on a more casual basis, Karen found that as the company grew, the need for a tighter system of compensation grew, too. She used surveys of the market rates for jobs to develop the company's pay structure. The company doesn't provide perks like company cars to anyone, including Karen, Frieda (now chairman), or Karen's sister Jackie, who serves as vice president.

Open communication among all family members in the business is key to developing a compensation policy everyone can accept. An outside consultant can be useful for mediating early discussions when a family business begins this process. Remember, family ties are strong and money is an emotional topic. When each person feels she has been heard, there is a much better chance of eventual agreement on a plan of action.

Pay Based on Company Performance

A compensation plan for family members whose fortunes are tied to the success of the family business should reward the overall profitability of the business. In this way, family members understand that the long-term success of the business relates directly to their personal pocketbooks. To do this, the plan should include more than just salary.

The compensation components for family executives can include such items as base salary, a shared-bonus incentive plan, and incentive pay based on individual targets. Each of these components can be tied to specific performance—of the company as a whole and of the individual. Salary, as we have discussed, should be based on market rates for the position held. If it is either too high or too low, the company will appear more or less profitable than it really is. If a family member is on track for eventually taking over the reins at the business, he could also receive stock options or shares as part of the compensation package. But ownership issues are not really part of basing compensation on performance, and you shouldn't confuse the two.

Evaluating Performance

When compensation for family members is based on their performance in the job, it is clear that some way to evaluate and measure that job performance must be instituted.

Job Descriptions

Job descriptions are needed for every position in the organization, so that everyone understands what is expected of each employee. Although it seems like a basic requirement in any business, many small family businesses neglect this step. Often, they are busy with the day-to-day work of keeping the business afloat. Job descriptions are one of those necessary evils that probably every company should have, but it can seem overly formal and not really necessary for a small family business. In a small company, people's jobs often intertwine, and it can be hard to delineate exact responsibilities, especially in upper management.

Writing job descriptions for every position in the company can be a daunting task. But you can only know how well someone is doing in the job when you know exactly what that job is. In a business, people need to know what is expected of them. If not, they assume that whatever they do is fine.

Performance Reviews

After clear job descriptions are written, each employee's job performance should be evaluated at least annually to determine how well she is doing.

In the smallest family businesses, this process is usually not formalized. The head of the company makes decisions because she is knowledgeable on a day-to-day basis with everyone in the organization. As the company grows, a more formal structure including job descriptions and performance reviews is important to ensure everyone is doing the job required.

Told You So!

When you require family members to undergo an annual performance review, you're not asking them to do anything more than a nonfamily employee has to do. If your nephew is performing his job well, he has nothing to be afraid of.

Although conducting a formal job evaluation of a loved one can seem harsh, this is another area where separating the family dynamics from the business is so critical. Most businesses can't afford to keep employees who don't perform well, and many family businesses have learned this lesson the hard way.

If at all possible, performance reviews should not be conducted by another family member. The direct supervisor should not be another family member. If need be, a manager from another area can be brought in to conduct the review, or someone at another level in the organization. It's better to give and receive feedback without the family filter getting in the way.

For the highest levels of management, the board of directors conducts performance reviews for the president, CEO, and perhaps other family members. Using the board in this way keeps the review process objective.

When done well, performance reviews can be an effective way to communicate with family members in the company. Goals are set and mutually agreed on. Later, the performance is reviewed to see if the goals have been met. This kind of job feedback is positive, is professional, and can build self-confidence. It also provides a clear rationale for pay and promotion decisions.

Some degree of jealousy among family members might still exist when many younger family members are vying for leadership positions in the family business. But setting up a clear structure that is used by everyone in the organization helps to alleviate some of those hard feelings.

Nonfamily members who are in the family business need to see that a fair compensation system exists. When family members are held to the same reasonable standards as nonfamily members are, employees have confidence in the objectivity of management.

The Least You Need to Know

◆ Separate business decisions from family decisions when it comes to money received as compensation for employment.

◆ Open communication among family members helps eliminate feelings of resentment when setting salary expectations.

◆ Everyone working in the family business needs to know how well they're doing.

◆ Clearly defined job responsibilities help everyone know what is expected.

Chapter 8

Communication

In This Chapter

- ◆ Keeping family member communication professional
- ◆ Family councils and family meetings
- ◆ Communicating with all employees, not just the family
- ◆ Reaching out to the media for favorable publicity

You might think that family businesses have no problem with communication issues. After all, family members have been talking to each other their whole lives. Who better to speak freely than family members?

That's not the case. In fact, having clear communication strategies and policies is probably more difficult in family businesses than nonfamily businesses. Family members have feelings and emotions and long histories with each other. Because of these family interactions, business communications can often be tough, as family members tend to make the business personal.

In this chapter, we discuss ways to help families in business with each other communicate more effectively. The more closely related people are, the harder it can be to say what you really mean. We'll get down to business on this topic.

Family Members Must Communicate

There are concrete steps family businesses can take to make communication in a family business go more smoothly. Communication concerns involve not only intrafamily dialogue, but also how family members communicate with other employees and the outside world.

Be Polite and Productive

Family members must adjust how they talk to each other in a family business setting. They must put aside their patterns of familial interaction, treat each other with respect, and try to listen as much or more than they speak. Words can hurt, and they can especially hurt in a family business setting. Both parties to a conversation should try to keep the dialogue positive and productive and focus on future plans rather than assessing blame for past mistakes.

There are specific ways to conduct business conversations between family members that can make the communication productive, not emotional.

Speak in the first person. Use the word *I* instead of *you*. When you start the conversation with a sentence like, "You are crazy for promoting Tim" the conversation is not off to a good start. The word *you* tends to put the other party on the defensive.

Suggestion Box

Talking with other family members in a business setting is difficult for many family members. Younger family members should be coached in how to have a constructive business conversation. That way, when a work issue arises, the family member will be prepared.

Emphasize how you feel, but ask the other person for his input. It might be better to say something like, "I'm uncomfortable with promoting Tim when he does not have the experience of the other candidates. What do you think?"

Be constructive and work with the other family member toward solving the problem. Trying to assess blame will not advance you toward a solution. But asking the other person if he agrees there is a problem will clarify the situation. If there is a problem, you can work on it together.

Listen more than you speak. Lots of family business problems occur because family members have preconceptions about what other family members feel and believe. If you listen intently, you might find what really drives the other person.

Find a few areas of agreement. Even if you still have a problem with the views of another family member, at least try to find some areas where you agree or your interests coincide, even if more meetings are required.

Parents should not address their sons and daughters by nicknames. They should not demean their children with phrases such as "You're not ready to take a leadership role" or "I'm the one who's paying your salary."

Family members should be educated about the value of in-office business communications being conducted on a strictly business basis. Family members should also talk as business colleagues. This businesslike approach is part of an overall communications plan to help family business members achieve unity about family business goals.

Mission Statement

If it doesn't exist, the family members should create a formal mission statement. A mission statement describes the goals of the business in a few sentences. This mission statement is an important document for family members, employees, and the general public. Often, family businesses put their mission statements on advertising because they want the public to know which values are important in their business. Creating such a mission statement is a great opportunity for family business members to get together and discuss family goals. Mission statements are discussed more fully in Chapter 5.

As part of this process, family businesses should consider developing a white paper to describe family wisdom and values. Don't assume that all family members are familiar with the history of the firm and its traditions. After a business matures, second- and third-generation family members might need to be reminded why the firm was started and what the goals of the firm have been.

Building Consensus

When family members are equal owners of a business, communication among them is paramount. Even though one family member might be CEO and have decision-making authority, key decisions should be discussed first among all the owners. Everyone who has an ownership stake wants to be informed and part of the ultimate decision. Building a consensus for the important issues will most likely be necessary in the ownership group—no matter how much day-to-day management responsibilities each person holds.

One 35-year-old partnership between two family members has lasted that long because of the partners' insistence on consensus for the key decisions. Their motto is "Each of us can do what we feel is necessary for the success of the business, but if one disagrees with something the other wants to do, we don't do it." With this credo, communication between the two partners is the key element that makes their partnership work.

Family Council

Creating the mission statement can be part of the task of a *family council*. A family council is a formal way to allow family members in the business to communicate with each other.

def•i•ni•tion

> The **family council** is the family group that decides family policy in a family business. A family council is separate from the board of directors, which makes business decisions. A family council makes family decisions.

The family council can perform a number of tasks for a family business. It can select board member candidates, determine employment practices, resolve family business disputes, and create a family business mission statement.

Family Council Meetings

In general, a family council should meet at least once a year. That meeting should include all family members 16 years or older, regardless of whether those family members own shares of the business or are employed in the business. The purpose of the family council is to make family decisions that affect the business and to ensure all family members understand what is going on in the business.

Family members or outside facilitators can conduct the family council meetings. The family council can be broken up into committees to address aspects of the family business. Members who work on committees can address the next meeting of the family council and report on their progress. If family members disagree on a particular issue, the family council can discuss it and even vote on which policies to pursue.

Family Council Decisions

The family council and/or the owners of the family business should decide and coordinate an ownership plan for family assets. It's important to have a policy decision on whether family members who do not work in the family business can own shares of the family business. Often, families make the decision that only family members who work in the firm can own business shares. Other family members can receive their portion of family wealth through gifts, inheritance, trust fund proceeds, or nonvoting shares.

As a family business matures and grows over time, some family members might not be able to rapidly advance in the company. When the business is in the third or fourth generation, there might be a number of cousins in the business who see obstacles to reaching a top management position in the company. Through the family council, these family members could be encouraged to try other opportunities, such as starting their own businesses or working for another company. The family council can encourage entrepreneurship by setting policies that loan money to would-be entrepreneurs for a stake in the new company. Such policies can be win-win, giving new entrepreneurs capital for new projects and creating new investment opportunities for the family business.

Communication with Employees

Handling communication issues properly benefits everyone in a family business. Studies have shown that communication is one of the strongest desires of employees, rivaling and maybe even surpassing pay and benefits. Employees want to be informed about what's happening in the business. Knowing how the company is making decisions is especially valuable to employees who are outside the family. Outsiders can be suspicious of family members' actions and decisions, often assuming family members are getting a better deal over the nonfamily member. When open communication with nonfamily employees is absent, rumors will fly.

By communicating to employees how management decisions are made and what criteria are used for promotions and pay raises, a family business raises the confidence and satisfaction levels of its employees.

Family Stats
Almost one half of family firms have a full-time employee responsible for human resource planning. (American Family Business Survey, 2007)

E-mail Communication

One way modern family businesses communicate is through e-mail and online chat, especially when the family business has several locations. In general, this has been a favorable development. E-mail is ubiquitous and online chatting makes face-to-face meetings less necessary.

Told You So!

Caution family members who have Facebook or MySpace pages that they should assume everything they put on the Internet is public knowledge. Embarrassing photos or messages posted on social networking sites can reflect poorly on the family business.

However, there are some things a family business has to look out for, especially in e-mail messages. E-mails tend to be very informal. And with a few keystrokes, e-mail messages can be sent to a large group of people.

The very ease of e-mail communication can be dangerous. Often, e-mail communications are terse. The meaning and import of such messages can be misunderstood. Also, many people use e-mail in a reactive way. If you are upset about something and write a snail mail letter, you should hold it for a day, think about it, and either revise the letter or not send it at all. People tend to react spontaneously with e-mail messages, and they often send messages they would not send on further reflection.

In a family business, these messages can be troublesome. When people communicate face-to-face, plenty of other messages are being sent beyond the words used. The emotion behind the phrases is communicated in the tone of voice and in facial expressions and body language. We have a fuller understanding of what someone really means when we hear and see the person in the communication process. E-mail has only the word component of the total communication package. Complaining about a family member in a face-to-face family conference is one thing. Doing it in an e-mail risks the e-mail being sent to others and causing hurt feelings.

Many family members are lax about controlling the distribution list of their e-mail communications. This can lead to inappropriate behaviors. And family members should remember that recipients can easily forward e-mail messages that should stay private.

Although e-mail is a great business communication tool, it is best for sending information to people quickly and accurately. But for family issues that are more delicate and emotional, e-mail is not the communication method of choice.

Family Business Meetings

Family businesses should hold family business meetings as a communication strategy to supplement e-mail messaging. Such meetings can take place around the dinner table. But it is better to have formal family-only business meetings at least twice a month to discuss how the business is doing. Each family member can discuss her area of responsibility. In larger family businesses, such meetings can be organized on a departmental level. But even in large firms, regular formal meetings of family members should be held to discuss firm issues and keep communication flowing among the members of the family.

Unless a family business crisis occurs, such meetings are best run with a definitive time period and a written agenda. By limiting the time for discussion of any one issue, the meetings become crisper and decisions get made and policy set. If more discussion time is needed on a particular issue, the parties whom the issue most affects can meet separately to hash out potential problems and opportunities.

Senior executives should always attend these weekly meetings, travel schedules permitting. Other employees can be invited to parts of the meeting when their input is needed.

Developing Communication Skills

Communication with other family members, other employees, and the outside world is important for a family business. Family members should be encouraged to receive training in communication skills.

Family business conferences often have special sessions or seminars on speaking skills. A number of universities around the country have family business centers that help build the presentation skills of family members. And public speaking courses are available from many commercial organizations.

To increase their communication skills, family members should be encouraged to join local clubs and organizations. Such organizations often give members a chance to make presentations to the group. The organizations also bring in outside speakers who can be role models for how a presentation should be made.

In addition to speaking courses, family members should be encouraged to acquire familiarity with presentation programs such as PowerPoint and Keynote. These programs enable a speaker to easily add photos, audio, and video to enliven a

Suggestion Box _____

Many studies have shown that public speaking is terrifying for many businesspeople. Family firms should make it a policy that executives should have to complete a course in public speaking as part of their job training.

presentation. Slides can also help cue a speaker to the content of the presentation, so the speaker does not have to rely too heavily on a written summary of the speech.

Family members who are trained in speaking before a group can assist the family when it needs to talk to the media. If a news story develops that affects the family business, a family member who has experience speaking can be assigned to handle the press.

Public Relations

Family firms are often involved in a news story that affects the family business, such as a fire at a warehouse, layoffs in the family business, a dispute with city government, or an employee in trouble with the law. When the media comes with questions, the family business should remember some important principles of dealing with the press:

- ◆ **Try to maintain good relations with the media.** Even if the story is not favorable to your firm, you have to realize that the media is only doing its job by trying to obtain facts.

- ◆ **Don't try to cover up or hide facts, because you will only hurt your firm's reputation.** A family business usually has a favorable public opinion. If something goes wrong in your business, the public might treat the business with sympathy because it is associated with a local family.

- ◆ **Try to remember that there is an upside to publicity.** The public will remember your company's name. Try to explain the news in a way that puts the best face on your company.

- ◆ **Consult with legal council because there may be liability in these type of events.** Management may want to consult with legal counsel before talking with the press in these types of situations.

Suggestion Box _____

If a serious scandal or very bad news affects a family business or its top executives, the family business should consult with legal counsel and consider hiring a professional public relations firm. A public relations firm can organize the response to the media and help develop stories to put the news in perspective.

Working with the Media

To avoid negative fallout from an unfavorable news story, companies should try to maintain a good relationship with the press. The Adolph Coors Company stayed out of the press for years after the kidnapping of a top company executive. The company instituted a policy that none of its top management team could speak to the press. This policy backfired when the company faced a bitter strike by the AFL-CIO. Because the company had avoided publicity for many years, the public had no knowledge of all the good things the company did for the community. The public was unsympathetic to the company as it faced a devastating strike.

A better policy with the press is to try to use the news media to promote your family business's image. If something good happens to the company, immediately send out a press release. If employees are promoted or make an important discovery, or if the company lands a big new contract or has expansion plans, send a press release.

Obtaining Favorable Publicity

Your family business should make top management available for press interviews. Executives should be encouraged to make speeches at events where there will be press coverage. Public relations can be even more effective than paid advertising in bringing out the strengths of your company to the general public.

Today, the public can be skeptical of advertising. A news story can give your family business a lot of credibility.

Developing Positive Stories

Here are some steps your business should take to make sure you are receiving the maximum amount of free publicity:

◆ Have top executives become involved in the local community. Make volunteer work mandatory for family members in the family business. Have the family support causes that are important to them.

◆ Join a family business forum at a local college or university. Family business forums can give your executives insights into the difficulties and successes other family businesses have had.

◆ Send press releases to newspapers, radio, and television stations on a regular basis. Media outlets are often hungry for news. Make sure you send a photo, if appropriate, and contact information in case the media has questions.

◆ When you do receive favorable publicity, make sure you reprint the articles, display the articles on your walls, post the news on your website, and send the articles to customers.

◆ Look for public speaking opportunities at local high schools and colleges as well as community groups and civic organizations.

Communication is an important strategy for any family business. Family businesses have to ensure that family members and other employees are informed promptly of events affecting the business. If the issue is important enough, customers and the press should also be informed.

Establishing good lines of communication is essential to keeping a family business healthy.

The Least You Need to Know

◆ Family members must develop good communication skills and be able to discuss and confront family and business issues in a businesslike way.

◆ A family council can set policy and give family members an outlet for issues that affect the family business.

◆ As a family business enters the third and fourth generation, family councils are helpful in keeping lines of communication open.

◆ A family business should develop a proactive approach to public relations.

Chapter 9

Marketing the Family Business

In This Chapter

- Branding the family business
- Choosing a family spokesperson
- Advertising the family business
- Marketing the family business on the Internet

During the Great Depression, there was a hot dog vendor who had a big sign on the side of the road that said "Frank's Hot Dogs Are Delicious! Turn at the next intersection and taste them for yourself."

Despite the Depression, the business was doing well enough that Frank could send his son, Frank, Jr., to business school. When he graduated, Frank, Jr., approached his father and said he wanted to join the family business. His father, impressed with his son's academic credentials, let him run the business.

Frank told his father that because the country was still in a depression, the business had to cut costs. First to go was the expensive big sign on the side of the road.

After the sign disappeared, revenues shrank and the business eventually had to close. Frank approached his son and asked him what happened.

"Dad," said the son, "I'm sorry the business had to close, but, you know, we are in a depression."

Whether we are in a depression, recession, or even when times are great, every family business has to market, advertise, and promote. You have to let the public know what your company does. When you stop marketing your family business, it will gradually fade away. In this chapter, we talk about how to make the most of being a family business in your marketing strategies.

Family Brand Marketing

Family businesses have several advantages over other types of businesses when it comes to marketing, advertising, and promotion. Although basic marketing ideas apply to all businesses, family businesses can capitalize on the unique nature of a family company to develop close connections with their customers.

def•i•ni•tion

A **brand image** is what an average consumer thinks of your company. A brand image consists of the ideas and experiences associated with a product or business in the minds of consumers.

A primary goal of all businesses is to develop a unique *brand image*—a way to separate what it sells from the products and services of its competitors.

Craig Kurz, head of The HoneyBaked Ham Company and grandson of the founder, understands the value of a brand for his family business. Although the company started with just one product and a patented slicing machine for spiral-cutting the ham, today's challenges and competition have forced the company to branch out into other food areas. When the patent on the slicing machine ran out in 1981, Kurz says the company was forced to talk not as a trademark, but as a brand. That meant it had to consider what was the essence of the business and find ways to extend along those lines. It determined that its brand was the quality of the product, not the way it was sliced. This helped the company broaden its product line to food that matched the hams in quality, value, and taste.

Brand Names

Creating a brand for a family involves some choices. First, there is the matter of the name. Suppose you are Josh Smith and you and your wife and children want to start a business selling widgets. You have leased a storefront but have to come up with a name.

Here are your initial choices for your name:

- Widget Workshop
- Widgets 'R' Us
- The Shop on the Corner
- Cheap Widgets
- Smith Widgets

Let's take a look at the list. Widget Workshop isn't bad (the alliteration is cute). Widgets 'R' Us is a rather obvious copy of a leading toy chain (you might even get sued if you use that name). The Shop on the Corner describes your location, but it doesn't do a good job of letting people know what your business is. Cheap Widgets gets the idea of low price across but might lead people to believe your widgets are not of high quality.

How about Smith Widgets? It should be a leading contender because it identifies your family with your company. If you're willing to put your name on the door of your business, it shows you have confidence in the products you sell.

All sorts of businesses have the name of the owner as part of the business name. Look around and you'll see Joe's Diner, Allen Lumber, Paul's Hardware, Alison and Paul Builders. All these are family businesses, and they're proud of it.

Many large businesses sometimes are named for their founders: Perdue Chicken, Wal-Mart (and of course Sam's Club), Ford Motor Company, Toll Builders, Johnson & Johnson, The Disney Company, and many more.

A family's name is enduring. It doesn't help to have a business named The Shop on the Corner if you move to the center of the block. Our hometown had a long-time business called The Downstairs Card Shop, located in the basement of a house. When the store leased space on the second floor of a retail complex, the name didn't make sense. It was eventually changed to The Downstairs Card Shop Upstairs, which led to some confusion. If the business moved again, would it be called The Downstairs Card Shop Upstairs Now on the Main Floor? If the owner had started with Ruth's Card Shop, she would never have had to change the name.

Told You So!

Don't pick a name for your business just because it sounds cute. For example, you might want to call your restaurant Anything's PASTAble, but not if your menu includes hamburgers as well as spaghetti. Calling it Bennett's Home Cooking incorporates a family name and is more appropriate for a restaurant with a diverse menu.

Creating an Identification Package

Choosing a name for your business is only the first step in establishing your brand. A brand is an image in your customer's mind of what your business represents. To complete the picture for the customer, you have to make sure your business has a color, a logo, and (if one fits) a slogan. These elements constitute the *identification package* of your business.

Choose a color for your business that will stand the test of time. The color you choose will be on your stationery, the signs outside your business, and the business cards you hand out. This color will stick with your business, so be wary of bright shiny colors and ones that seem blah and dull.

def•i•ni•tion

An **identification package** consists of the color, logo, and slogan for your business. These elements will reinforce your brand image and create a lasting impression of your business.

A **graphic artist** is a professional designer who assembles images and text to create a piece of commercial art.

Choose a color that everyone in the family is comfortable with. The color you choose will be tied to the family in the public's eye, so if Mom hates orange, don't choose that color to represent your business. A color can also represent the type of product you sell. For example, Ralph Lauren has Purple Label clothes that sell for much more than his regular clothing. Purple is the color of kings and conveys a feeling of quality and luxury.

You may also need a logo—a graphical representation of your store's name. If you are using your family name, such as Rodd Roofing, you can choose a typeface you think looks nice. A better bet would be to find a *graphic artist* who can translate your color(s) and name into an interesting visual image. Some family businesses create a logo that features members of the family or the family dog or cat. If people associate a certain image with your particular family, make it part of the family business. Some money spent designing your image will be money well spent if it helps the public form an image of your enterprise.

You might want to choose a slogan for your business. If you choose to have a slogan, it should be specific, not general. For instance, a slogan like "Service is our #1 priority" is too generic. It could apply to any business. On the other hand, a slogan for a family lumber business such as "120 years and still building" fits the business and conveys a feeling of trust that the business must be doing something right if it has been around that long. The lumber business could also advertise the fact that the business has been in the same family for all its 120 years, further conveying to the public a sense of continuity.

After you have your name, color, logo, and slogan, your family is ready to present itself to the world. Here's how you should do it:

As a family business, you should choose themes that convey what your business is all about. The Copps Family Supermarkets in Wisconsin had cartoon images of animals based on the Keystone Kops as a takeoff on the family name. The Copps, like their namesakes, would rush around the store putting away groceries, helping customers, and marking down prices. The image of the Copps was so warm and fuzzy and met with such a favorable consumer response that Copps kept the animated animals in its advertising for many years. Copps even created dolls and coloring books of the animals to sell to their customers.

Suggestion Box

Find new ways to use the family logo and slogan to advertise the family brand. Try giving away magnets, pens, notepads, and other small merchandise to help implant your family brand in your customers' minds.

Family Spokesperson

The spokesperson is the human face of the business. For someone to take on the role of spokesperson, that person must be willing and able to represent the family in any contact with the public or the media.

The role of the business spokesperson is an important one. A spokesperson conveys the idea to customers that they are dealing with a person, not an impersonal business.

Requirements of the Spokesperson

The family spokesperson must have the ability to talk comfortably to the press. If the public should know certain information about your business, the spokesperson is the one to deal with the media.

Told You So!

Some family members are naturally shy. If you don't like the spotlight, don't apply for the spokesperson job. The family spokesperson must show a willingness to be a public personality.

Other family members will have to realize that much of the credit and blame for the family business will fall on the shoulders of the spokesperson. Fair or unfair, the spokesperson represents the family.

There are many reasons for having a spokesperson. That person can articulate the values of the family firm. That person can be the face of the firm, someone to get in touch with if you have a problem. That person can also explain why the firm is having a big sale or introducing a new product line.

Choosing a Spokesperson

Usually, the choice of a family spokesperson is easy. It's the CEO or president. If Jane Rowe is the boss of Rowe's Furnishings, Jane Rowe is a natural to be in front of the camera and tell everyone why they should buy their furniture at her store.

But what if Jane Rowe doesn't want to be in front of the camera? She might be shy. Or she might prefer that her daughter Amanda take the leading role. If Amanda is comfortable speaking and can communicate family values, she might be a good choice to be the public face of the Rowe family.

A more difficult decision is to use a nonfamily member as the spokesperson of the family business. If family members are still involved in the management of the business, it might be strange to use a nonfamily spokesperson. Such considerations are not as crucial when you are dealing with a Fortune 500 company, but for most family firms, it probably makes sense to feature a family member as the spokesperson.

Or maybe several family members think they are the right person for the job and there is no way to pick one out without creating a lot of family tension. Here are several ways to deal with this situation:

- Ditch the notion of a family spokesperson and do other forms of advertising and marketing.

- Choose another type of spokesperson (such as a cartoon character or even a family pet) with characteristics that represent the family's values.

- Share the wealth and have several family members represent the family (a great old-time example of this is the brand image of the Pep Boys: Manny, Moe, and Jack).

The family spokesperson should appear on as many of the local media outlets as time and budget permit. These include: television—both local stations and cable TV—radio, newspapers, and direct mail. The company spokesperson should give a consistent message, emphasizing family values and traditions as well as sale and product information.

Advertising the Family Business

When you have your name, brand image, identification package, and spokesperson identified, you're ready to start advertising. A family business has specific points it can advertise to the public that a nonfamily business can't. Make the most of them.

Marketing Local Ties

One of the most important values a family business can advertise is its roots in the community. If your family has operated your business for 75 years, has hired 100 local workers, and is involved in many community activities, you should feature these ties to your community. These include plenty of things to highlight: your profits are not traveling to some distant headquarters; you've invested in the local community; and you have had close community ties for a number of years. Many of your customers will consider these points good reasons to do business with your firm.

But be careful of stressing your ties to the local community if you have any intentions of moving or selling your company. One large company that exemplified local commitment was Anheuser Busch of St. Louis. For five years, Anheuser Busch has been rated by *Fortune Magazine* as the no. 1 company in the beverage industry in "America's Most Admired Companies" and the "World's Most Admired Companies." Anheuser Busch is everywhere in St. Louis: it has sponsored the law school building at Washington University, the August A. Busch Conservation Area, and the city's ballpark. The company has 6,000 employees in St. Louis.

Anheuser-Busch's recent sale to InBev of Belgium generated waves of surprise in the St. Louis community. In the first couple of months following announcement of the sale, more than 67,000 signatures were gathered online to protest the sale of St. Louis' iconic company. One of the downsides of a strong local involvement is shock and resentment when a family business is sold or moves.

Communicating Family Values and History

Besides community support, your family firm can advertise other values to the community. You can talk about your quality of customer service; your "family" of employees; your support for local charities, causes, and organizations; and your ties to the traditions and history of the town.

These values should be communicated in all your business advertising. If the story is interesting enough, you could prepare a handout or brochure describing the history of your family business and how you have grown to be the company you are today. Many long-standing family businesses have a timeline on their websites that highlights the major events of the firm's history. Such a document further reinforces the feeling of family and continuity for the business.

A marketing advantage for family businesses can come when they are recruiting employees. For example, Major Brands, Inc., is a family business of more than 500 employees that distributes premium wines and spirits. Each year the company recruits at major business schools, especially in Missouri, where it is headquartered. The company incorporates the fact that it's a family business with family values in marketing to potential employees. That family focus has enabled it to attract top recruits over major companies such as Coca-Cola and Procter and Gamble.

The Family Business Anniversary

One aspect of your family business that you will certainly want to celebrate is your business anniversary. Whether you've been in business for 5 years, 50 years, or 100 years, an anniversary is a great time to have a party for your customers.

Suggestion Box

Don't forget to include your suppliers in your family business anniversary celebration. They might contribute to your advertising costs. Also, if you are having a party, invite your main suppliers and their families.

If your firm has not been celebrating its anniversary publicly, now is a good time to start a new tradition. If you don't have the records of when your family business anniversary occurs, pick August. August is a great month to have an anniversary sale: people are gearing up for the fall and no national holidays occur in August.

When you have a big anniversary to celebrate, such as 25 years, 50 years, or 100 years, you should plan your anniversary celebration months in advance.

This is a time to prepare a history that emphasizes your family's longstanding ties to the community. You can also prepare a month-long celebration of the family business anniversary, with special sales, entertainment, and surprises at the business.

Advertising on the Internet

More and more family businesses are turning to Internet advertising. Internet advertising gives these businesses more bang for the advertising dollar and space to explain all the special aspects of the family business.

Internet Advertising Advantages

The Internet is an ideal place to market and advertise a family business. Advantages to Internet advertising include

- ◆ Almost unlimited space to give a complete family history

- ◆ An opportunity to provide biographies and other information about family members

- ◆ A way to explain and illustrate family values and traditions

- ◆ An opportunity to connect with customers and let them express their loyalty to the family business through testimonials and other communications on the website

- ◆ A way for a family business to grow domestically and internationally

E-mail is an advertising medium particularly well suited to small family businesses. Family businesses can use e-mail as well as Internet-based communication devices such as blogs, frequently asked questions (FAQs), and live online chat to stay in contact with their customers. Also, the ability of home-based family businesses to sell products through Internet sources such as eBay, Amazon, and Google is giving new entrepreneurs a virtual marketplace in which to sell merchandise.

Suggestion Box _____

Your family business should have a website. If you can't afford a professional website developer or you like to do things yourself, you can explore developing your own site. Many sites on the Internet can help you create a website for your family business for little or no money.

Growing the Family Business on the Internet

Having a website can be an important way to grow a family business. In many cases, family businesses are comfortable in their current location. They know the area, the people, the challenges, and the opportunities. Expanding to other regions and especially to other countries can cause rifts in family unity.

The start-up costs of an Internet-based business can be far less than a bricks-and-mortar building. The Internet is the place where the family can test whether its products will be popular in other places besides its one location.

The web is the great equalizer. Small companies with great products can compete with the giants of industry. Dorothy Lane Market, a small, three-store supermarket chain located in the Dayton, Ohio, area, has developed a worldwide following for its specialty food products. A family business founded in 1948, its current CEO, Norman Mayne, has leveraged the power of the Internet to build Dorothy Lane's reputation much further afield from its Ohio roots.

The company sells its "Killer Brownie" and other food products very successfully through its website.

A website can open up a traditional family business to national and international commerce. For example, James Candy Company is a relatively small fifth-generation family business located in Atlantic City, New Jersey. It has an interesting history— legend has it that sea water foam washed over the original owner's candy stock and he fortuitously named his wet candy "salt water taffy"—and the name stuck. The James Candy Company website tells that story, as well as featuring the company's history, its family ties, and its commitment to the local community through charitable causes. In addition, the website lets customers from all over the country purchase its candy products.

Loyalty Marketing Programs

Another way family businesses have found to advertise is through loyalty programs. Loyalty programs give rewards to customers based on their purchase histories. The more a customer spends, the better the rewards he receives. Rewards can include tangible benefits such as better prices, but they also can include benefits such as recognition and better service.

The creation of a rewards card can reinforce the "family" brand. For example, in our family clothing business, Gordon's (named after my uncle Milton Gordon, one of the co-founders) in New Jersey, we had a gold card for customers who shopped in the Ralph Lauren department. These customers received discounts based on purchases. They also got advance notice of sales, private sales, and other special opportunities based on their participation in the loyalty program. One year, Gordon's teamed up with Ralph Lauren to host an actual polo game (the Ralph Lauren logo is a person playing polo). The customers were invited to free seats at the match, a luncheon, and a fashion show at halftime featuring the latest Ralph Lauren fashions. The party was by invitation only, and only Gordon's gold card customers were invited. The gold card for Ralph Lauren clothing at Gordon's meshed the two brands together for our customers. We benefitted from identification with the high-end clothing line, and it was one the most successful customer programs ever at Gordon's, driving sales for many years.

The Least You Need to Know

- A family business can use the family connection to create identification in the public's eye.

- A family spokesperson who is comfortable in the public spotlight can effectively communicate the family business values to the public.

- The Internet provides family businesses with growth and diversification opportunities.

- A loyalty program will encourage your best customers to spend more with your family business.

Part 3

Unique Challenges of the Family Business

Family businesses are known for having caring, comfortable workplaces, where family members and outsiders alike are treated fairly—"like family." But family businesses must pay careful attention to the needs of nonfamily employees and offer them enough opportunity to keep them satisfied.

This part explores the unique challenges family businesses face and gives you ideas that will help you solve your family business issues.

Chapter 10

Balancing Home and Business

In This Chapter

- ◆ Keeping the home place separate from the work place
- ◆ Women's new opportunities in family businesses
- ◆ Keeping your children informed
- ◆ The supportive role of grandparents
- ◆ Bringing faith into the business

One of the toughest tasks for a family business is to keep a balance between home and business. When the family's income depends on the family business, it is easy to think of the business as equal in importance to any family member. It's hard not to talk about the family business around the dinner table, or at family holidays, or whenever the family gets together, because so many people in the family are part of the business.

Today more than ever, husbands and wives work together as partners in the family business. It can be exciting and fun to grow a business along with a family, but the balance between work and family life can be difficult to maintain.

In this chapter, we examine how participants in a family business approach the challenge of creating a warm home environment as well as a successful business climate. We look at women's expanded role in the family business and how that might add even more stress to family life. We also take a look at how grandparents can help with aspects of home and business life and the role a family's faith can play in a family business.

Home Place vs. Work Place

When a family also has a family business, the two entities are closely related. Mom and Dad are in charge of the family affairs, and they're also in charge of the company. Kids do some of the household chores at home, and at the family business, they start to take on more tasks as they grow, learn, and mature. Grandma and Grandpa might have been the originators of the family business, and their roles in the family might be similar, too, as the historical leaders of the family. No wonder so much business talk spills over into the home turf for family businesses!

But a separation between home and the office is necessary for the sake of everyone in the family—not to mention for the nonfamily employees in the business as well.

Families with children in the family business often strive to make a distinction between the workplace and the home. For instance, children who work in a business might be more comfortable calling their parents by their first names at work, rather than Mom and Dad.

Adult children must be treated with respect in the office environment. A father or mother who remembers his or her child as a little boy or girl must set those feelings aside and treat the child as a colleague at work.

Business Success Does Not Necessarily Come Home

A successful family business does not guarantee a successful home life. Skills that work well in a business don't always translate to family skills, and money doesn't ultimately drive home success.

Businesspeople who are used to commanding others in an aggressive business environment can't use that same style to manage situations at home. The type-A businessperson might have to be calm and considerate at home. After all, employees are being paid and need the job, so they will put up with a difficult boss. Kids are another story altogether!

Keep Family Business Discussions Businesslike

Most people who own and work in their family businesses would recommend that families find ways to separate work life from home life. One way to maintain that separation is by having clear discussions about the family business with family members in a businesslike manner. Families should meet to discuss the family business on a periodic basis. Isolation can make individual family members work at cross-purposes. Basic family finances should be shared with the children, as should parents' expectations about their children working in the family business.

The discussions between parents and children should be concrete. This is especially crucial if the children are currently working in the business. When they are starting out in the business, children should be told what the parents' expectations are and what opportunities are available if they stay in the business.

The family should also consider putting its values in writing. The writing can be in the form of a mission and values statement, which outlines what the family is trying to accomplish with the business. Such a document can be valuable in giving new employees an understanding of the principles that guide the family business.

Keeping a Far-Flung Family Informed

To make a clean split between business and family decisions, many larger family businesses are now creating the role of the *family president* who is in charge of family matters.

The family president communicates with the CEO and top company managers to ensure that family issues are considered when the top managers make business decisions. "If you want a healthy family business, then you need to devote the time and resources to developing a healthy family," says Sarah Schmidt, the family president of the family that owns U.S. Oil Co., Inc., in Wisconsin.

def•i•ni•tion

The **family president** is a family member who is in charge of matters related to the family. The family president is in touch with the CEO and other top management officials as a representative of family interests and values.

U.S. Oil has put Ms. Schmidt in charge of communications with family members. Because family members are scattered throughout the country, Schmidt travels to personally hear the concerns and opinions of family members. She then communicates family members' concerns and feelings to the CEO and other top business managers.

To keep family member owners who do not work day-to-day in the family business informed about family business decisions, many businesses have annual or semiannual family meetings. These meetings provide family members a forum where they are informed about where the family business is headed. They can also participate in committees that address such issues as working in the family business, succession, distribution of family wealth, and philanthropy. By keeping family members apprised of the direction of the family business and involved in some of the decisions, more trust often exists among family members.

Opportunities for Women in Family Businesses

The role of Mom, creating a secure home life to balance the stresses of family business life, was a traditional role for women. But this has changed. Today's women have the same opportunity for involvement in their families' businesses as their male relatives. Here are three prototypes of women and the way each participates in her family's business today—quite a departure from 30 years or even 15 years ago:

◆ **Liza Leader.** Liza's father started a construction business 30 years ago. Today, Todd's Construction has 44 employees and specializes in school construction. Liza, now 28, worked summers doing some bookkeeping for the business while in high school and college. In college, she developed an interest in green construction and eventually convinced her dad to offer green alternatives to school systems planning new buildings. After working for one year after college in a sales job at a department store, Liza joined the family business and set up a green building department at the company. Now Todd's Construction is one of the country's leading experts on green construction and Liza gets invited to speak at trade associations on her specialty. Although she has a younger brother in the business, the family council recently decided that Liza would be the firm's CEO when Todd retires in three years.

◆ **Olivia Owner.** Olivia is one of three children of an entrepreneur who started a chain of car washes. The business expanded rapidly and now includes 15 car washes in three states. Although Olivia worked several summers in the family business, she eventually decided she was interested in education, went back to school, and earned a Master's and Ph.D. She now teaches English literature at a state university. But Olivia, 35, has stayed interested in the family business.

She attends family council meetings every six months. Recently, she was asked to help draw up guidelines on how family members could and should work in the family business. Olivia owns 15 percent of the company through stock she inherited, and she plans to stay active as an adviser to the business.

♦ **Cindy Carefree.** Cindy has never been interested in the family clothing business. Now 24, Cindy has worked winters at ski resorts and summers as a waitress. Cindy's family had a policy of children either working in the business or receiving a cash settlement reflecting the value of their share in the business. Cindy took the $300,000 she received, put most of it in the bank, and now is thinking about whether she wants to have a steady job or continue her current lifestyle. She has no interest in ever entering the family business.

These three prototypes of women represent some of the choices women now make with regard to their families' businesses. Women have a variety of opportunities to interact with the business, from a management role to an ownership role to a recipient of the wealth of the business.

New Choices for Women

Let's examine the factors that have brought women to the top of 24 percent of all family businesses today. The trend for women leaders in family businesses reflects women's increasingly important role in many areas of society. Half the new lawyers and doctors in the country are women. Two-income families are the rule, not the exception. And a recent survey of college and graduate students showed no difference in the percentages of women and men who wanted to enter a family business.

Women are achieving greater responsibility and success in family businesses for many reasons:

♦ Societal acceptance of women as leaders

♦ Women's success in other leadership positions, such as politics and higher education

♦ Increasing numbers of women completing college and graduate school

♦ The need for women to take leadership roles in second- and third-generation family businesses

> **Family Stats**
>
> Women in family business are no longer just the powers behind the throne. Over one third of family businesses are now preparing to have a woman in the leadership role as president or CEO.

Many women who stepped out of the workplace to raise their children are now jumping back in. Many have started home-based businesses, using the Internet and new communication devices to start firms that would have been difficult to put in place 20 years ago.

> **Told You So!**
>
> Why Women Become Entrepreneurs:
>
> ◆ A desire for self-determination and more flexibility in working and family life
> ◆ A wish for freedom
> ◆ Wanting to do things better than they were done at the previous workplace
> ◆ Hoping to use their own creativity to see a business grow

Continuing Problems for Women

Even though the outlook for women in family businesses is greatly improved, there are still some perceptions that have to be overcome and some challenges that are gender-specific. Many women would still say today that the business world is a man's world and women have to work harder, longer, and smarter to stay on par with their male counterparts.

> **Family Stats**
>
> Women make 77 cents to a man's dollar, according to U.S. Census statistics from 2005. African-American women earn 72 cents to the dollar, and Hispanic women fare even worse, earning only 59 cents for every dollar a man earns. At the rate the gap has been closing over time, the Institute for Women's Policy Research estimates equity will not be achieved until 2057.

Many professional women on the way up feel they have to prove themselves—not just to their colleagues, but also to themselves.

Many women attempt to be superwomen, trying to perform all the traditional family tasks while maintaining a high-powered job. At times, something has to give, and without a spouse willing to share equally in family responsibilities, this type of woman can feel that she is always working and living on the edge.

Women still dominate jobs that are relatively low-paying and not perceived as prestigious as male-dominated professions. In 2006, 96.7 percent of secretaries and

94.6 percent of childcare workers were women. By contrast, 78.5 percent of first-time jobs for Ph.D. holders in math-related fields went to men. This disparity continues, despite many recent studies that show women perform equally well on math ability tests as their male counterparts. Is there still a gender bias that keeps women from seeking and obtaining higher-paying jobs? The statistics show this might still be true.

Women more than men might also be pulled by the separate demands of family and business. They might feel a need to be a nurturer and caretaker in the family while performing simultaneously as a no-nonsense leader at work. Issues such as putting the children in daycare or trying to organize family meals might sometimes conflict with the demands of running a business. Making a business out of a family and a family out of a business can be a burden.

Family Stats

A recent survey of women showed that some personal costs and difficulties are associated with women rising to the top. Ninety percent of women surveyed believed they had to go to great lengths to prove themselves. And 80 percent reported difficulty balancing work and family.

Why Women Join Family Firms

Despite some significant problems, more and more women are joining family businesses. Some of the many reasons women seriously consider working for the family business include

- **Flexibility.** Family firms are often more aware of a woman's need to balance her family obligations with attention to her job. A family business is more likely to accommodate a family member who needs flexible hours to take care of the kids or aging parents or who wants to further her education. Many women start part-time in a family business and gradually transition to a full-time role as their children grow up or as they become more integral to the success of the business.

- **Comfortable environment.** Many women (and men) feel more comfortable in a family environment. There is often more of a balance between family needs and business needs than there is in a nonfamily firm.

- **Creating for future generations.** In a family firm, your efforts at work not only benefit you via a paycheck, but also help preserve the family business for future generations.

What Children Should Know

The roles parents take in the family business can have a tremendous impact on how children are raised. The accepted norm these days is for both parents to work, especially in a first-generation family business where there is much to do and not enough time to get it done.

Perhaps because of the increasing role of women in the day-to-day life of a family business, children today sometimes say they know their teachers better than they know their parents. But even though children might resent parents who neglect some aspects of family life because of business demands, studies have show that children are proud of their parents' business accomplishments.

Even when family businesses go through difficult periods, children tend to not focus on the negative aspects of a family business. In fact, many see the business as a security blanket. They see the money that flows from the business, and they do not concentrate on the hard work that goes into producing the money.

Learning the History of the Family Business

It is important that children know the lore associated with a family business—how it started and how it has grown. The family business is an important part of the family history that every child grows up with. Also, children's attitudes toward accountability, teamwork, and work ethic are partially formed by seeing how her parents perform in the family business.

 Suggestion Box _____

Try creating an album with information about the family business, including newspaper articles, brochures, photographs, company information, letters, and so on. Make the album available to children so they can become immersed in the history and accomplishments of the family business and family business members.

It is not crucial that children show interest in the family business when they are young. Many children basically ignore the family business until high school or later. Yet these very same children often decide in college or even years after college that they want to make a career in the family business.

Explaining Money Matters to Children

At some point when a child is growing up, the parents should explain to him what happens to the assets of the family business. In some families, only children who work in the family business receive stock in the business. Often, those families compensate for children not in the family business by providing other assets.

On the other hand, some families distribute ownership rights in their family business to all their children, regardless of whether they are employed by the business. In these cases, children who are not in the business are sometimes assigned nonvoting stock and the children in the business receive voting stock. As the children grow up, they should understand the arrangements made for them.

The Challenge of Stepchildren

The role of children in the business can become much more complicated when two people marry with children from previous marriages. A family's emotional ties can interfere with working relationships. Parents might be slow to accept the competence of their stepchildren. Ideally, blended families should work as a team, with everyone understanding the goals and objectives of the family business.

With stepchildren in the picture, it is often wise to set rules ahead of time and behave consistently toward all children in the business. Both parents must work together to ensure that all children feel they are being treated fairly in the family business.

The Important Role of Grandparents

A big help to parents in the raising of children in a family business can be grandparents. Grandparents add perspective to the task of raising children as well as running a family business. Grandparents can experience many of the joys of child-rearing without the full-time responsibilities of being a parent.

Grandparents are often less controlling of their grandchildren than parents might be. Usually, they find a niche for each of their grandchildren without playing favorites. There is often a sense of easy companionship between grandparents and grandchildren.

In addition to tending to grandchildren when parents are overwhelmed with family business and other obligations, grandparents can instill business virtues in young children. If the grandparents were involved in the family business, they can bring their historical perspective to the next generation.

Faith in a Family Business

For many people, religious faith is a big part of their lives. Some family businesses try to create harmony between their domestic and business lives by bringing faith into their family businesses.

For instance, the family that owns Chick-fil-A, a chain of fast-food restaurants, keeps its restaurants closed on Sundays because of its religious beliefs. Many other families believe their religion precludes them from operating the business on the Sabbath. Some Hassidic Jews consult their rabbis on the right thing to do in a given business situation.

The Effect of Faith

In some family businesses, religious beliefs are of paramount concern. Such faith-first families can be more functional than secular families who might not have a strict moral conscience. These religious families live out their credos and pray when the business experiences problems. These families take seriously the notion of stewardship—that they have a moral obligation to conduct their business according to the values inherent in their religions.

There are some possible downsides to trying to make a family business an extension of a family's religious life. Some religious families might have a fear of individuation, intolerance for dissent or different lifestyles, and sexism, and might even confuse a parent's will and God's will. In some cases, religious families might show self-righteousness, but also an ambivalence about whether it's permitted by their religion to seek wealth.

Instilling Moral Values

Although some family businesses are faith-first, the vast majority practice their religions in quieter ways. Religion can give a family a strong value system that motivates it to act out of generosity and love. From this foundation to do good work, a family business can have at its core positive virtues to treat customers fairly, give good value in its products, and maintain high standards.

Even though many family businesses do not adopt the faith-first approach, many family business executives believe it is important to bring the moral character of the family to the workplace. Jon Huntsman, founder and chairman of Huntsman

Corporation (one of the world's largest chemical companies), believes that the workplace should be an extension of the home.

In his travels around the world, Huntsman says families from different countries all have the same root values. Their concern is first and foremost their families, not their jobs. He believes that in a family business you must check your ego at the door because the business relies on trust, respect, and love. He also thinks everyone in a family business should be a cheerleader for other people. They should seek good fortune for the other person first. He believes most family businesses end in disarray because of the selfish interests of one or more siblings. His namesake building at the Huntsman Cancer Institute has the quote "Selfless giving unto others represents one's true wealth."

The Least You Need to Know

◆ For most family businesspeople, a separation between business and home is healthy.

◆ Women have a vast array of opportunities in family businesses and are increasingly taking the helm.

◆ Challenges for women include achieving a balance in their home and business lives, especially when they have young children.

◆ Grandparents can help ease the burden of parenting and at the same time help instill family business traditions and values in their grandchildren.

◆ Faith can bring a clear sense of moral purpose to a family business, but there are some dangers in bringing religion into an office.

Chapter 11

Expansion of the Family Business

In This Chapter

- ◆ Ways to grow the family business
- ◆ Creating new opportunities for family members
- ◆ Encouraging family members to become entrepreneurs
- ◆ How expansion also increases opportunities for nonfamily members

Just as strong families grow over time, a family business grows as it becomes more successful. Expanding the family business is an exciting time in the lifecycle of the business. You've reached the point where you're ready to grow, but there are so many issues: how to finance the project; what the scope of the new enterprise should be; who should run it; and so on.

In this chapter, we look at the who, what, when, where, why, and how to expand a family business. Some of the issues are similar to the original founding of the business, but as the family grows more complex, so, too, does the family business.

Growth Opportunities

If a family business is successful, those at the helm will want to see the business grow. A business must be strong to weather the storm of being passed to the next generation. If the head of a family business has inherited it from his parents and wants to pass it on to his children, the goal is, naturally, to send it on in better shape than it was before. Such strength is often achieved through growth.

The family business can become stronger by decreasing reliance on any one customer or product, thereby diversifying the business's revenue base. It can improve its in-house systems to obtain better profitability within its price structure. But it can also seek to become a larger company, so that it is a bigger player within its industry.

Early in the lifecycle of a family business, growth is a fairly simple proposition. It usually involves increasing the inventory of products carried or adding more services. For example, a dry cleaner could add tailoring services and offer rug cleaning as ways to increase business. These new products and services can probably be handled by existing staff and equipment.

But at a certain point, a family business that has the capacity to grow will want to make a more substantial move. Some of the more common ways expansion can take place for a family business include:

- Establishing an additional location

- Acquiring another existing business, usually a smaller one

- Establishing dealerships or distributorships of the product

- Offering franchise ownership of the business concept to others

- Joining an industry cooperative to save money in areas such as purchasing or advertising

- Developing a catalog or other new marketing methods

- Becoming a public company

Any of these expansion alternatives is daunting for a family business to consider. And before it undertakes any kind of expansion, family business management should make sure the business is capable of handling the stresses that will occur with growth.

Sugar Bowl Bakery is a family business that has expanded tremendously since its modest founding in 1984. The five Ly brothers have used several of the methods previously listed to grow the San Francisco-based business from their original $40,000 investment to today's company with more than $42 million of annual revenue and 400 employees.

As immigrants from Vietnam, the brothers pooled their savings to purchase their first location. The family, including spouses, provided the personnel needed to run the operation. Their first expansion was to add Vietnamese food to the bakery/coffee shop operation. After two years, the business had generated enough money that the brothers knew it was time to grow. They collectively decided to add a second location and purchased the real estate, using their savings to finance the expansion of the business.

A third location was added four years later. With each new location, some of the family members branched out to run the new operation. Over time, they have diversified their product lines, usually in response to customer requests. They have also added to their distribution channels by becoming suppliers of baked goods to other retailers, including large hotels as well as supermarkets. Each expansion has required some juggling of roles, but family members remain in control of the business.

The business started as a partnership but shifted to a corporate structure in 1993. They are able to acquire other companies more readily and continue to consider the option of going public in the future. Sugar Bowl Bakery tries to be responsive to its customers and keeps its management structure simple. The next generation of Lys is now working in management positions in the family business after growing up in the bakeries. Opportunities are made available to them, but they must prove themselves capable of handling the positions.

The story of Sugar Bowl Bakery is one of rapid growth—an average of 25 percent per year since its founding. It illustrates how, through careful expansion, a family business can continue to include family members in the decision-making process so that the growth is handled smoothly. In fact, the business has been so successful it was chosen Small Business of the Year by the Small Business Administration in 2008.

Determining the Right Time

How does a family business decide whether the time is right for expansion? Generally, you're open to the concept of expansion when your business is already successful. Sometimes forces outside your business spark the idea—a new location becomes available, a competitor decides to sell, or a customer asks for a new product. If the idea comes from outside the business, you need to do some business soul-searching to ensure the new opportunity fits with your goals and strategy. This can take the form of meetings to discuss the underlying vision of the family business and how the proposed expansion helps to realize that vision.

A family-owned and -managed salsa business, Renfro Foods of Texas, found itself in a situation where an international expansion opportunity came to it unsolicited. A Vancouver-based distributor wanted to bring its products to Western Canada. Although the Renfros hadn't considered that market for their products, they evaluated the opportunity and determined that it would be a way to introduce themselves into the international market with little risk. Following that success, they decided to grow their Canadian business further, which required a deal with a distributor for Eastern Canada. This time, the expansion was initiated by the Renfros. The deal took two years and a lot of consumer education efforts, but the sales increases made the venture pay off. Since then, they have expanded into additional international markets, using what they learned in their first foray into Canada to bring their products to other countries, including several in Europe.

Expansion ventures might come to you, or you might develop the ideas for expansion yourself. In either case, it is important to evaluate whether this is the opportune time to make the investment, move, hiring decisions, and whatever else it will take to make the new venture a success. A marketing plan for the new project should be created, just as it should at the start of any new business. Key considerations include evaluating your financial situation and determining how the new project will be funded, who will run the new venture, and how it will be marketed to customers. Probably the most important consideration—and one that often gets overlooked—is how the new venture fits with the current successful business. How does this expansion opportunity further the goals of your family business?

New Roles for Family Members

Expansion of a family business requires personnel changes and, often, new employees. In a family business, some family members will be eager and willing to accept the new responsibility.

When a business is expanding, hiring decisions are of utmost importance. In many cases, the head of the company shifts her attentions away from the core business to the new venture. The central business can suffer unless a qualified person has been given authority to handle it. A trusted family member who has been second in command will likely fit this description and provide that person with a chance to show her management skills.

Sometimes the need to create new space for family members in the business will be the incentive for growth in a family business. Young people in the next generation will require new opportunities, and often, the previous generation is nowhere near retirement age. Creating a new division or product line can provide the management opportunity necessary to keep the young family members excited about the family business.

VP Records started in 1979 as a small music studio in Jamaica. As the market for Caribbean music grew, so did the record company. Patricia and Vincent Chin began the company and catered to independent stores who agreed to carry their records. As the business grew, their son Randy joined them and took the enterprise global. Five offices around the world are part of the expansion of the company in the past 30 years, as the record label signed recording artists who had some big hits.

Told You So!

When you're considering expanding your family business, you'll need to delegate more. If you are a hands-on manager, you might have trouble handling everything when the business grows unless you learn to hand over some of the details to others.

Today, Randy's brother, sister, and brother-in-law have top management positions, and Randy's nephews work in the business, too. With more expansion planned, Patricia is moving on to a new fashion design project along with Randy's wife. The growth of VP Records into *Billboard Magazine*'s Best Independent Record Label has provided new opportunities for many members of the Chin family.

Diversification

Adding new product lines or a new location provides new management opportunities. In a family business, such growth can be instrumental in keeping next-generation family members active in the business.

S&S Worldwide has been a family business for the Schwartz family in Connecticut since the company's founding in 1906. But the products it started producing at that time bear little resemblance to the products the company carries today. Growth for S&S has been sustained by the strategy of diversification.

It began as a small leather goods company, producing items such as change purses, suspender fittings, and hair curlers in the early years. When second-generation management took over during the Depression, the business diversified into kits to assemble small leather products for the vocational rehabilitation market. The business grew with large national customers. It diversified further to items used by recreational programs and camps. Over time, it has continued to add more and more products to meet the needs of its growing customer base, which now also includes such diverse industries as hotels, amusement parks, and daycare centers.

Today, with management from the third and fourth generations of the Schwartz family, the company has grown into a $60 million business with 350 employees. Products are displayed in large catalogs and on the company's website. When you look at what it offers, you begin to understand how diversifying the product mix has enabled this family business to thrive for more than 100 years.

Acquisition and Consolidation

Acquiring other businesses is an important way for a family business to achieve its expansion goals. Acquisition of a competitor can help a business strengthen its position in the marketplace by making it a bigger firm that owns more of the market share.

Most family business owners will not make many business acquisitions over the lifespan of the company. But if your family business is ready to purchase another company to add to the value and strength of the business, there are a number of important considerations.

Merging a company into an existing business is a strain on everything, so be sure your new acquisition will be worth it to your business. Be careful that the debt service doesn't overwhelm your ability to pay. And don't neglect your core business as you integrate the new business into your operation.

Suggestion Box

Make sure you understand the culture of the business you intend to acquire. Family businesses are shaped largely by the owner in the way that people work together, how they serve customers, and a host of other interpersonal considerations. The business you acquire must be able to mesh with yours to make the acquisition successful.

An interesting example of a family business that has grown through acquisitions is in an industry that might not seem the most logical—funeral homes. However, Service Corporation International (SCI) has grown almost completely by buying other existing funeral homes. Its expansion has been enormous, from its start as a family-owned mortuary founded in 1925 by the grandmother and father of SCI's current chairman, Robert Waltrip, to today's public company with more than 1,600 locations; 13,000 employees; and a net income in 2007 of $248 million.

In 1962, Waltrip decided that the funeral business was ripe for some consolidation. He began buying mom-and-pop funeral homes in the Houston area. Most of those businesses were family-owned organizations in their third or fourth generation of ownership. At that point, often no one in the family was available or interested in the funeral business, and owners who wanted to pass the business on had nowhere to go. Waltrip found that there were strong economies of scale to be achieved by having one fleet of limousines servicing several funeral homes or one back office handling all the administrative work for several homes.

In 1971, SCI bought its first network of funeral homes, acquiring 26 at one time. In 1981, it bought its largest competitor in the business, purchasing 91 funeral homes and 22 cemeteries in one deal. Waltrip's goal from the beginning was to build a national chain of funeral homes, much like a hotel chain. He sought acquisitions in geographical locations with large populations of older people and targeted the largest funeral homes for purchase. Interestingly, each funeral home purchased has retained its name and, often, its management. This allows a sense of personal attention and community continuity, which are key to a funeral home's success. The name SCI doesn't appear anywhere at the funeral homes.

SCI's purchase of many family-owned funeral homes has allowed those family businesses to survive and thrive. Many of the homes now owned by SCI are still run by the original founding families of those homes. They note that they could not have expanded without the investment from SCI.

SCI, a public company since 1969, has less than 10 percent ownership by the Waltrip family but has tried to retain family values. Robert Waltrip is CEO and his son Blair is executive vice president. A Waltrip son-in-law is also in the management of the business. For now, SCI has the character of a family business—one that has grown exponentially in the past 40 years by purchasing smaller family businesses.

Creating New Entrepreneurs in the Family

Most people who are part of an ongoing family business will tell you that they "grew up" in the business. When the family has a business, usually young members of the family are encouraged—if not expected—to help out in the business as soon as they are old enough.

To sustain operations across generations, the family business has to grow. Families must teach the next generation how to grow the business if it is to survive. The entrepreneurial spirit that gave rise to the family firm by Grandpa has to be developed in the grandchildren to create new family business entrepreneurs.

Culture of Innovation

The foundation of developing entrepreneurs in the next generation is the family itself. A loving, supportive family that fosters cooperation yet allows for individualism will be the seed for new innovators in the family business.

Within the family business, the culture must encourage innovation and creativity. A budding entrepreneur will be shut down if presented with too many roadblocks when the situation requires speed and flexibility.

Too often, the second and third generations in a family business are reluctant to risk trying something new in a successful family business. They are likely to continue what has worked well and are less willing to gamble on the untested. But when a family has encouraged experimentation, learning, and innovation, young people in the family business might see new business ventures with an entrepreneur's eye. This can be key to a family business's growth over the years.

Spreading the Wealth—Encouraging New Ventures

Expanding the business offers opportunities to family members currently in the business and, sometimes, to ones who aren't yet in the family firm but are looking for a new venture. A successful family business can provide such opportunities within the structure of the company, encouraging family members to stay or join the business, as well as further strengthening the overall company.

When a family member has specialized skills, perhaps after a training program, college, or graduate school, she might offer a new idea to the family business that creates a growth opportunity. Many family businesses have dipped their toes in the technology waters in just this way. Son or daughter comes home from college after majoring in information technology and has a brainstorm about how computers can be used to build the business. This kind of situation can be a win-win for everyone: the family business includes a family member who is energized about her role in the company, and the business is enhanced by the new innovations.

The Bastianich family is a great example of how expansion can bring more family members into the family business. Mother Lidia Bastianich started a modest restaurant in Queens, New York, in 1971. Ten years later, she opened the successful Felidia restaurant in Manhattan, drawing on her reputation as an accomplished chef. Several other restaurants were opened across the country in the ensuing years. Her children, Joe and Tanya, were drawn to the family business over time, after careers in other fields. Son Joe developed a love of wine, and through him, the family business now includes a vineyard in Italy and a retail wine business. Daughter Tanya developed a travel company that grew from Lidia's customers wanting to go with her on her trips to Europe. The travel company specializes in tours of Italy that combine art, food, and wine. Tanya has also been involved in the development of Lidia's website as well as a line of food and lifestyle products.

The Bastianich family empire is highly diversified, but all the areas of business stem from the initial interest in Italian food. Both first- and second-generation family members have contributed to the growth and success of the company. Their far-flung ventures are drawn together, not surprisingly, by a weekly family meeting that revolves around a hearty meal!

Their efforts typify a growing movement within companies known as *intrapreneurship*. A family business can promote a culture that encourages new business ideas from within.

The more flexible and less bureaucratic nature of family businesses helps to encourage intrapreneurial ideas. When discussion of the family business is a regular

def•i•ni•tion

Intrapreneurship is working within an existing company to develop innovative new business ventures, using the financial backing of the existing firm.

dinnertime event, family members often become interested. Both Joe and Tanya were working outside the family business originally, but their interest in the Bastianich restaurants grew to inspire their new ideas for the family business expansions.

Family business leaders must be open to new ideas, not shut them out. An autocratic family business leader will not encourage other family members to bring up new business concepts. What a mistake that would be for many family businesses!

Dangers of Expansion

Expanding a business can be a dangerous undertaking for a family business. It's similar to the decision to start the business in the first place, but now other people are involved and dependent on the operation of the business. Much more can be at stake when you expand than when you first founded the business.

Family Conflict

The decision to expand will be made by the family business's management group. This can mean the CEO acting alone, the board of directors, the management committee, or any combination of people who weigh in on company decisions. Expansion plans are often discussed with retired family members who are no longer part of the day-to-day management. Because such family members are probably owners of the company and likely to be on the board of directors (if one exists), they will think they have a right to have a say in the decision.

But if those family members are no longer involved in the workings of the company, they might be making decisions from the heart, not the head. Expansion needs to be thoughtfully considered as part of the company's business strategy.

Financing Considerations

Financing an expansion project can be costly. If a family business is to grow, it often has to take on debt through a bank or another financial institution. The growth of the business has to add sufficient revenue to the company to pay its debt service.

Told You So!

Don't undercapitalize your expansion project. It can take as much or more time and money than your original business required to make the new business plan a success. Arrange your expansion financing carefully.

Family-owned Hull Printing in Vermont was forced to close because of an expansion decision that didn't work out. Needing additional space, the company decided to expand its business at the same time by buying new equipment, hiring more employees, and increasing printing capacity. When its sales did not grow, it began to have trouble meeting payments to the bank. Eventually, the business closed.

Including Nonfamily Members in Expansion Plans

One of the best ways to reward and retain nonfamily executives in a family business is to grow the business. Because many nonfamily employees sense a *family ceiling* for their long-term prospects with the company, being able to manage a new acquisition or a new division gives them a reason to stay with the family firm.

In fact, including nonfamily members in the family business's expansion plans is almost always a smart move. You'll get an outsider's perspective on the value of the strategy to the company, and you'll increase management opportunities for valued nonfamily employees. A good management team is hard to build, and if yours includes folks who aren't family members, you'll need to create reasons for them to stay with you.

def•i•ni•tion

The **family ceiling** is the limit at the upper level of management that a nonfamily employee can move to in a family firm, where all the highest-level management jobs are reserved for family members.

Family members aren't always available for growth ventures in a family business. The Gilbane Building Company provides a good example of a family-owned firm that understands the value of nonfamily members in its management team.

Gilbane was founded in 1873 by brothers William and Thomas Gilbane as a carpentry business. Over its 130-year history, it has grown into a very large construction firm, with $2.5 billion in sales and offices in 24 cities. But it remains a family-held company with Thomas Gilbane, Jr., at the head.

The firm was forced to rely on nonfamily management when it established its first office outside New England in 1976. Family members on the company's board of directors understood that they would lose their best nonfamily employees if they didn't offer opportunities for advancement. Today, most of the company's regional management is made up of nonfamily members. Family comprises primarily corporate management and understands that the company's phenomenal growth could not have been achieved if they had restricted all the management positions to Gilbane family members.

One of the potential weaknesses of family businesses is that a close-knit management group can become insular and unaware of changes in the industry. Where a nonfamily firm might see opportunities for expansion because the management group is more diverse, the management of a family business might be of such a like mind that new ideas are less obvious to them. A research department can help the family business be on the lookout for growth opportunities.

Suggestion Box

Brainstorming sessions with nonfamily employees, customer focus groups, and regular attendance at trade shows and seminars will help a tightly knit family management team learn from outside perspectives. This way, the family business will be less likely to miss growth opportunities that might come along.

The Least You Need to Know

◆ Expansion can open up opportunities for family members who might be attracted to a new venture.

◆ Expansion can help retain valued nonfamily employees by providing them with new responsibilities.

◆ There are many ways to expand a family business, but you must evaluate how such growth meets your goals for the company.

◆ Most successful family businesses must grow to continue through more than one generation.

Chapter

12

Nonfamily in the Family Business

In This Chapter

- ◆ Using nonfamily members to provide vital management skills

- ◆ Recruiting nonfamily executives

- ◆ Consider the nonfamily employee's "family ceiling"

- ◆ The high value of outside board members

A family business wouldn't ordinarily seem the best place for any outsider. Family businesses tend to promote from within the family and often want to compensate family members more generously than other employees. In addition, nonfamily members often encounter a *family ceiling* in a family business: outsiders can advance, but only so far. Nonfamily members can easily be caught in the web of family disputes and jealousies, forced to take sides in a fight in which they have no real stake.

In this chapter, we discuss how the family business deals with the non-family employees. Unless the business is extremely small, outsiders will be part of a family business. Family members must be able to work well with them, provide them with sufficient incentives and responsibility to retain them, and (sometimes) treat them like family.

The Varied Roles of Outsiders

Nonfamily members can perform invaluable roles for family businesses. In fact, enlightened family businesses make it a point to recruit talented nonfamily members and to reward these outsiders generously.

Suggestion Box

Family members should try to achieve consensus on bringing in outsiders to fill top management or board positions. If the family is not united in accepting outsiders, the nonfamily members will probably not be able to accomplish difficult tasks for the family.

Some of the ways outsiders can benefit a family business include:

◆ **As consultants or mediators.** Outsiders can be brought in to help the family with a business problem or to help settle a family dispute or organize the family for appropriate interaction with the business (see Chapter 15).

◆ **As key managerial employees.** Up to and including taking on the role of the CEO of a family business.

◆ **Working in interim positions.** In a family business, nonfamily members can help out when there is a short-term family need or problem, for example, during the sudden loss of a family member who is a key manager.

◆ **As members of the board of directors or board of advisors to a family business.** Some of the board members should be outsiders to give the board(s) a fresh perspective.

◆ **As investors in the family business.** Outsiders can provide crucial financing and should be kept informed of major family decisions.

Outsiders on the Management Team

Perhaps the most crucial role an outsider can play in a family business is becoming part of the family business's management team. Hiring a nonfamily executive is difficult and can be costly. Some family members might be disappointed that they did not get the job. In addition, outsiders might be worried about family politics and the difficulty of advancing in a family firm.

Skills Necessary for Outside Managers

Before hiring a top manager, a family business should consider the corporate objective in hiring someone outside the family. Does the outsider have skills or experience that no one in the family has? The family should focus on what it is trying to accomplish with the new-hire rather than on personalities. For example, if a family business wants to develop a new line of business and no family member is interested in taking on the new responsibility, the business can search for talent outside the family.

If the family business is facing a problem that might require outside help, the management should put a dollar value on how much the problem is costing the family business. It is expensive to bring in someone new. If the cost of the problem far exceeds the cost of a new-hire, an outsider should be actively considered. The family managers should determine which skill sets are needed to solve the problem and whether any current family members can accomplish the task.

Recruiting an Outside Manager

When recruiting a nonfamily member, it pays to consider the candidate's needs. Newcomers to a family business are often concerned that there will be a permanent glass ceiling in the family business. That might be true; the highest levels of management in many family businesses are closed to outsider employees. For a talented outsider, the family business must offer other types of compensatory benefits.

The advantages of working in a family business can be stressed, including its tight-knit culture and strong sense of security and stability. The long-term growth horizon of the typical family business is another selling point. Many family businesses are less concerned about quarterly profits than nonfamily firms because family businesses tend to be privately held and have fewer obligations to public shareholders. This gives the outsider employee a more secure feeling, knowing that day-to-day profits are likely to be less important than annual or five-year goals. For many people, a company that has a longer-term vision is an appealing employer.

The Interview Process

As in any company, when a family business needs an executive, the requirements of the job must be carefully considered. The family members hiring the executive should focus on the critical skills necessary to perform the job and know what they need in fill the job. Ideally, the considerations should be the same, whether a family member or nonfamily member is being considered for the position.

Nonfamily candidates should be introduced to top family business owners and managers. There should be an interview by one or, at most, two family executives. It's often valuable to schedule an activity with the candidate (such as visiting a plant) before the interview. This gives the candidate the opportunity to talk about the visit during the interview.

Suggestion Box _____

After the interview, it is important to schedule another short event with the candidate. You should make sure you disclose any family situations that could impact the job. You should ask the candidate whether he has anything to disclose to you.

Interviews do not always reveal whether a candidate will have the skills necessary to do a great job. The best questions focus on integrity, ability to work with others, creativity, and problem-solving. The candidate should also be questioned about what he thinks is necessary to be successful in a family business.

A candidate for an important family business position should sign a waiver letting you check any and all of his references as well as verifying all educational and certification accomplishments.

Working with a Search Firm

Working with a good search firm can help a family business select the right candidate for a sensitive job. The search firm working with the family can develop a list of target companies where someone capable of solving the family business needs might be currently employed.

Think of a search consultant as an important recruiting resource. She will go to candidates you cannot directly approach. When you help a search consultant define the person you want, you should focus on the positive aspects of the job you are offering. These include information about your company, the responsibilities and potential the job holds for the candidate, and future growth opportunities in your company for the candidate. You should also let potential candidates know why the position is open.

The title and responsibilities of the job are crucial to attracting candidates. You might have to boost compensation 25 percent or more from the candidate's current job to attract interest in the job you are offering. You might also want to offer a performance bonus if the candidate successfully accomplishes the tasks assigned.

Some families have had good success in hiring nonfamily managers and CEOs. Decagnon Devices, Inc., a manufacturer of scientific instruments and sensors located in Pullman, Washington, has more than 70 employees and revenues over $8 million. The company tries to ensure all employees feel like family members.

> **Family Stats**
>
> Sixty-four percent of family businesses give family members a position with the company without measuring them against outsiders. And only 14 percent of family businesses hire a CEO from outside the family. But when they take that step, most family businesses are satisfied. Seventy-one percent of family businesses that did hire an outside CEO rated their experiences as "extremely successful" or "very successful."

The company has a ping-pong table and slot-car track, and employees play soccer together on their breaks. The company pays 100 percent of the healthcare premium for employees and their dependents. The company also tries, when possible, to hire family members of outsiders.

Companies like Decagnon Devices do well because they extend the virtues of a family business to outsiders. The family atmosphere can attract many qualified nonfamily employees.

Why Bring In an Outsider?

The reasons to bring in an outsider for an important family firm position include ...

- ◆ When no family member has the management skills needed to lead the family business to the next stage, an outsider might be necessary to fill the position.

- ◆ When significant disagreement exists in the family over which family member should take the reins, an outsider should be considered. Sometimes the family members cannot reach consensus on one family candidate, so the best solution is to look outside the family.

- ◆ If the family business has been floundering, or if the business is desperately in need of fresh ideas, an outsider can be essential for the family business's survival.

> **Family Stats**
>
> Fifty-five percent of family business CEOs older than 60 who expect to retire in the next five years have not picked a successor. Bringing in another executive to share some of the management burden can free up the CEO's time to work on succession issues.

Another reason to look for outside help is when the business's CEO has not prepared the family firm for his retirement. An outsider taking some of the day-to-day stress off the CEO can help the family firm start planning for a successor CEO.

Dividing Family and Business Responsibilities

Laird Norton Company, LLC, a family business with almost 400 living family members who are owners of the company, has taken a unique approach to running its business with the help of outsiders. Founded in 1858 as a logging company, Laird Norton has morphed into a financial, real estate, and investment firm. To keep the business successful, but also to keep the family successful, Laird Norton decided to have a president of the family as well as a company CEO. In 2001, Laird Norton hired the first nonfamily CEO in the company's business and, at the same time, created a family president. The family also decided to put two outside directors on its 10-member board of directors.

Creating a family president is an unusual step, but it makes sense for Laird Norton. The company keeps close contact with far-flung family members through an Internet site and an annual family get-together, which more than 60 percent of the family members attend. The company keeps even its young family members involved by providing education about the family business and participation in shareholder meetings at an early age.

By dividing business and family responsibilities, the company has created a situation in which family members can have their needs met by a full-time family representative. Putting a nonfamily CEO in charge of the company for the first time in the family's history was less traumatic because of the creation of the family president post.

Helping a Family Firm Expand

Sometimes, a family business reaches the point where no family member has the skills necessary to move the business forward. In that case, looking for a professional manager outside of the family makes good business sense. One firm with a successful experience with a top nonfamily manager is Dudek and Bock, a spring manufacturer in Chicago with annual sales of $42 million. A 50-year-old family business, the family leadership recognized its need for professionalism to grow. After an executive search, they settled on Dave Sindelar as the company's chief financial officer (CFO).

Sindelar enabled the company to rethink many of its business decisions. He encouraged it to expand into Mexico to keep down costs and obtain new business. Sindelar communicated constantly with family members, some of whom were initially skeptical that an outsider could work well with a business populated with a number of family members. But Sindelar's persistence and good ideas helped turn all the family members around.

Although Sindelar may never become CEO, he is compensated at a level that makes up for that lost opportunity. And when the company did expand to Mexico, Sindelar was named chief operating officer (COO) of the company's Mexican venture.

Alternatives to Hiring Outsiders

Because hiring a top family manager is such a lengthy and expensive proposition, the family business owners should consider alternatives to a full-fledged new-hire. Maybe a consultant can be brought on temporarily to work on the problem. Or maybe an interim manager can handle the task. Outsourcing the problem to a specialist firm is another way to handle a challenge, as is a strategic alliance with another firm that can do the work.

An interim executive can be a valuable asset to a family business when business problems remain unsolved for months. Often the interim executive is a former business owner who has solved the same challenge in her business. Interim executives tend to be older, and many are retired. They like helping another business but don't want to commit to the business for the long haul.

Interim executives are not consultants. They do not give advice on how to fix a problem. Rather, they immediately become part of the team, get their hands dirty, and try to employ strategies to help get the family through a current difficulty or help with upcoming issues such as succession planning. Interim executives can take any position with the family business, including CEO, CFO, COO, or president. Sometimes an interim CEO is appointed when the family business CEO dies or becomes sick and the next-generation family member is not yet ready to take the helm of the business.

The interim executive advises the owners of the family business on available options and works in the business to fix deficiencies and enhance profits. An interim executive can help run the company while a long-term person is being recruited to fill an unexpected vacancy in the company. Like an interim football coach who is hired for the remainder of the season when the coach has been fired, an interim executive helps a family business get through a short-term period when there is no leadership at the top.

Creating a Stimulating Environment for Outsiders

If a family business decides to hire outsiders for key jobs, it must make the work environment stimulating for the new employees. A family business can make the newcomers feel welcome by doing the following:

- **Recognizing employees when they do a job well.** A simple compliment will suffice most of the time. All new employees want feedback, and outsiders in a family business especially need to see that they fit in and are meeting expectations.

- **Showing a commitment to excellence and quality.** Turnover and absenteeism are much lower in family businesses that stress the importance of quality. Nonfamily employees recognize that everyone in the company, family and nonfamily members alike, must reach for that high standard.

- **Encouraging outsider employees to grow personally and professionally in their jobs.** When employees are encouraged to try new challenges, creativity increases and new ideas and products come into being.

Told You So!

It is important that nonfamily employees be kept out of family disputes. Nonfamily employees want to take up family values, but they should not be brought into the middle of arguments among family members and forced to choose sides.

- **Allowing nonfamily employees to participate in decision-making as often as possible.** Employees want to feel involved in making contributions to the company.

- **Involving nonfamily employees as part of teams set up to solve important issues for the family business.** Working as part of a team fosters identification with team and family business goals.

Hiring a Nonfamily CEO

The biggest job in a family business is the CEO position. When the family business owners decide to hire a nonfamily member as the CEO, the family should make sure that the outsider views his role as a *steward* of the business.

def•i•ni•tion

A **steward** is a leader who is more concerned with making a contribution to the organization than of benefiting personally. Stewardship occurs when the goals of the family business align themselves with the goals of the CEO.

The concept of stewardship can be difficult to instill in a nonfamily leader because that leader might have trouble understanding all the family values, history, and customs. Most family business leaders are seen as agents for the family, who try to do the right thing for the business but also are very concerned about their own compensation and stature in the industry.

To pick a steward, a family business has to choose someone whose character and integrity are just as important as his business skills. This kind of leader has to have a clear awareness of family issues and family personalities. The CEO must manage the business for the long-term interests of the family as well as navigating short-term business concerns.

An Independent Board of Directors

The support of a strong board of directors or board of advisors is necessary for the success of a nonfamily CEO. Situations arise that can cause conflict between a non-family CEO and some family members. For instance, the CEO might want to fire or discipline a family member. Only a strong board can give the CEO the comfort level to make such a decision.

But no matter how comfortable a nonfamily CEO becomes, the family owners will almost always find it easier to replace a nonfamily CEO than a CEO who is a family member. The removal of a nonfamily member is much less likely to have a long-term negative impact on family dynamics.

Finding Outsiders for the Board

Family businesses that are growing can benefit from outsiders on their boards of directors or boards of advisors. With the growth of the Internet and globalization, family businesses need the intellectual resources and experience that nonfamily members can provide.

An independent board can be an invaluable asset as a family business grows. In pick-ing members of the board of directors or advisory boards, family businesses should look for

◆ **Business judgment.** A board member must have the capability of understanding the business challenges and opportunities a family business faces.

◆ **Management expertise.** Family businesses should choose candidates that have faced decisions similar to those confronting the family business.

◆ **Leadership.** Simply picking board members who will agree with whatever top management proposes will not keep family management on its toes. A family business that is comfortable with its management decisions will want an inde-pendent board that can stand up to management if it thinks management is making a bad decision.

◆ **Crisis experience.** When the business faces a crisis, a board can help give guidance to the family business management team. If changes in the CEO or other top management are necessary, a strong board can implement the changes that might be necessary for a family business' survival.

Told You So!

Some CEOs try to pick a board with directors who will rubber-stamp all the CEO's decisions. Not only is this counter to the family's long-term interests, but it exposes board members to possible lawsuits if the CEO's actions are in opposition to the business's well-being.

◆ **Strategy and vision.** The board should not get involved in day-to-day management decisions. The board should be more concerned about long-term results and how the family business' strategic plan is being implemented.

In addition to having these strong personal characteristics, board members should have some familiarity with the industry of the family business. Board members should be on friendly terms with family members, but they should try to avoid being thrust into the middle of family issues.

Outsider Board Members Help with Planning

Some important family business issues require the expertise of board members. Board members can help the CEO and other managers of the family business develop a succession plan for the business. Family members must answer the fundamental question of whether they want to continue the family business.

If the family members do not want to continue the business, the board members can help with sale arrangements. If family members want to continue the business, board members can become active in managing the process by which a new CEO will be chosen. Boards can also help family members develop ways of comparing candidates for the CEO and measuring the effectiveness of the leader of the company.

Sometimes no family members want to take over the helm of the family business. In that case, the current family ownership can begin to view the business more as an investment than as a long-term family holding. The family could promote a non-family member who is currently in the business to the position of CEO. Or the family could look for an outsider to run the company. Another alternative is to pursue the sale of the business.

If a sale is not imminent or even possible, the family owners and managers must make other provisions to protect their stakes in the company. To protect the family interest in the business, the ownership can make profit distributions at greater levels to ensure that family members profit from the continuing success of the family business. Family owners and managers can also make improvements in the business in the hopes of attracting an outside buyer or improving the business so much that the business continues to grow the family wealth and provide current income to family members.

The Least You Need to Know

- Outsiders can perform a valuable role by performing tasks family members do not have the skills to accomplish.

- Creating a congenial atmosphere with generous compensation is necessary to attract talented nonfamily members to key manager roles.

- If a nonfamily CEO is hired, she should be a steward of family values.

- An independent board of directors or board of advisors with several nonfamily members will provide a needed independent check on family managers.

Part 4

Outside Advice

As a family business continues its growth, it will face new challenges. Some outside specialists can help guide the business through the situations that arise.

Financial planners can help the family business keep much of the wealth in the family while still providing incentives for the next generation.

Lawyers and insurance agents help the family business avoid some of the pitfalls of running the business.

Family business consultants and coaches can help improve communication in a family business.

This part helps you decide when you'll need outside specialists and how to choose people who can work well with your family business.

13

Financial Decisions

In This Chapter

- ◆ Financing a family business start-up
- ◆ Family help in financing
- ◆ Using loans
- ◆ Attracting outside investors

Financing a family business involves different challenges and opportunities than in a nonfamily business. In the early years, financing a family business is often a more personal affair. As the business grows, financial decision-making becomes more difficult, as the needs of family members involved in the business often diverge from other family members who are not working day-to-day. Finally, as the family business matures, its financial needs and resources begin to resemble other nonfamily businesses.

In this chapter, we look at the ways a family business can fund business needs. Beginning with the business start-up and moving through several phases of growth, we examine the various financial alternatives family businesses use to reach their business goals.

Financing a Start-up Family Business

The early years are often a challenge for the family start-up business. Like other businesses, the family business has a need for financing but does not have much to offer. It has no track record, no customers, and no *collateral*. Going to a local bank with a great idea is tempting, but the bank will be reluctant to finance a start-up on the basis of a good business plan alone.

def•i•ni•tion

Collateral is security for a debt. If you default on your debt, the lender can sell any property identified as collateral to pay back the debt.

Initial Financing

Suppose you and your family want to start a car wash business. You call the business Karen's Car Wash. You will manage the business day-to-day, your husband will do the bookkeeping, and your two college-age kids will work at the business during the summer. Hopefully, one or both or your children will take over the business eventually if it becomes successful.

You've done a lot of investigation and figure you need $150,000 to start your car wash business. You have $20,000 in savings you can apply to the new business but no idea how to proceed.

Bank Financing

Your first inclination might be to go to a bank. Most people think of a bank as the first option for borrowing money. However, banks often are a difficult way to raise money for a fledgling business. Your new family business will probably not be approved for a traditional bank loan. However, it is still worthwhile to check with a local banker. If you had success in other business enterprises, the bank might be interested. If some of the $150,000 you need to start your business will be used for assets such as car-washing equipment, you might be able to finance that portion of the funds you need with a loan from a bank.

If you have assets that can act as collateral for your business, such as a house or other real estate, the bank might lend you money using those assets as security for the loan. The banker might also help you with the checking account and other banking arrangements you need to run your business every day.

Suggestion Box

Even if you are unable to take out a bank loan immediately because you are just starting out in your family business and have no assets, meeting with your local banker can still be a good idea. The banker you approach might have other ideas for how you can raise money, such as a government loan for small businesses or other local community resources for small businesses. Your local banker can be a useful resource and source of funding for you as your business grows.

Other Sources of Funds

If you are unable to secure your funding through a bank loan, there are other sources of capital for your new family business. One is through the provider of equipment for your business. Of the $150,000 you need to start the business, suppose $100,000 of the cash is needed for car-washing equipment. It might be possible to lease the equipment, or maybe the equipment manufacturer will finance a large portion of the equipment. That will ease your immediate cash needs and let you pay off the balance of the loan as business comes in.

Self-Financing Your Business

Suppose you either lease the equipment or convince the equipment company or bank to finance most of your equipment needs and you reduce your initial cash needs from $150,000 to $70,000. You only have $20,000 in savings, so where will the additional $50,000 come from? You need the additional cash to hire help, lease the real estate where you are going to locate your car wash, buy uniforms, buy supplies, and so on.

Told You So!

Be careful about relying too much on equipment companies and other third parties to finance your business. Interest rates can be high, and repayment terms can be difficult. Consult with a lawyer and/or an accountant before you agree to any third-party financing deal.

One possible funding source is your house. If you have equity in your house, you might be able to borrow money with an equity line of credit.

Another possible funding source is credit cards. Many first-time business owners borrow against the line of credit on their credit cards. This process can be very risky, though, especially if you have to pay a high rate of interest on your credit card obligations.

An additional source of funds might be your life insurance policy. Life insurance policies—especially whole life policies—often have a cash value. Often, you can borrow against this cash value of life insurance policies.

Family and Friend Financing

If your own personal sources of funds do not yield enough cash to start your business, you can do what a lot of family businesses do: go to family and friends to borrow the money you need to finance the business.

The Delicate Nature of Family Financing

Going to family (and friends) and asking them to loan or give you money to start your business is a delicate proposition. On the one hand, for fledgling family businesses, the family might be the only source of financing readily available. Often, family members want to help, especially if they are in a financial position to loan or give money to a new business. But because it is your family, you have to make sure you start your financial relationship with other family members on firm footing.

If you think asking family members for money is going to cause rifts in the family, you might want to reconsider the idea. It might be better to work for another firm in the same or a related industry until you have the capital necessary to start your own business without the aid of other family members. You don't want money to be the cause of acrimony in your family.

If you need to borrow money from other family members, you might want to consider a third-party resource to help with the transaction. Websites such as www. virginmoney.com help family and friends make borrowing or loaning money a better experience.

But family members are usually more than willing to help another family member in need. Your parents might have adequate resources both for their retirement and to help you get your business off to a good start. Your brother or sister might be independently wealthy. You might be the favorite niece of an unmarried aunt who wants to help you in your new endeavor.

Paying Back Family Members

Even with these supportive family members, though, you should be careful that everyone is aware of how, if at all, the money will be paid back. You must determine whether the money is a gift, or a loan, or an investment in your business.

For example, suppose Aunt Esther hands you $20,000 to put into your business. When, if at all, does Aunt Esther expect to be paid back? Will you be paying her interest? Suppose your business does extraordinarily well and you eventually have 10 car washes. Does Aunt Esther profit from your success? Is she an investor who is entitled to a share of your success? Or would she be happy just to have her invested capital back?

Documenting Family Loans and Investments

To ensure Aunt Esther is happy every year when she meets you at the Thanksgiving dinner table, you should clear up the financial arrangement immediately. You should have an accountant or a lawyer prepare a short document that describes your financial arrangement with Aunt Esther. The document should describe how much Aunt Esther is giving you, what the terms of the loan or investment are, and when Aunt Esther is going to be repaid. You might think that such a document is unnecessary when dealing with a close family member, but an agreement will help clarify when and if Aunt Esther will be repaid.

Such a document will not only help the relationship between you and Aunt Esther, but will also protect you if Aunt Esther were to die or become unable to look after her own affairs. Some other family member or a lawyer or an executor of Aunt Esther's estate might want clarification of your financial arrangement with her. By having a clear, precise document that spells out what Aunt Esther gave you and what she expects in return, you will be able to show third parties the clear arrangement with Aunt Esther.

Family Debt vs. Equity

In general, when you're starting a business, debt can be better than equity. Debt is more straightforward. If someone lends you $20,000 for 10 years at an agreed-upon interest rate, you or your accountant can easily figure out how much your payment will be every month. However, if someone invests $20,000 in your business, the relationship can be much less clear. That person, especially if he is a family member, might expect to be treated as an advisor as well as an investor, and you might suddenly have a partner in your business.

After you have achieved the initial capital requirements of your business, you then face the day-to-day financial challenges of running a business. As your business becomes successful, you can deal with the challenges of your next stage of financing.

Suggestion Box

Although debt is preferred by many family businesses, it is not for everyone. Some people become extremely concerned about taking on debt. If you will be upset about having significant debt in your business, you should consider having a partner. You might make less money in the long run, but you'll sleep better at night knowing your debt is manageable.

Your Financial Team

Before you go on to the next round of financing, you must line up the best financial team for your business. Even if you are running a relatively small business, you need a part-time and eventually a full-time bookkeeper. The bookkeeper will keep track of the bills you need to pay and your *accounts receivable*. Your bookkeeper will also make out the weekly payroll.

def•i•ni•tion

Accounts receivable are money owed to you by your customers. If your customers owe you a lot of money, your business might suffer. Keep up with customer debt by sending monthly bills and following up with phone calls to late payers.

Keeping Proper Records

Having your records in good working order is invaluable for a business. First, you need to keep accurate records to determine whether your business is profitable. If you are running a profitable business, obtaining financing from outside sources will be much easier.

The IRS will be very interested in your business. If you keep proper records, you will be able to answer any questions the IRS might have. In a family business, it is easy to entangle personal and business checkbooks. By keeping track of your bills and your deposits, you will ensure your business is on sound financial footing.

Hiring the Right Accountant

Early in your business's lifestyle, you should establish a relationship with a certified public accountant (CPA). A CPA is an accounting professional who can set up your bookkeeping system. The CPA can make sure you set up your business properly from a financial perspective. Many businesses are on the accrual method of accounting, which means they recognize income and expenses the year the income is earned or the expenses are incurred, no matter when the income is received or the expenses paid.

Other family businesses are on the simpler cash method, which recognizes income only when you receive the actual cash and recognizes expenses only when you actually pay them. Your accountant can tell you which business accounting method is best for you.

Hiring a good accountant is necessary for a family business. If you have family members who are investors in your business, they will want to know that your finances are checked by an accountant. The extra layer of professionalism an accountant brings to your business finances can help defuse potential disputes about the profits or losses of the business.

Told You So!

Many family businesses start out with sloppy bookkeeping. Not only can bad recordkeeping lead to trouble with the government, but it can also impair your efforts to receive funding for your family business. Start your business with a good financial team— it will be cheaper in the long run.

Phase Two Financing

After you've established good financial recordkeeping and your family business begins to have some success, you will be ready for phase two of your financing.

Karen's Car Wash business turns into a great success. You've opened five car washes, and you have nieces and nephews clamoring for summer jobs. Your son has decided to join the business, but your daughter is pursuing an advanced college degree. Your son wants to expand your firm. Even though your cash flow is good, you are worried about raising the money for a major expansion.

Nonfamily Business Financing

Here's where a family business can differ significantly from nonfamily businesses. At this phase of your business cycle, many nonfamily businesses are ready to seek *equity financing:* they are willing to give up a share of the business for more outside financial help. They see wonderful growth opportunities if they can leverage their business, but they don't have the financial resources to finance the growth themselves.

def•i•ni•tion

> **Equity financing** is giving up some ownership in your business in return for cash. Equity financing is different from debt financing, which involves receiving money in the form of a loan.

Many owners of nonfamily businesses are leery of too much debt financing. If they owe a lot of money that has to be paid with interest, they feel as though their business might be pressed to pay back the borrowings. They would prefer to give up a degree of control in the business to investors. Investors are people who are paid back only when the business is profitable (through dividends) or when the business is sold.

In fact, if the business were profitable enough at this stage, many nonfamily firms would consider a public offering as a way to raise a substantial amount of money. In a public offering, the company puts together a detailed prospectus that describes the firm's prospects and capital needs. The general public is invited to invest in the company and receive shares in the company. All the companies listed on the major stock exchanges have raised capital this way.

Family Business Financing in Phase Two

Many family businesses are unwilling to go public or try to attract other equity investors such as venture capitalists. Here are some reasons why:

- In family businesses, the owners of the business are often also the top management. Most of the top executives are usually family members as well. When a family business gives up some control by allowing outsiders to purchase ownership share of the business, other people have a role in running the business.

- Family businesses have great flexibility in giving jobs to family members, often wanting to ensure that the family business offers opportunities to the family. When outsiders have a say in running the business, they will question hiring decisions that involve family ties.

- Family members can draw great salaries and have other perks because they own and run their own business. Having equity partners decreases the ability of family members to set their own salaries and receive the perks of ownership.

So what's a family to do if it wants to expand and yet is unwilling to take on outside investors? Let's go back to our car wash business and see what other alternatives are available.

Bank Financing for the Family Business

At this stage of the business, bank financing becomes an attractive alternative to equity financing for many family businesses. The car wash will likely find banks that are willing to finance its expansion.

A bank will be interested in the fact that the business has a track record. Suppose the business has been operating for eight years, has hired a good accounting firm, and has good financial records. The bank can see the pattern of sales growth and measure the profitability of the business. More importantly, the bank has assets, such as buildings, equipment, and receivables, that it can use as collateral against loans.

The bank will also be comforted if it sees a plan for growth that is consistent with the business that has been established. The bank will be more likely to loan money to finance more car washes than if the company decided it wanted to venture into the restaurant business.

Drawbacks of Bank Financing

Bank financing, though often less intrusive than equity financing, does pose risks. The bank requires payments of principal and interest, which will have an impact on the company's cash flow. Also, if for some reason the company falls behind on principal and interest payments, the bank will want to know why and will often want new

Suggestion Box _____

Financing your business during a strong growth phase is one of the biggest challenges a family business will face. It is also an opportunity to lay the ground-work for a long-term successful business. You might want to reach out beyond the family for outside, impartial advice on how to best finance your growing family business.

information from the business. If the company's financial troubles continue, the bank can even seize its business assets.

One group of family members who might not be thrilled with new bank financing is family members who are partial owners but who don't work in the business. Family businesses typically use part of the proceeds from bank financing to keep salaries high. So the family members who are working day-to-day in the business will potentially benefit more from bank financing than family members who own a share of the business but are not actually working it.

Financing from Cash Flow

To avoid the problems with bank financing, some family businesses decide to self-finance most of their company's own growth. In other words, they only grow when they can afford to, using cash generated from the business and other less intrusive financing alternatives such as equipment financing from a manufacturer. These companies take a conservative approach to growth that involves much less short-term financial risk but might impair the company's long-term ability to grow or be competitive.

In this second stage of financial development, family businesses and their nonfamily counterparts are still significantly different in terms of financing. However, during the next stage of financing, the differences between family-owned businesses and nonfamily businesses tend to disappear.

Third Stage of Family Business Financing

The third stage of financing involves companies that are really on an upward trajectory. They have survived the start-up phase and have done well on their initial expansions. However, as a firm does well, it often needs a great deal of extra financing to meet the needs of expansion.

At this point in its history, the firm might need to get bank financing and search out equity investors. Success brings opportunity, but it also brings financial needs.

Selling Equity in a Family Business

When a family business sells equity to investors, it has to reassess its priorities. At this point, it is on the way to becoming a large business with responsibilities to shareholders as well as family members. No longer can family needs always come first. Family members might not always run the company, and a board of directors with outsiders will be watching management's moves. What's best for the family might not always be what's best for the company, and vice versa.

In fact, when a family business becomes very large, it starts to resemble other large businesses more than other family businesses. Wal-Mart is more similar to other large businesses such as General Electric, Coca-Cola, and Mobil/Exxon than it is to the mom-and-pop family business, although that's how it began. The management team running Wal-Mart does not consist primarily of family members. An outside CEO and outside board of directors set policies and make strategic decisions. Although the Walton family is the largest stakeholder in Wal-Mart, it is not the primary driving force in the business.

Advantages of Equity Financing for Large Family Businesses

This widening of the family business from the family sphere to the general public sphere has its advantages for some second-generation and most third-generation and beyond family members.

For one thing, if these family members have stock in the corporation, it gives them a public market in which to sell their shares. Shares in a private family-owned business usually have little to no market, and family members who want to sell their ownership positions and cash out of the family don't always have a ready way to do so. Also, family members who do not have a large management role in a family business but do have a financial stake often do not have much of a say in the management of the corporation, particularly with regard to corporate expenses. When a family business becomes a public company, there are more external checks on management.

Preserving the Family Fortune

As a family business becomes large, the family has ways to ensure that it still prospers regardless of how its business fares.

One way to preserve family capital is to start divesting the family fortune from the family business. As a business grows, it will issue stock. Much of this stock will be in the hands of family members. Many family members will sell at least some of their stock for cash or for a chance to invest in unrelated enterprises. This diversification will help ensure the family's wealth is no longer tied exclusively to the company it might no longer control day-to-day.

Suggestion Box _____

Your family business can conserve its income while still making significant contributions to charitable organizations. Consult with your accountant to find out some of the positive financial benefits of philanthropy.

At this stage, many former family business executives either move to another challenge or, if they have accumulated significant wealth, enter the philanthropic phase of their lives. These individuals have plenty of money to live out their lives in a pleasant fashion. Many of them turn to estate planning to ensure their children and grandchildren have trust funds to help them in their business careers and private lives. Many former family business employees also start giving money to charities and other worthy causes.

The Least You Need to Know

◆ A family business start-up often has to look to family resources to fund the initial phase of the business.

◆ A family business should create clear, legal documentation for investments and loans by other family members.

◆ As the family business grows past the start-up phase, it might be able to secure bank financing for future expansion.

◆ After the family business achieves considerable success, it may consider becoming a publicly financed company.

Chapter 14

Protecting the Family Business

In This Chapter

- ◆ Structuring the family business to protect the business and family members
- ◆ Incorporated family businesses must act like corporations
- ◆ Passing the business and financial assets to subsequent generations
- ◆ Using insurance products to protect business and personal assets

Family businesses are delicate creatures. Matching the soul of a family with the combativeness of a business can lead to difficult situations. Lawyers and insurance agents help family businesses prepare for the worst while planning for the best.

Most people resist going to a lawyer as long as possible. Professional advice can be painful and often costs a lot of money. The supply of lawyer jokes seems boundless. Most are of the variety "Question: Why won't the shark eat the lawyer? Answer: Professional courtesy."

But family businesses will find the need to hire a lawyer on occasion, and in this chapter we help you make the most of your meetings with counsel.

We also discuss how other professionals—accountants, human resources specialists, family business advisors, and insurance agents—can help you make the best decisions for your family business.

How Lawyers Can Help

For the family business, a lawyer can perform the yeoman's task of making sure the family survives despite the occasional pitfalls inherent in running a business. Providing that protection comes with a price: legal fees. However, those fees can be worth their weight in gold if they help a family avoid financial problems or future litigation.

Here are some of the areas where lawyers can help protect a new or growing family business:

- Help the family decide the best legal structure for the business.

- Protect the family name from competitors or after a sale of the business.

- Protect intellectual property rights.

- Help the family develop procedures to deal with claims of sexual harassment, divorces in the family, family members who want to start competing business, and other family business situations.

- Advise families that form corporations on how to structure business transactions without incurring personal liability.

- Advise families to plan for the future by putting together succession plans, estate plans, formalized compensation plans, and other business documents.

When You Don't Need a Lawyer

Not all families need or can afford all the services lawyers provide. However, most family businesses will profit from seeing a lawyer before the business starts operating and using a lawyer to help the business grow successfully.

Some legal protections can be obtained without hiring a lawyer. For example, every new family business today should consider acquiring a *domain name(s)* to do business on the Internet. Even if the family business does not need a website when it begins its operations, it should plan for the future. Registering domain names is relatively inexpensive, and it helps protect the family from future disputes as to who has rights to the family name.

def•i•ni•tion

A **domain name** is the name used by a family business on the Internet. Usually, the best domain name for a family business is the name of the business. If that name is not available, try to relate the name to what your business does.

Creating the Right Legal Structure

You might be able to start a corporation or other legal structure to run the family business without using the services of a lawyer, depending in which state your family business resides. But not having a lawyer do the initial formation work might be penny-wise and pound-foolish. You should consider having a lawyer (and/or an accountant) explain the advantages and disadvantages of various business structures. The type of legal structure you use to organize your business is important for the future of the company, and it's a decision you should not make lightly.

When your business is organized but is still small, you might not have to use lawyers very often. But legal situations can occur fairly soon, and you should be prepared.

If you have organized as some form of a corporation, which many businesses do to protect their personal assets, you will have to issue shares. It could be that, in the beginning years of the family business, you will give shares only to immediate family members. But as the family business grows, shares might be given to other members of the family and even outsiders.

At that point, you will have to consider what rights your minority shareholders will have. You might not want to give those minority shareholders any rights in the management of the business, but under some states' laws, minority shareholders who are ill-treated might be able to force a sale of the family business or at least a repurchase of their stock holdings.

Suggestion Box

Many family businesses give stock in the company only to family members who work in the business. This might be a good policy to follow to minimize family disagreements. Family members who don't work in the business could be given cash, real estate, or other compensation as part of a will or trust.

To prevent a possible future lawsuit, you should draft a buy-sell agreement that will be binding on you and other shareholders. Such an agreement gives all shareholders certain rights to sell their interests. In many family businesses, other family members are given the first option to buy the sellers' shares, usually at a price set by a market appraisal of the family business. If other family members do not want to buy the shares, the minority shareholder may be given the right to sell the shares to an outsider.

Told You So!

If you are interested in prenuptial agreements, be sure to check how your state's courts treat them. Some state courts strictly enforce prenuptial agreements. Others are more skeptical of such agreements, especially if they seem coerced.

Another legal protection that some family businesses opt for is having family members who are planning to get married enter into prenuptial agreements with their future spouses. Divorces are tricky affairs for many family businesses, which do not want a disgruntled ex-spouse to have a significant stake of a family business. By having family members enter into prenuptial agreements, family businesses can help ensure that family business shares remain within the family.

However, prenuptial agreements do have a downside. They have to be entered into before a marriage, and many future spouses view such agreements with distaste. Here, the conflicts between the business side and the family side of a family business are most evident. Some families dispense with the idea of prenuptial agreements just because they tend to make people unhappy or even distrustful at a time when they should be most excited about the future.

Protecting the Corporate Structure

After a family business is up and running, the management should make a concerted effort to ensure the company runs as a formal corporation, if a corporate structure is chosen for the business.

Following Corporate Rules and Regulations

Sometimes, corporate rules and regulations are ignored to the financial detriment of family members. Many family business owners naively think that because they have formed a corporation, their personal wealth is safe.

But a family business that is incorporated must follow the rules. These include issues of debt management, compensation of officers, shareholders' rights, business capitalization, taxes, and more.

However, courts often *pierce the corporate veil* and hold individual family members liable for corporate debts or obligations if the court feels the corporate status of the family business has been abused.

def•i•ni•tion

> **Piercing the corporate veil** is when courts rule against family members when they find the corporation those family members have started is a sham. If family members fail to observe corporate rules and regulations, unduly enrich themselves, undercapitalize the corporation, fail to reveal the corporate structure, and generally disregard the corporation, those family members can be personally liable for debts.

The actual legal doctrine of piercing the corporate veil occurs either when owners have a corporation that is too thinly capitalized for the type of business it is in or when the owners of a corporation do not treat the corporation as an entity separate from themselves. This can happen in a family business where creditors or suppliers think they are dealing with family members and do not realize there is a corporate structure. Family members should be sure to enter contracts and other legal agreements in the corporate name and should be diligent about revealing the corporate name to third parties. If the family members do not act as if a corporation exists, a court might eventually decide the corporate structure was a sham.

When the Corporate Structure Fails

In one case, a family business owner who failed to submit the paperwork to renew his company's corporate status was held personally liable for debts the corporation would ordinarily be liable for. In another instance, a court held that a minority shareholder was entitled to a piece of a family business even though some family members testified that she had relinquished her shares. Because the corporation did not have annual meetings and the recordkeeping was faulty, the court said that it would give the benefit of the doubt to the minority shareholder.

In other instances, courts have ruled against the corporate status of a family business because the family members received "excessive corporate distributions." Creditors of the business, which had gone into bankruptcy, were allowed to recover salary and dividend payments that the court viewed as excessive.

Family members are personally liable for withholding taxes and other governmental obligations. If a family business fails to pay withholding taxes on employees' wages, for example, the owners of the business will be personally liable for the taxes and could face possible criminal charges for not paying the taxes when they were due.

Sexual Harassment and Discrimination

Another area where family businesses must be careful is sexual discrimination and sexual harassment. A lawyer or human resources professional can help a family business create a policy to deal with sexual harassment, as well as policies to prevent such problems from occurring in the company.

Told You So!

A family business faced with a sexual harassment or sexual discrimination claim against a family member should hire an impartial outside person to conduct an investigation. Such claims must be taken seriously if the family wants to avoid an expensive lawsuit.

Sexual harassment cases involve unwelcome sexual advances or verbal or physical conduct of a sexual nature. Sexual discrimination cases can involve instances when women in a firm are treated unfairly compared to men or men are treated unfairly compared to women. Issues include equal pay for equal work and equal opportunities for advancement for women. Companies should ensure that all employees understand they have the opportunity to advance based on their potential, not on their gender.

Family firms should follow these steps to help prevent sexual harassment lawsuits:

1. Family businesses should have written guidelines on what constitutes sexual discrimination and sexual harassment, and those guidelines should be communicated to all employees.

2. Any complaint about sexual harassment or discrimination should be promptly investigated.

3. Key employees should be informed about the progress and results of the investigation.

4. Disciplinary action should be taken against any employee found guilty of sexual discrimination or harassment.

Claims of sexual harassment or discrimination can be particularly troublesome for a family business. If a family member is accused of sexual harassment or discrimination, nonfamily supervisors can be reluctant to thoroughly investigate a claim against a family member for fear of retribution.

Representing Competing Family Interests

Hiring a lawyer to represent the family business might not solve all of a family business's legal needs. Family members frequently have disputes over a financial or ownership issue. The family business's lawyer might feel uncomfortable giving advice to two different family members without signed authorizations by each family member saying they are aware of potential conflict of interest.

If the dispute is a major one, each party to the dispute should be represented by a separate attorney. This can be expensive, but it might be the only way major differences can be resolved. Lawyers often represent clients with a common goal but differing interests. However, when those differing interests flare up and threaten the harmony of the family or the family business, it is a lawyer's responsibility to step back and say she cannot represent both sides.

Family Business Planning

Lawyers can be helpful in guiding a family business through the planning process. They function as an outside voice that provides an important perspective for many decisions that can have an emotional family overlay.

The Value of Hiring Family Members

As we discussed in Chapter 7, family businesses often have to make hard decisions involving whether to favor family members over outsiders when making management and promotion decisions. Legal advice can be helpful in establishing company policies that address hiring and other employment issues.

Family businesses, by their very nature, have to face charges of unfavorable nepotism: the idea that some family members can rise in the business because of their family connections and not because of competence. If such negative feelings of nepotism pervade a family business, the business might have a hard time attracting and keeping nonfamily members as employees. Family businesses that favor unqualified family members might eventually lose their competitive advantage because of unqualified management.

Many family businesses see value in retaining family members as employees. The wealth generated in the business is kept inside the family structure. Family members are often best able to ensure that family traditions and family values stay alive in the business. But family businesses need to ensure that qualified outsiders have a fair opportunity to advance in the business.

To preserve the integrity of the hiring process, a family business can work with a lawyer or a human resources professional in several areas:

◆ Drafting a succession plan for the business to determine how future CEOs are chosen

◆ Developing a compensation plan for key employees

◆ Developing an organizational chart with clear delineation of employee responsibilities

◆ Helping draft strategic plans for the business

◆ Developing guidelines for family members, which can include several years of working outside the business before joining the business and having rules on ownership for family members not working in the business

By working with a lawyer or human resources professional to develop these plans and goals, a family business shows its commitment to fairness to all its employees, regardless of family membership.

Family Business Estate Planning

Another way lawyers and accountants can be helpful in the family business is by developing estate plans for top family executives. If a business is doing well, an estate lawyer can help the business owners pass on the ownership and value of the business to future generations while minimizing the effect of estate taxes.

One of the key aspects of any estate plan is to take advantage of the estate tax laws. For instance, it is probably not advisable to have all the family business stock in the name of one spouse. If the estate is split up, each spouse can qualify for an estate tax exemption. This can result in substantial tax savings upon the death of the second spouse. In many states, how a couple owns its home can have major implications in the event a successful lawsuit is brought against one of the spouses. A tax lawyer or experienced accountant who is knowledgeable about your state's regulations will guide you for your specific needs.

Selling the Business

Lawyers are especially valuable at the time of the sale of a family business. Important considerations include whether the sale is a stock sale or assets sales, what happens to the family name, and whether family members will continue in the day-to-day management of the company. Another important matter to consider is the negotiation of noncompete agreements.

One key consideration for family businesses is how the family name will be used after the business is sold. If the sale is to another family member, the new family owner will probably want to keep the family name on the business. However, even nonfamily owners might want to keep the name—especially if the family name has accumulated goodwill. A family business might want to spell out how the name can be used and possibly limit the type of products or services that can be sold using the family name. The family also might want to ensure the family business name is not being used in a manner inconsistent with the political, social, or religious beliefs of the owner or other family members. This is a matter for negotiation, and a lawyer can be helpful in structuring a transaction that makes sense for both sides.

The Living Trust

Some financial planners recommend transferring interests in a family business through a living trust. They claim that such a trust will avoid probate, keep family assets private, and lead to lower tax burdens for family businesses. However, setting up a living trust can be a complicated affair, and no family business should attempt one without consulting the family business lawyer and accountant.

Insuring the Family Business

Hiring or consulting with lawyers and accountants is not the only way a family business can protect its assets. For many business risks, insurance can help the family business weather business storms.

An Umbrella Policy for Personal Risk

One of the most basic insurance tools family business members should think about is an umbrella insurance policy. Because many family businesses are intimately tied to the personal finances of the family members who own the business, the last thing the business needs is a personal financial crisis by one of the owners.

An umbrella policy can add millions of dollars of personal coverage on top of automobile and homeowner's insurance. This policy can be an effective and inexpensive way to protect against many personal lawsuits.

Disaster Planning

Another insurance need that is important for many family businesses is business interruption insurance. Hurricanes, tornadoes, fires, and other natural catastrophes can stop a business from functioning for days, weeks, or even months. Some family businesses cannot reopen if the losses from a natural disaster are severe. Business interruption insurance can provide a safety net while a business recovers. Make sure your inventory and other assets are valued at market value rather than cost because that is what you'll have to pay when you rebuild.

Many family businesses plan for a disaster by having substantial financial reserves ready for an emergency. Even when a business is covered by insurance, disagreements with the insurance company on coverage or delays in settling a claim can be a financial hardship on a business. Some companies set up a strategic reserve to cover foreseeable disruptions. These reserves help a company through economic slumps or increased competition in their business sector. Family businesses that have not taken on equity investors have more flexibility in keeping significant funds in reserve. Third parties might characterize such reserves as excessive, instead of as a prudent way to prepare for a possible emergency.

Another way a family business can do advance planning for a disaster is by making sure vital business information is backed up and stored offsite. Many computers offer backup software that allows a company to retrieve vital information if a computer malfunctions or a hard drive crashes. But if a fire or another disaster strikes the family offices, computer storage onsite is not enough. Not only will the computer be destroyed, but all the onsite backup will also be lost. Take the additional step of storing key information offsite. It is inexpensive and a small but necessary protection for vital family business information.

Life Insurance

Life insurance, especially on the CEO of the family business, can be valuable in case of an unexpected death. Sometimes the CEO is so vital to the business that significant financial losses will occur if the CEO dies. Life insurance policies on key personnel can help a family get through the financial problems of an unexpected death.

Some ideas for protection of the family business do not involve an insurance policy. For example, some family businesses make it a policy that key executives do not travel together. Losing one brother in a family firm in a car or plane accident is a horrendous loss. Losing the three brothers who run the company in the same accident might mean the end of the company.

Along the same lines, it is helpful for managers in a family business to learn each other's jobs. That way, if there is a death or serious illness in the family, another family member can take up the task.

Health Insurance

One of the more pressing concerns for family businesses is healthcare. Because of the expense of healthcare, many family businesses prefer to set up a health program at their businesses.

Employer/Employee Considerations

A family business has to balance several competing priorities when setting up a health plan:

- **Employees want a quality health plan.** They view health coverage as one of the most important considerations in choosing a job.

- **The cost of providing health insurance has increased.** Health insurance costs have risen substantially more than any other business cost over the past 20 years. Now more family businesses are requiring employees to pay more for their health benefits. Deductibles have increased and some services have been dropped.

- **A business health plan might be a better option.** Family businesses whose employees are primarily family members should probably opt for a business health plan because a business plan is likely to be much cheaper than any health insurance family members could obtain outside the business. But health insurance for a business must be offered and available to all the employees of the business. When a number of nonfamily employees are involved, the family members should have a serious discussion with their financial advisors to see which type of health protection they can afford to offer.

Long-Term Health Insurance

As part of their health insurance planning, family businesses should investigate the possibility of long-term healthcare insurance. It is more likely that a relatively young family business owner (in his 40s or 50s) will have a long-term health issue than die. If an owner is in a car crash that causes severe but not life-threatening injuries, having long-term healthcare can alleviate some stress during a traumatic time for the family and the family business.

Having long-term care insurance satisfies the family member who is nearing retirement as well as the younger generation. For the family business leader looking toward retirement, long-term care insurance helps ease the concern about financial security if a catastrophic illness occurs. And having the long-term care insurance in place will be a comfort to the next generation in the family business, knowing that cash won't need to be drawn out of the business to pay healthcare expenses should a severe health problem occur.

Malpractice Insurance

Being a member of the board of directors for a family business presents unique challenges. Often, family business decisions are made for the sake of the family, and sometimes a conflict occurs between family needs and best business practices.

Larger family businesses with an outside board of directors will confront these issues from time to time. Family business directors have to walk a tight line between family interests and business interests. To attract the best outside directors, a family business ought to give those directors malpractice insurance for decisions that might prove controversial.

The Least You Need to Know

- ◆ Lawyers are an expensive but vital resource for family businesses.
- ◆ A lawyer can help you structure your business to avoid problems from the government, suppliers, employees, and disgruntled family members.
- ◆ Lawyers can help an established family business set up effective wealth preservation practices.
- ◆ Insurance policies can help protect a family business from disasters and provide employees with vital health insurance.

Chapter 15

Consultants and Mediators

In This Chapter

- Resolving disputes and planning for the future
- Choosing a well-credentialed consultant
- The need for consultants' objectivity
- Mediators as impartial observers

A father hands over the day-to-day management of the family business to his daughter. However, the father keeps ownership control of 51 percent of the stock in the business. The daughter wants an ambitious growth program for the business, involving a heavy investment in new technology. The father demurs, claiming that a more conservative approach would preserve his comfortable retirement. The daughter argues that if the family doesn't grow in a new direction, the business could die.

How can the family business resolve such a disagreement? A paid family business consultant often is the best answer. In this chapter, we discuss how to decide when the family business needs outside consultation. We look at the kinds of consultants and mediators who can help the family business and the kinds of services they offer.

When a Consultant Should Be Hired

Sometimes even the best of family businesses hits a roadblock. It could be competition. It could be a slump in the economy. Many times the trouble exists within the family.

When a problem in a family business is not solved, the business can suffer. Tempers can flare. Relatives might stop talking to each other, and the problem can move into the workplace environment. In these types of situations, it is often a good idea to use consultants to help get the family business back on the right track.

Suggestion Box

One of the biggest barriers to a family hiring a consultant is the fee a consultant charges. Contact your industry's trade association or related professional associations to find out typical fees for consulting services.

Consultants can even be valuable when there is not an actual dispute. A family business might want to start a family council or set up a succession plan. The business might be considering expansion and might need help in obtaining financing or writing a business plan.

The Types of Consultants

There are many types of consultants, and they handle different situations. Consultants can be internal. For example, a large family firm might have an in-house lawyer who can help the family through a difficult situation. Or the firm can have an accountant who is a whiz at getting through financial impasses.

Sometimes, the consultant is a hired gun, a specialist called in for a specific problem. The arrangement can be temporary or, if the problem is difficult, a consultant might work with a business for months or even years. In addition to lawyers and accountants, family business consultants can help with a variety of family business difficulties. There are also family business-trained psychologists who specialize in handling some of the personal issues that can arise when family members work together.

Many times, a team of consultants is necessary if a problem is multifaceted. In that case, one of the consultants acts as the team leader and reports directly to the family business CEO or another top management official.

Consultants Work on a Variety of Business Problems

The types of problems consultants handle are varied. They include:

◆ **Developing a succession plan.** A consultant can help a business devise standards to pick the next CEO. The consultant can even help make an evaluation if several candidates are vying for the top job. A consultant can assist in managing a sharing of power if appropriate. In addition, a consultant can give advice on how the transition from one generation to another might take place.

◆ **Helping a family business develop a sustainable governance structure.** When a family business first starts, the business can be adequately managed by the CEO with the support of other family members and outside employees. However, as the business grows, an independent board of directors is often helpful to give advice and approve management decisions. A consultant can help a family business develop a strong governance system that includes not only an independent board of directors, but also a family council in which family matters are addressed and a strategic business plan is developed.

◆ **Management of conflict among family members and various stakeholders in the business.** Sometimes, family members have disagreements that cannot be resolved among the parties. The disputes might be about how the business is run, who is responsible for certain decisions, or salary issues, to mention just a few. A consultant can help a family business work out disagreements before they need to be mediated or litigated.

◆ **Handling labor difficulties.** Labor problems can escalate to impasses and strikes. It is better to deal with labor issues early, and a consultant can help a family business understand which issues are important to workers and how the family can make its nonfamily employees happy.

Steps to Hiring a Family Business Consultant

Before hiring a consultant, defining exactly how the business will benefit from a consultant is helpful. The first step in this process is to write down the problem the consultant will be hired to address with you. If you cannot write down the problem, you are not prepared to face it. The consultant might not totally agree with how you describe a problem, but doing so is a necessary first step.

Next, the family business needs to build a consensus that a problem exists and needs to be solved. The family must also acknowledge that a problem exists and that it needs fixing. Without the family's involvement, the consultant is doomed to failure.

Determining the Problem and Who Should Be Involved

The family must also determine the parties who need to be involved in the consulting effort. Should the consultant deal with only the owners of the business? Or do other family members need to be involved? Should the management team be brought into the process? Think through your problem and decide who should be included in its resolution. Sometimes the consultant can help you with this process!

Told You So!

Hiring a consultant when some family members feel a consultant is unnecessary most often leads to failure. In fact, many reputable consultants will only work for family businesses in which consensus has been reached that the family needs a consultant.

Care should be taken to find the right type of consultant. Is the problem legal? Financial? Managerial? Psychological? Or is it a complicated problem that will require a multidisciplinary team of advisors? Figuring out which type of consultant is necessary for this particular problem is important to do before a consultant is recruited.

Finally, the family should seek referrals. Managers can ask other family businesses whether they can recommend a particular consultant. Trade and professional associations often have lists of consultants. The Family Firm Institute, Inc., a professional association of consultants and advisors who work in the family business field, could be of assistance to you.

Picking the Consultant

Consultants can play a large role in the success or failure of a family business. Because they help address some of the most important decisions of a family business, considerable care should be taken to choose the right consultant.

Some things to consider when selecting a consultant for a family business include:

◆ **Credentials.** A consultant should have the right type of education and training to solve the specific task for which he is hired. In addition to academic degrees, a consultant should have practical, hands-on experience working with family businesses. A consultant should supply a list of references, and those references should be thoroughly checked.

◆ **Overall competency.** An initial meeting should be scheduled for consultants the firm is considering. How a consultant handles the family members at this meeting should help determine whether he is hired. The consultant should describe the types of situations he has dealt with and the results.

◆ **Experience with the family's issue.** Even though a consultant can have be very competent, he might have no experience with the particular issue your family is facing. If the issue is highly technical, look for a specialist rather than a general family business consultant.

◆ **Price.** Consultants charge in a variety of ways. Some charge by the hour; some charge by the task. Others want to be put on a monthly or yearly retainer. A frank discussion of money should take place immediately to lessen the chance of future disagreements about fees. Check with your trade association, professional associations, other family businesses, and other consultants to determine whether the fees your consultant wants to charge are in line with industry norms.

◆ **Values that match those of the family business.** One of most important distinguishing characteristics of a family business is its values and traditions. Make sure the consultant understands those values and traditions. You want a consultant who is empathetic with your business plans and needs.

◆ **Personal chemistry.** If you like the consultant, it will be far easier to work with him. A consultant with a flip or superior attitude may have the intellectual framework to help your business, but if you don't like him, you and your family will have a hard time accepting his recommendations. You don't have to be best friends with a consultant, but you have to respect and get along with anyone advising you about your business.

After a consultant is chosen, the family business managers must develop a working relationship that is based on trust and respect. However, a family business's use of consultants is rife with potential pitfalls.

 Told You So! _____

Watch out for conflicts of interest. Some consultants, especially financial advisors, want to sell products as advice. This can be counterproductive because the family business member will wonder whether the consultant is giving impartial advice or merely pushing a product he will profit from. Ideally, you should pay consultants only for their advice.

Potential Pitfalls of Consultants

Keep in mind that the managers of a family business should not expect miracles from the consultant. Inflated expectations can make the consultant's job more difficult. A consultant cannot fix all of a business's problems. What the consultant can do is help identify solutions the family business managers can implement. The consultant is not a business manager. The consultant is a facilitator to help the mangers institute a workable solution for family difficulties.

How Not to Use Consultants

Problems with consultants can occur because some managers are looking for validation of decisions they have already made. They are looking for a friendly pat on the back and reassurance that they are doing things correctly. Reassurance is not the proper role for a consultant. A consultant is usually hired to help fix a particular problem or help with familial relationship problems. Propping up egos is not a proper role for consultants.

Likewise, some managers want the consultant to be the keeper of family secrets. They want to confide in the consultants because they do not want a family confrontation. They'd like the consultants to manage change but not reveal the secrets. This puts the consultants in an awkward position. It is better to discuss problems with family members openly, with the consultant available to help facilitate agreement or reconciliation.

Similarly, some managers hire consultants to be ambassadors to the rest of the family, or allies against them. They want an outside person to validate their arguments against other family members. But the more a consultant is seen as favoring one family member or one point of view, the less effective that consultant will be.

However, consultants can play a valuable role in getting family members to sit down and talk to each other. This is especially true when there is a generation gap in the family. The second or third generation might feel that their older relatives and other older managers do not give their generation proper respect or authority. A consultant might be able to bridge that gap and provide a mechanism for members of different generations to begin talking with each other.

Why a Family Business Might Not Want a Consultant

The use of outside advice does not necessarily have to be in the form of a consultant. Many family businesses ultimately decide that hiring a consultant is not the best solution for their company. Reasons not to hire a consultant include:

◆ **Cost.** Consultants can be expensive. Some consultants want long-term contracts because their experience shows that family businesses have a hard time quickly resolving issues such as family disputes and succession. Also, the consultants believe a longer-term contract will show the family's commitment to making important changes.

◆ **Privacy concerns.** No matter how reputable the consultant, many family business managers are reluctant to go outside the family to discuss important business matters. These family members can be concerned about a consultant inadvertently leaking family secrets, or they might feel that family members are better positioned to solve internal problems.

◆ **Other available alternatives.** Some family businesses meet with other businesses in share groups set up to solve common family business problems. Other family businesses have the ability to use the resources of a nearby university or college that has started a specific program to help family businesses. A local university might offer courses that can help businesses deal with the financial or legal problems family businesses must confront. These programs often also focus on the family side of the family business.

◆ **Inappropriate use of consultants.** Some family businesses insist on telling the consultant what the problem is. Consultants should be hired to get to the root cause of the problem. Another mistake many companies make is hiring a consultant just because she has experience in the family business's industry. Consulting is a specialized skill and requires people skills as well as knowledge of an industry.

Alternatives to Consultants

If a family business decides not to hire an outside consultant, it must then decide how to solve family business problems. One route can be to take family problems to the family council, if one exists. If no family council is in place, this might be the right time to set one up.

If the problems the family business is facing are not personal, family problems, the family might be able to arrange for outside help that is not as expensive or intrusive as a consultant. For instance, suppose a family business wanted to explore marketing alternatives on the Internet. A local university business class on marketing can take on the problem as a case study, or the university can supply some interns to work with the company to develop a marketing strategy. This approach can be far less costly than hiring outside consultants, and it might lead to the eventual hiring of the interns or other employees to initiate the marketing program.

Also, the family business might decide to enroll some family members in a management training program so they can be taught to handle the problems the family business will face in future years. If the problems are long-term (such as succession issues and future direction of the family business), a program lasting several months or several years might provide the future leaders of the family business with the expertise to deal with the family's long-term challenges.

def•i•ni•tion

A **share group** is a group of business owners from your industry who meet periodically to discuss common business problems and opportunities.

Networking is another alternative to consultants. There are likely to be other businesses in your industry that you do not directly compete with because of your specialty, products, or location. These other businesses can join with you and other noncompeting businesses in your industry as a *share group*.

Your industry trade association might offer you or help you put together a share group. Share groups are helpful because they let businesses with similar goals help each other with problems they have successfully solved. Sometimes a share group uses the services of a consultant if there is an issue they all want to learn more about.

 Told You So!

Your share group can discuss a variety of issues, but your group must take precautions that it is not viewed as an anticompetitive gathering. There might be some antitrust problems to consider when setting up a share group. For example, pricing discussions can lead the government to conclude that the purpose of the share group is to minimize competition. It is better to avoid talking about pricing altogether in an industry share group.

Using a Mediator

Sometimes the difficulties within a family business become so painful that hiring a consultant is not enough to fix the problem. Tensions among family members might have become so great that at least one family member or family member grouping has threatened or instituted a lawsuit. Family members might not be talking with each other, and a poisonous attitude might have set in at work. In such cases, litigation might seem necessary, but there can be an alternative: *mediation*.

Mediators are trained professionals who are brought in by a family business to help resolve serious disputes. Unlike consultants, mediators do not attempt to solve future problems. Mediators are there because a major problem has erupted. Rather than provide a solution to the problem, mediators help family members achieve a resolution to which all parties can agree. The problem might still remain to be solved, but the mediator helps the parties avoid an expensive and protracted legal fight.

def•i•ni•tion

Mediation is the process of solving serious family disputes that are in litigation or headed for the courts. An impartial third party helps the parties understand the dispute and helps the parties work through some sort of settlement of family differences.

Problems for a Mediator

Examples of problems in family businesses that mediators can help solve include …

- Arguments over payment of dividends.

- Succession issues.

- Disagreements over the future direction of the company.

- Severance pay disputes.

- Problems caused by a divorce of one of the principals of the family business.

- Disputes among siblings about roles in running the business.

The problems mediators face might seem similar to the problems consultants are brought in to solve. However, a mediator is brought in later in the game, when the situation has deteriorated. Because the parties are threatening or might have actually instituted litigation, a mediator is often the last recourse before the family dispute is aired in public in a courtroom.

Advantages of Mediation

Mediation has become a popular way to resolve serious family disputes for several reasons. The earlier a dispute is resolved, the less financial and emotional damage the dispute causes.

The individuals involved in a dispute are best able to come up with a solution to the dispute. If the parties to the dispute do go to court, they are putting their fates in the hands of a judge or jury. If the issues are close, they are risking many thousands of dollars and many months or years on what is essentially a coin flip. The parties involved in a dispute know the issues far better than an outside judge or jury. A mediator can help the parties get to the core disagreements that have fueled the dispute and help the parties come to a sensible solution.

> **Family Stats**
>
> Mediation has a good success rate. About 80 percent of disputes that go through mediation are resolved. Considering the high cost of litigation and the amount of time litigation takes, it makes sense for parties to try mediation even if they believe their disputes are intractable.

Family members usually have personal feelings that can impair communication during a dispute. An objective third party can help with the give and take. This is often the best path to preserving a relationship among the parties. If the dispute does go to trial, one party will never be satisfied.

A mediator has no stake in the outcome of a family problem. A mediator does not have any authority to force the parties to a dispute to come to an agreement. What a mediator does is help family members come up with their own solutions to disputes.

How Mediation Works

When mediation takes place, it should occur at a neutral site. If a lawsuit has already been filed, the parties to the lawsuit can bring their attorneys.

The first step in the actual mediation process is for both sides to tell their stories. Then the mediator comes up with a problem definition. This is a crucial part of the process. Often, parties cannot effectively verbalize what the dispute is about. By making the dispute concrete, the mediator can help the parties understand the real nature of their disagreements.

The mediator then works with both parties and discusses the strengths and weaknesses of their respective arguments. The mediator does not offer an opinion or advice, but helps the parties understand better the basis of their conflict and how it can possibly be resolved.

For mediation to be effective, all relevant parties to a dispute must be involved. That means spouses should attend the mediation sessions, even if they do not presently work for the family business.

The attorney for the family business is often the one who recommends mediation. If a serious dispute occurs among family members, the family business attorney is often put in a precarious position. If the attorney sides with one side, he can risk the wrath of the competing faction. If the attorney wants to continue being the family business attorney, another party should be chosen to conduct mediation.

In the end, all a mediator can do is help ensure the parties in a dispute recognize how an independent observer sees the dispute. Whether the dispute gets settled amicably can be a reflection of how the family business normally handles disagreements.

Styles of Dispute Resolution

Some family businesses rely more on collaboration, compromise, and accommodation. These businesses will have the best chance of avoiding litigation in the first place or working effectively with a mediator in a major dispute.

Other families rely on competition and avoidance. These families might have a strong CEO who tends to impose her will arbitrarily in family disputes. There might be a strong culture of avoidance among other family members, who try to patch over hurt feelings. In such a culture, when a dispute does break out into the open, it might be much harder to solve because family members are not used to working together effectively.

The Least You Need to Know

- Consultants provide expert and outside approaches to family problems or disputes.

- Choosing a consultant means considering the fit of the consultant's values with family values as well as an examination of the consultant's credentials.

- Alternatives to consultants include educational training for family members and share groups with similar businesses.

- Mediators are brought in as a last attempt to solve problems when a family business dispute has gone or is about to go to court.

Part  5

Taking the Family Business into the Future

This part of the book helps you wade through the thorniest issue of all for family businesses—succession of the business ownership and management to the next generation. Everyone has heard the story of the family business president who never thought about who would run the company after she was gone. When that president was suddenly unable to work, the business was in real trouble.

We don't want this to happen to your business. These chapters bring you through the whole process of succession, from the founder to the next leader or next set of leaders, and then into the third generation and even beyond.

Chapter 16

Sale of the Family Business

In This Chapter

- ◆ Planning for the sale of the family business
- ◆ Determining the value of a family business
- ◆ Selling versus gifting the business to the next generation
- ◆ Plans that reward employees and let family owners cash out of the business

One successful business owner wrote a book about his family business. He called his business a "member of the family" that had to be brought up, fed, and taken care of. The relationship with the business was so personal that he was upset for weeks when he had to sell the business. It was like giving up on a member of the family.

Many family business owners have similar feelings about their businesses. Especially difficult when the founder is still involved with the business, it can be nearly impossible to have to give up your "baby" at any price. In this chapter, we discuss all the considerations that go into knowing when it's time to sell your family business and how to make it the best transaction it can be.

The Right Time to Sell

The family business is an integral part of family life, and it may be difficult to part with. Yet business owners become convinced that the right thing to do is to sell the family business for many reasons.

Factors to Consider Before a Sale

There are many reasons the time might be right to consider a sale of the family business:

♦ Family members may want the members of the next generation to own the business, and a sale to them makes the most economic sense.

♦ The family business owner might be tired of the stress of running the business. Some owners lose interest in the business or just realize it's no longer fun.

♦ The business requires a significant financial investment, and the family does not want to take the risk of such an investment, or doesn't have the liquidity, or cannot raise the capital.

♦ The value of the business is high, and the owners are concerned that the business will decline in value in the future. The owners could also want the capital from a sale for other activities or to start another business.

> **Family Stats**
>
> Selling a family business is usually a complicated affair that can take from 6 to 12 months. That is one reason planning for a sale should start years before the business is actually sold.

All these and many more reasons might convince owners of a family business that it is time to sell. The decision to sell should be a family decision. If significant dissension exists among family members, potential buyers will sense that something is not right and might not be willing to pay a good price for the company.

Selling During Good Times

All family businesses should keep in mind the possibility of a sale. But many family business owners will not consider the possibility of a sale for the wrong reasons.

Family business owners are reluctant to sell when the business is growing. The business is providing jobs for family members and the future looks bright. However, when things look the brightest, selling might be the smartest thing for a family to do.

Think about it. Will someone want to buy your company when there's no growth and the prospects look gloomy? Maybe. But you'll receive the highest price for your company when the skies are sunny and there are no obstacles in sight. Your company has to do an evaluation of the benefits of continuing in business versus the advantages of selling at a premium price.

Don't Wait Too Long for the "Right" Time to Sell

Another reason people don't sell is that they think the business climate might improve. That is a tricky proposition. You don't want to sell your family business at the bottom of the market. However, many business owners have turned down good offers for their companies because they thought things would improve. When the promised upturn does not occur, prices can plummet. Some of the brightest managers on Wall Street in recent years have seen their firms' values reduced to virtually nothing after they turned down good offers for their companies.

Another reason owners give for not selling is that they want to sell in the future, but "just not yet." Often, owners of family businesses feel such affection for their businesses that they just cannot take the final step to make a sale. That reaction is understandable from an emotional point of view, but family members should try to take the emotion out of business decisions.

Told You So!

People often only consider selling the family business if it is doing poorly. If your business is doing well and has good prospects, your family should at least consider the possibility of a sale. Its value will be the highest when everything is going well.

Determining Whether to Sell

Family business owners can have legitimate reasons for not wanting to sell their businesses despite a legitimate offer. Perhaps second- or third-generation family members have the capacity and desire to continue to run the business profitably. Conditions in the industry might be rapidly improving, or a product the company is developing might have a chance for rapid growth. Many family businesses that are in a favorable sector of the economy have seen the value of their businesses grow exponentially when investors realize the growth potential of what the company is doing. A company might be negotiating a new and large source of business and might want to postpone selling until this new business is firmly in place.

The Antinori family traces its roots in winemaking back to the year 1389. Their current wine business, Marchesi Antinori, was founded in Italy in 1863. Today, Piero Antinori, along with his three daughters—Albiera, Allegra, and Allesia—continue the tradition of 26 generations in their ownership and management of the business. Piero insists that "we think this is the best solution for us" to continue as a family business for now. It seems to be a smart decision for them—their business extends well beyond Italy to wine regions of the United States, Chile, Hungary, and Malta. In fact, they sold 49 percent of the company in 1983 to a British beer brewer but eventually bought their interest back.

Questions to Ask Before a Sale

In determining whether to sell a family business, the family members should ask themselves some important questions. The first is, "How important is the company's legacy to the family?" If the legacy is important, will it be preserved despite a sale?

Another question to ask is, "What are non-negotiable issues?" For instance, some families do not want new owners to take the family business into new business areas. They are reluctant to associate the family name with enterprises that might leave the public with negative associations.

Suggestion Box

Involve all family members who work in the business in the sale process. When family members feel they have a voice in the decision-making process, they will be supportive if the sale hits any snags.

A third question is, "Who is going to negotiate the deal?" Sometimes, it should be the CEO. But often a family would be better off using a third party. That way, the CEO and other top management can step in and help save a failing deal or veto sale conditions the family finds too onerous.

Prepare to Sell

Preparing to sell the family business might be a multiyear process. First, consensus should be reached that the business should be put up for sale. The advantages of selling the business must be weighed against the benefits of keeping it in the family. Do any second- or third-generation members want to carry on the business? If so, then if there is a sale, perhaps a financial arrangement can be made to pass on the business without making it too costly for the next generation of family leadership while giving the retiring family members a financial cushion. Unless there is family unanimity on a sale, problems might arise that will cause bitter family feelings or make the sale process far more difficult.

Some family businesses are run fairly casually—after all, it's all in the family and who cares if a few corners are cut? But to prepare a family business for sale, the business must ensure the financial books are in order and that the business is being run professionally. Lawyers and accountants might be necessary to supervise this process.

It's also important to consider when it's appropriate to tell employees who are not family members about an impending sale. You should tell them early enough so they can decide if they want to stay under new ownership, but not so early that you jeopardize the deal.

Transition Plans

Family members who have been intimately involved in the business have a tough transition to make when they sell. The jobs they have had (in many cases, for most of their adult lives) will be gone, and with them, the prestige, responsibility, and excitement. Even when sellers welcome the deal, they can be confused about what to do when they aren't in charge of their company anymore. Sellers must be prepared to handle the transition away from the family business.

If they are young enough, they should think about another potential career. For many family business owners, the thrill is in the start-up. Entrepreneurs are usually bubbling over with business ideas. The sale of a successful business has provided the seed money for many new businesses to get started. If the sellers are older, they should think seriously about whether they want to retire or plan alternative activities to fill their lives. After reviewing the alternatives, some potential retirees might discover they would rather stick with their business. This can mean continuing to work in the business after it is sold, working for another similar business, or perhaps not selling the business after all.

Negotiating the Sale

A key concern when faced with a decision to sell the family business is keeping the negotiations private. Families thinking about selling a business may want to have a buyer sign a confidentiality agreement. Such an agreement is crucial if word of a pending sale might hurt the company's viability in the marketplace. Because the average sale of a family business takes from 6 to 12 months to complete, confidentiality of the transaction is an important consideration.

Visits from Buyers and Sellers

Sellers might want to visit the buyers' offices and talk to other companies the buyer has bought. Although it is common for a prospective buyer to visit the seller's business (there can be several visits before a sale), it is rare that a seller visits the buyer's offices. However, such a visit might give the seller helpful information about the strength and culture of the company with which it is dealing.

Working with Professionals

Before the sale of the family business, a professional accountant should make sure the financial records of the company are in good order. Any sale will be contingent on the family business providing full and complete information about the financial health of the firm. If there are any financial problems with the company, the company must disclose them before, not after, a sale.

The company should also consider hiring a professional *mergers and acquisitions* firm to conduct the sale of the firm. A mergers and acquisition firm might be able to attract new potential buyers so the company can increase the price it will get from the firm.

def•i•ni•tion

Mergers and acquisitions are the buying, selling, and combining of companies that can finance or help a company grow rapidly without having to create another business entity. A *merger* is the combination of two similarly sized companies to form a new company. An *acquisition* occurs when one company purchases another and becomes the new owner.

The family business may also want to work with a family business consultant during the sale process to address family concerns about the sale and discuss appropriate parameters for keeping family and nonfamily employees informed about sale discussions.

Completing a merger or an acquisition is usually a long process. It starts with a series of informal discussions between the companies and their advisors, followed by formal negotiations. Then when a deal is struck, there is a letter of intent, *due diligence*, a purchase or merger agreement, and finally the execution of the deal and the transfer of payment.

A firm that really wants to sell and receive a good price from the sale might want to be flexible on the terms of the sale. Depending on the strength of the buyer, the selling firm might want to do an installment sale, in which family members are paid over time for the value of the firm. In addition to helping to achieve a higher sales price, this type of transaction can have tax advantages for the selling family members.

def•i•ni•tion

Due diligence is a reasonable investigation of a proposed investment deal before the transaction is finalized. The investigation is usually done by the investor's attorney and accountant to check out the investment's worthiness.

Valuing the Family Business

If a family business does make the decision to sell, it has to determine the value of the business. This is best done by an outside firm that specializes in assessing valuation of businesses.

Valuation Factors

A number of factors determine the valuation of a family business:

- **The size and potential of the markets for the family business.** If the family business sells a specialized product to a small niche, it might have limited growth potential. However, if the business has a new product in a large market segment, it could be worth significantly more.

- **The size and diversification of the customer base.** Buyers worry about taking over a family business with just a few large customers. The less dependent the business is on any one customer, the higher the valuation another company will put on it.

- **The quality and depth of the management team.** This can be a considerable worry to the buyer of a family business. If key family members are not interested in continuing to work for the acquired business, the business might be worth less to a potential acquirer.

- ◆ **The state of the economy in general.** When the stock market is going up and the future seems bright, companies tend to receive higher valuations.

- ◆ **The fortunes of the industry sector.** More important than the health of the economy as a whole is how other companies in your industry are doing. If the industry sector in which the family business operates is doing well, there might be great interest in buying the company. In fact, in sectors that are experiencing good profits, a competitor can prove to be the best buyer. It will value the company more highly, especially if cost savings can be put in place by merging the two firms.

- ◆ **The effect of government policy.** If the industry is heavily regulated, governmental action (or inaction) might contribute significantly to the value of the firm.

A potential buyer of a family business will consider most of these issues. But the buyer can have a completely different idea of the worth of the family business than the business itself has. If that is the case, a third-party valuation is definitely in order.

Suggestion Box

If your business has a proprietary product or service, your valuation might be less dependent on industry sector valuation or the state of the general economy. If outside economic conditions are poor, you might want to hold on to your business until your proprietary product or service is recognized by the market.

Periodic Valuations

Some family businesses have periodic valuations of their businesses by objective third parties even if the business is not being sold. One advantage of such an evaluation is that it gives a realistic picture of the firm's value. Family members can then make an informed decision about whether, based on that valuation, now is a good time to sell. Secondly, such a valuation can impact family distribution and investment programs. If the valuation is high, the family can distribute income and make new investments more readily than if the valuation is disappointing.

Remember that even though the valuations can be helpful, they can also be costly. And the valuations might have estate tax consequences.

Valuing the business could potentially create problems with family members who are minority shareholders and are not working in the business. If the valuation is high, those shareholders might have stronger arguments when they petition to have the family business distribute part of its wealth to shareholders. For these reasons, many family businesses decide not to have periodic business worth evaluations, even if these valuations might help determine whether the company is ripe for sale.

Retaining Ties with the Business

Even if a sale of the family business is completed, some family members will retain ties with the sold business. The sale could be for less than the whole company, so family members will still own part of or have a significant stake in the business after it is sold.

It may be that the sale is made in install-ments. Depending on how the deal is structured, family members' ultimate profit in the sale might hinge somewhat on the future profitability of the firm.

Family members might sign employment contracts and noncompete clauses with the new owners. These types of agreements can keep alive the relationship between the buyer and seller.

Told You So!

Many employment contracts with previous owners do not work out. Family members don't like the loss of authority, and new owners and employees might be suspicious of family members.

What Can Go Wrong

There is always the possibility that something goes wrong after the sale and the buyer and seller become embroiled in litigation. If the buyer thinks that not everything was disclosed before a sale, the buyer could sue.

Likewise, the seller might believe the buyer has violated the written sales agreement. Potential violations to the sales agreement include using the family name in an unau-thorized way and not making the required payments on a mortgage or installment sale. Although litigation is time-consuming and costly, it might be necessary when either the buyer or seller thinks it has been misled.

When the seller continues to work with the acquiring company, it can be difficult to be an employee rather than an owner. In many cases, family members do not work out their complete employment contracts, preferring, instead, to leave early to pursue new opportunities.

A Family Business Sale That Worked

The family business VitalChek, founded in 1987 by Herb Barrett and his son Michael, provides a good case study of how a successful family business should go about the process of a sale. The company provides fast retrieval and delivery of personal records, such as birth, death, and marriage certificates. State governmental agencies are big users of their services. After 10 years, the Barretts had grown the business to 62 employees and $50 million in annual sales. At that point, Herb decided he was ready to take some cash out of the business to provide financial security for the future. But he couldn't do that and continue to invest in the business, although that's just what it needed to take advantage of opportunities for growth.

VitalChek looked at the idea of selling the business to a large public company, but that plan was discarded. The Barretts wanted their employees to continue in their jobs and their business to grow, and they felt a huge company would be less likely to keep their business intact. Instead, they began to plan for the sale by increasing revenues to make the company more attractive to potential buyers. The market for their services increased after the 9/11 terrorist attacks, and a number of bids were entertained. In the end, the Barretts chose to be purchased by another entrepreneurial company, Choice Point, that was in a similar line of business and would maintain VitalChek as a way to strengthen its business. The deal was completed in late 2002, seven years after Herb Barrett first began to consider selling the company. All the firm's employees continued in their jobs, and the three members of the Barrett family in the business received three-year employment contracts, plus $120 million in cash.

Retirement of One Partner

When one of two partners in a family business decides to retire, difficult situations can arise. Do the sons and daughters of the partner who stays in the business have preference for top management positions? Who takes over the responsibilities of the retiring partner? How should the retiring partner be paid for her share of the business?

To avoid having these problems come to a head when one of the partners is thinking of retiring and selling her stake in the business, communication among family members is essential. Families should take specific actions to avoid problems when this situation occurs.

Have a clear policy on the hiring of family members. Partners should consider a policy of hiring their own sons or daughters only with the approval of the other partner.

Buy-Sell Agreement

Keep the *buy-sell agreement* up-to-date. The buy-sell agreement should describe in full detail the procedure for the sale of a retiring partner's stake in the business. The agreement usually calls for the remaining partner to have the first right of refusal for buying the business at market value or a specified discount from market value. The buy-sell agreement also describes the terms of the sale, including how long the acquiring partner has to pay off the cost of the business.

The buy-sell agreement should also contain a procedure for valuing the family business. Usually, an impartial person agreed to by both partners should perform the partnership valuation.

def•i•ni•tion
___

A **buy-sell agreement** is a document that sets the terms on how a business will continue when an owner wants to retire. A buy-sell agreement includes a mechanism to fix the value of the business.

Finally, the buy-sell agreement should delineate what happens if the surviving partner(s) do not want to or cannot afford to buy out the retiring partner's share of the business. Alternatives in this scenario include letting the retiring partner sell his share to an outside investor or another family member or to put the entire business up for sale.

Agreeing to the procedure ahead of time for the situation in which one partner wants to sell out is invaluable. Trying to put a procedure in place at the last minute can lead to misunderstandings and hurt feelings.

Diversifying Assets

Another factor partners in a family business should consider is diversifying assets to pay for the retirement of a partner. If all the family business assets are tied up in family stock and family holdings, funding a retirement is often difficult. However, if a substantial portion of the family business assets is invested in other, liquid assets, funding a retirement can be much easier.

Family members in a family business should think about what happens to the next generation when one of the family business members retires. It might not be fair or right for the business to automatically assume that the children and/or spouses of the family member remaining in the business should run the business after retirement.

The nieces and nephews of the remaining partner might be more qualified than the sons or daughters or spouse. Or it might be the case that a nonfamily member would be a better steward of the firm in the future.

> **Told You So!**
>
> As a business grows, diversification becomes crucial to family members' financial health. By keeping all family money and assets in the family business, family members are taking a huge gamble and won't be prepared for a significant downturn in the family business.

The Succession Plan

Partners in a family business should agree on a succession plan before a retirement is in the works. This removes a thorny issue for the retiring partner: how to ensure his children receive a fair shake in the ongoing business.

Most importantly, a family partnership should try to operate as a team. If teamwork can be established before a retirement takes place, much drama can be removed from the family business. The more communication lines are kept open, the better able a family business will be to handle the stresses of a retirement.

Transferring the Business to the Next Generation

Often sellers decide to transfer their family business to the next generation instead of looking for outside buyers. The owners of the family business have several options when contemplating this transfer of business assets:

- They can give the business outright to the next generation.
- They can give gifts of a portion of the business to the next generation over a series of years.
- They can sell the business to the next generation.

The financial health of the selling family business members, the acquiring family business members, and the family business all have to be considered in deciding how the business will be transferred.

If the selling family members are not independently wealthy, an outright gift of the family business will probably not be appropriate. The family business might be necessary to fund the owners' retirement.

Gift vs. Sale

Even if financial considerations permit it, an outright gift of the family business might not be practical or even advisable. Gifts to children often have financial, tax consequences, and emotional strings attached. An outright gift might provoke feelings of guilt in the next generation: they have not earned the ownership of the business.

Gifts also have another intangible problem. It is difficult to be a family hero if you are just receiving the business for free that your parents or grandparents created. If you buy the business, you are creating a new era in the business, in which you can create new family traditions and legends.

Gifting the entire business makes estate planning difficult and complicated for the departing owners. How much should the children or grandchildren not in the business receive from the estate? Should children or grandchildren who receive a gift of the business be excluded from the estate? Such problems can create ill feelings even in a close-knit family.

Suggestion Box

The gift-versus-sale debate hinges on the needs of the selling family owner. Owners should use conservative valuations to determine whether they can retire in comfort. Once you give away something, you cannot easily get it back.

Gifting over Time

Gifting a business or part of a business over a number of years might make more economic sense. Because the departing owners retain some control and stake in the business while the business is being gifted, they can receive benefits during the gifting period that will make their retirements easier.

Smaller gifts to family members who work in the business are seen as rewards for service rather than as an unearned handout. Pushing the gifting period outward in time also makes it more possible to develop a plan for relatives who are not in the business to receive an adequate portion of the estate.

Selling to the Next Generation

Selling a family business to the next generation can come at the suggestion of the departing owners or upon request by the next generation to have more of a role in the fortunes of the business.

What Sellers Need

When a business is sold to the next generation, the owners have to measure their cash and future payout needs against the ability of the next generation of the family to pay for their retirement. Often, the younger generation wants to pay out the price of the sale over time. This can be appropriate, but the selling generation might want to institute protections if it needs the income from the sale to retire. Precautions could include:

- Personal guarantees from buyers
- Life and disability insurance on the buyers to protect the income stream of the sellers
- Measures to restrict buyers from taking on too much debt
- Provisions against the sale of assets by the new owners
- Prohibitions against acquisitions by the new buyers for a specified period
- The right to renew finances
- Restrictions on the amount of salaries the new owners can pay themselves and their family members during a specified period

These and other even more restrictive provisions make it clear to the acquiring family members that the previous generation is serious about collecting the money due it from a sale.

The Downside of Restrictions

But if the next generation does not have the ability to repay or the business goes sour, or if the next generation is devious about hiding or squandering money, the selling generation might find itself in a difficult position. Even suggesting serious restrictions on how the next generation handles the business can cause difficulties among family members.

In most instances, a sale to the next generation goes smoothly. But if such a transfer cannot be worked amicably, an outright sale to a third party can be beneficial.

Told You So!

Restrictions on the new generation of family business ownership can create significant tensions within family businesses. Avoiding family tensions through a third party sale might have long-term benefits for all family members.

Ownership Transfer Through Employee Stock Ownership Plans

Another alternative to a sale to a third party is an *employee stock ownership plan (ESOP)*. In that plan, ownership of a business is gradually transferred to the employees. Employees might be given shares of the business after a certain period of time, or they might buy shares of the business.

Benefits and Dangers for Employees

Some studies have shown that employees who own businesses are happier and more productive. Because of the improved productivity, the business becomes more profitable. And part of the profits of the company can be shared with employees.

In an ESOP, the employees can elect some or all of the board of directors. They can also elect the leadership of the firm. Critics of ESOPs often point to slow decision-making as a disadvantage to this form of ownership. Also, employees at ESOPs can have a large portion of their personal wealth invested in the firm. This can be disastrous to employees at firms like Enron and WorldCom that went bankrupt and destroyed the financial equity of many employees.

def•i•ni•tion

An **employee stock ownership plan (ESOP)** involves the transfer of a business to its employees. For a family business, this transfer gives a stake in the company to outsiders as well as family members. Profits and productivity can increase for firms instituting an ESOP.

Owners Can Profit from ESOPs

For owners of a family business, having an ESOP can accomplish several goals:

◆ It can motivate employees to become more productive.

◆ It can enable the owners to reward nonfamily employees with a stake in the business.

◆ It can enable the owners to sell a share of their business but leave in place the traditions and employees of the company.

ESOPs are especially valuable to large family businesses and public corporations. There might be fewer advantages for smaller family businesses.

Most family businesses will eventually be sold. That is why family business owners should always be mindful of maintaining the market values of their firms. Families that use a family business as a cash cow or employment firm for relatives with no other prospects face the risk that they will gradually destroy the equity of the business. If they do that, the opportunity to sell the business can evaporate.

The Least You Need to Know

◆ The best time to sell a business depends on market timing and the needs of the current owners and the next generation.

◆ Valuing a business depends on the economy and industry sector as well as the actual worth of the company.

◆ A sale to the next generation might work better for a family business than an outright gift of the business.

◆ Selling at least part of the business to employees over time might be a better alternative than selling to outsiders.

17

Succession Planning

In This Chapter

- ◆ How to transfer assets to the next generation
- ◆ Planning for the next leader while the current one is healthy
- ◆ The best successor isn't necessarily the heir apparent
- ◆ Resistance to succession planning

The issue relating to family businesses that gets the most attention is that of *succession*. This is when the head of a family business steps down and hands over the leadership of the business, usually to one or more family members.

Every business, whether family-owned or not, turns over its leadership periodically. But in a family business, the choice of a new head of the firm brings potential family conflict and struggle. Indeed, an all-too-common situation for a family business is this: the head of the company keels over at his desk one day. No one has been designated to take over, and the battle among top management ensues.

Some prior planning for succession would have gone a long way toward alleviating this problem. In this chapter, we discuss how family businesses choose the next leader of the company. We examine the best ways to plan for succession and how to decide when the next generation is ready to take the reins. We also look at why so many family business leaders don't plan for their successors, and the problems this can cause in the business.

Succession Objectives

One of the fundamental missions of a family business is to pass the business to subsequent generations. That's usually part of the definition of a family business itself—keeping the business in the family across generations.

But most experts would agree that family businesses do a worse job of planning for the transition to the next generation of leadership than nonfamily businesses do. There's a lot of family baggage that can get in the way of successfully planning and carrying out succession of the family business.

The two main goals when planning for succession in a family business are as follows:

♦ Distributing assets from one generation to the next in a fair and efficient way

♦ Passing control of the leadership of the business to the person or persons who will do the best job of maintaining the success of the firm

> **Family Stats**
>
> Only 29 percent of U.S. family businesses have a written succession plan. Only 41 percent have actually identified a successor. But when a successor *has* been named, nearly 90 percent say that the new leader will be a family member. (Source: Laird Norton Tyee Family Business Survey 2007)

The people who receive the company's assets (that is, stock) are not necessarily the same as the person or persons who take leadership of the company. The two goals are different and should be considered separately as a family business prepares for succession. The objective is to maintain family harmony, although that can be difficult to do if emotions are allowed to get into the process.

Ownership Considerations

The first decision that should be made in planning for succession in the family business concerns the future ownership of the business. Who should be able to own stock in the company, and how should be it distributed?

Passing the assets of the business fairly within the family can be tricky because everyone's idea of fair is different. For many families with businesses, the business itself is the family's main source of wealth. The business assets might be Mom and Dad's main legacy to hand down to the next generation. Often, it's a delicate balance to pass the business ownership to the next generation in a way that best serves the interest of the business as well as the family members.

Should Family Ownership Continue?

Before any other decisions are made concerning succession planning, the family business must first determine whether ownership of the business should continue in the family. This can sound like a given for a family business, but it is not. For some family firms, the next step for ownership and management is to move the company out of the family's hands.

The company might be at the stage where it is ready for a big infusion of financing, and the strategy is to go public and have many outside shareholders purchase a majority of the business. Or perhaps the time has come to dissolve the business. Although Granddad started the company 60 years ago, maybe no one in the family lives near the business or is interested in running the business. In such a case, the best strategy might be to sell the business and divide the proceeds among the family members, who can then take the money and use it for other projects.

There are plenty of reasons for a family business to decide that it's ready to become a nonfamily business. Many family businesses make the assumption that the family must own the business forever, but the decision should really be considered based on the current condition of the business and the interests of the family. The owners of the business must confront this issue and make a decision for the future of the company.

Locking Up the Stock into the Future

Some family business founders make it clear to successive generations that they will continue to be in charge of the business in the future by restricting future sale of stock outside the family. This is done through trusts and restrictive sale agreements that can considerably reduce the ability of up to two future generations to dispose of company stock.

It's an estate-planning tactic that also sends a strong signal to the next few generations that they are expected to be stewards of the family business. Sam Walton famously did this before his death, maintaining a large portion of Wal-Mart stock in his family's hands.

This kind of collectivist succession strategy binds the family and business closely together. When a family has members in the next generation who enjoy working with each other and have a strong family identity, it can be a successful way to pass on ownership and control of the family business.

Sometimes stock is held in a voting trust for up to 10 years to let the next generation grow into adulthood before it has full control over the business. This can be a good strategy when no one in the next generation is ready to take charge of the family business when the current leader is ready to retire.

Empowering the Next Generation

A different succession strategy is based on the idea that conditions change over time and what is right for the family and the business now might not be right in the future. These plans place no future restrictions on the sale of stock. The retiring generation sends the signal to the next generation that it must make decisions for the company based on the business climate at the time.

Of course, this is a strategy for succession that gives the next generation more latitude with regard to company ownership. It comes from a point of view that the next generation has been prepared well and can make its own decisions that will be for the good of the company and the family.

This strategy for the future of the family business is individualistic in nature. Family members might not necessarily join the business in the future. The company could be sold or broken up to provide the next generation with a whole different set of business opportunities. Such a strategy could be a good choice when siblings in the next generation have never been close or have always been in conflict.

Keeping Ownership in the Business

Another issue when passing stock from one generation to the next is whether stock ownership should be limited to family members who work in the business. Many family businesses make this a rule to ensure that ownership of the company remains in the hands of those who really care about the business. The owner-operated family business has been shown to be a successful model for running a company.

In some family businesses, every family member who works in the business holds an equal share of ownership, no matter what his position in the firm. But this can cause arguments among family members. The sibling who is CEO and feels he contributes the most to the success of the business often feels resentful of siblings or other family members who have equal ownership shares of the company when their responsibilities with the firm are not as great. In other family businesses, the stock is apportioned based on job responsibilities, which can help with the fairness issue. But many parents still want to leave stock equally to all their children, no matter their positions within the family business.

For some types of family businesses, it is important to keep ownership in management's hands. A high-risk, entrepreneurial business that requires family funding or collateral makes sense to be owner-operated.

Although no one plan is best, how the ownership of the firm is passed to the next generation is a decision that should be made early in the succession planning process. This way, everyone involved understands and agrees on the ground rules.

Finding the Next Leader

After the decision has been made how to best distribute the family business assets to the next generation, the second objective of succession planning must be met: that of finding the best person to lead the company after the current CEO or president leaves that post.

This is different from ownership considerations, although they are often interconnected. The successor of the family business must have the necessary skills to lead the business successfully into the future.

Raising the Issue of Succession

In the ideal world, when the family business leader reaches a point when she is ready to retire from the business, a successor has been identified, approved, and groomed. But in most family businesses, this isn't the path that is followed.

Many family business leaders would rather die with their boots on than prepare for a graceful exit from the firm. And indeed, this has often been the plan of succession in family businesses—no plan at all. It's an all-too-common story about how a family business flounders when the leader suddenly dies without a successor identified or named. One famous example of this, which has a happy ending, is the *Washington*

Post story. The publisher, Phillip Graham, committed suicide and Katherine Graham took over. Although she had very little business experience, she decided to become publisher in order to keep the business within the family. However, the transition was very difficult.

There is no one best time to begin the process of planning for succession. But the head of the company must agree to tackle the issue before any progress can be made. Often, a reminder of one's mortality is the impetus to starting the planning process—for example, the founder has a heart attack that lands her in the hospital for a few weeks, a colleague leading another business dies and reminds the CEO that she is also vulnerable, or a bitter family dispute forces the president to examine the possible candidates for succession.

The process of finding the right successor can take years, so beginning it while the leader is healthy and the business is successful is the best approach. It takes cooperation and commitment from all the people who have a stake in the family business. The process will require family members to examine some difficult areas—aging, death, inheritance, and choosing among members of the family, to name a few.

Developing a Decision Process

The first step toward creating the way the decision will be handled is to ensure the leader is fully in agreement with finding a successor. Sometimes other family members try to start the process, but unless they are very powerful in the organization, they will likely get nowhere with their attempts.

One possible start is to have the head of the company agree to a retirement date, to drive the decision process forward. Announcing a date can help keep the founder from changing his mind about stepping down.

As part of the planning process, the family should evaluate the future of the firm and why the family wishes to maintain the business. When everyone agrees on the shared family values of the family business, making the transition to a successor is easier.

Suggestion Box _____

When beginning to think about succession planning, it is helpful to imagine the business ten to fifteen years in the future. Try to figure out what challenges your business might face in the future and whether your firm is ready to meet those demands. Ask yourself whether the leader of the business is so tied to the identity of the business that another leader will be difficult for others to accept. These are hard issues to consider, but they're important for determining who would be best to run the company in the future.

The start of succession planning can be the right time to develop some of the organizational structures discussed in previous chapters, such as a family council and board of directors, if they don't yet exist. The family council is the place to address the wishes of individual family members with regard to succession issues and to iron out whether the firm should be kept in the hands of the family. Because the family council is separate from the day-to-day operation of the business, these issues can be discussed without affecting the operations of the business.

Family businesses often establish their boards of directors in response to the start of the process of succession planning. For many businesses in the first generation of leadership, this is the first critical decision for the company for which the founder wants outside help. The board can consist of several directors who are not in the business, to provide an unbiased perspective. Several family member directors can be part of the board as well to weigh in on succession.

Another group that can be formed at this time is a succession task force. This group will develop the details of the succession plan, and therefore needs to be intimately involved with the company. The leader is usually part of the task force, along with likely successor candidates and other senior executives who might not be under consideration for successor, perhaps because they are not family members. Ideally, this group will look at least five years into the future of the company and identify other managers who have potential to lead the business and consider the training they will need to help them grow into new roles.

Assessing the Future Needs of the Family Business

Before potential candidates for succession can be identified, the needs of the company should be considered. The succession task force should do this by formally listing the managerial strengths, talents, and abilities that will be most important for the company in the future. For example, is a specific technical skill critical for future expansion of the firm? Will financial expertise be paramount as the company grows? Or are international plans so key to the firm's future that the next leader must be skilled in dealing with people from other countries?

If the company periodically develops a strategic plan, its direction will already have been set for at least a few years into the future. The senior management who are part of the succession task force should look further down the road for the company and try to foresee what it will need in the way of management talents in the next generation's leader for the company to thrive. Making these assessments isn't easy, but in the family firm, long-term planning is often key to the firm's growth and stability.

Choosing the Successor

The next step for the succession task force is to identify multiple successor candidates—not just one. Many founders naturally gravitate to a child who is working in the business. Some ethnic biases point toward the eldest son for the continuation of some family businesses. But today's family business must discard those old-fashioned practices and be more inclusive in their consideration of a number of possible successors to find the best fit.

Evaluating several candidates is the best method to ensure the company eventually selects the right successor. It is another useful way to define the qualities needed by the company, by comparing the abilities and talents of several candidates.

There are pros and cons to whether a successor should be identified and announced far in advance of when the leader actually steps down. If one heir apparent is identified early, this limits the company's choices and keeps qualified potential successors from being considered. There is the danger that the successor who is considered a shoo-in by everyone can feel entitled to the job and become complacent, which might keep the successor from further learning and development. Many business leaders prefer to keep an open mind about the next successor as long as possible, to better evaluate all the candidates until the choice must be announced. But on the pro side, if there is one obvious choice for the next leader that people openly acknowledge as the best candidate, announcing the choice early can be fine. It will send a strong signal both inside and outside the firm that the company is in control of its destiny and has made preparations for its future.

When a group of potential successors is identified and groomed, the company has the flexibility to take another route to succession if necessary: a team approach to leadership. This can be a good option for the family business, especially if several well-qualified family members in the next generation work well together. H. J. Russell & Company, a family-held construction and real estate conglomerate in the Atlanta area, has taken the team successor approach. Herman Russell's two sons have split the responsibilities of leadership, with one as CEO and the other as president and COO. Herman Russell's daughter chose to leave the company management to run the family foundation.

Told You So!

Try to keep your succession candidates from feeling overly competitive with each other. It should be a way to compare among qualified people, not a winner-take-all horse race.

There's a famous story about how Reg Jones, as chairman of General Electric, evaluated succession candidates. He would appear at the candidate's office door and ask, "You and I are flying in one of the company's planes and the plane crashes. Both of us die. Who should be the next chairperson of GE?" He would do it once, and then ask the same question again of each of the candidates three months later. Then the last time he asked it, the question changed slightly: "We're flying in the plane that crashes. I die but you live. Now who should be chairperson?" Jones would also ask the question of senior management who were not in contention for the top job, but whose counsel he valued.

Suggestion Box

If possible, do an outside search for a CEO when looking at family members within the firm as possible successors. It will help you understand more fully what kinds of qualities your company needs for its next leader, and it can give you important marketplace compensation information as well.

After a group of candidates have been identified by the succession task force, their progress and performance should be carefully watched. Specific performance measures should be instituted, with performance quantified in numbers as much as possible. Comparing increased sales rates across product lines or cost reductions achieved is easier than discussing more qualitative measures such as being innovative or a good manager. These kinds of more subjective measures can also be included through performance evaluation interviews or even surveys with peers who work with the candidate. The idea is to establish a file of information on each potential successor so her business performance can be reviewed by the group choosing the final successor.

It is important that each of the possible successors be given real jobs to perform, not figurehead-type positions that don't allow the person to show her true skills. This will help her acquire the abilities she will need in the future and will give the task force something real to assess. Because young people are growing and learning in every new position, it will help to try them out in a number of positions. The best will learn from their mistakes and use the knowledge to enhance their performances on the next job. Give each of the candidates enough time to really show what she can do. This is a process of years, not weeks or months.

Potential candidates might be sent to formal schooling programs as part of their evaluation and training while being considered as one of the possible succession candidates. An executive MBA training program can be appropriate, or courses to enhance technical skills, financial knowledge, or other programs to round out the candidates' skill sets. Although only one of the candidates is likely to be chosen for the top spot, the other candidates will benefit from the training, and in a family business, they are likely to remain with the company as part of top management.

Involving the board of directors is a good idea for lending more impartiality to the search process. Outside directors have experience from other companies that can be useful in providing comparisons among candidates. Another idea is to use outside assessment centers that administer testing on management skills such as team building and decision-making.

Making the Process Work

We've outlined a long-term process for finding a successor in a family business. It might seem overly complicated and involve too many people—especially if your family business is small. But every family business can fit these ideas to its own structure to improve how it chooses the best leader.

Communication to Stakeholders

Even in a privately held family business, there should be some transparency about the succession plan. This assures interested parties that the business will continue into the future. Customers, suppliers, and creditors want to understand that the family business has taken steps to ensure that its leadership transition to the next generation has been thoughtfully considered and will be handled professionally.

Exact details of the process do not have to be disclosed. But letting those stakeholders know that the business is carefully managing this critical task will allay fears about the future solvency of the business.

A side benefit of informing outsiders that the business is planning for leadership succession is that it might help to keep everyone in the company on task. Many family businesses begin the process of succession planning and encounter so much resistance or internal struggles that they simply give up on the process. If others outside the firm are expecting to hear of a successor named within a stated time frame, the company will be much more likely to keep the work on track.

Contingency Plan

As part of the succession planning process, the family firm should also prepare a contingency plan. Because the process usually takes several years or more, emergencies can happen during the intervening time.

If the leader dies before a successor is chosen, the company can be thrown into disarray. A contingency plan, perhaps bringing in a trusted director to lead the company temporarily or naming a nonfamily manager CEO until the ultimate successor is identified, will ease the company through the rough period.

Choosing a Nonfamily Successor

This chapter has focused on succession planning when the family business expects to elevate a family member to leadership. But the process outlined here will also help a family business choose a nonfamily member, if the business is willing to entertain outsiders as potential candidates for succession.

There might not be a likely family candidate for successor when the leader is ready to retire. Or a trusted nonfamily employee might be best suited for the job.

Some family businesses make specific plans to go outside the family for a new leader. The family-owned company Hollar Seeds has chosen a son-in-law, Andy Medina, over other family members to succeed the president of the company, Larry Hollar.

The succession plan that has been developed will take more than four years to implement and includes the eventual transition of company ownership to the new president. When Hollar's son made it clear that he would not join the company, a search for a successor was started and Medina was identified. Hollar insists that the choice of his son-in-law is "based on who he is, not who he married."

Family Stats
One in four (25 percent) family businesses say they plan to name a nonfamily member as the next CEO of the company. (Source: Marquette University's Center for Family Business)

At Henningson Cold Storage Co., a family business based in Oregon and recipient of several family business awards, the chairman and president of the company, Mike Henningson Sr., decided to take himself out of the succession process entirely. When it was time to begin planning for a new leader of the company, Henningson turned the entire process over to a task force that consisted only of nonfamily directors of the company. He wanted the process to be seen as completely objective, and he knew that several good candidates worked at the company, including both family and nonfamily members. Ironically, the successor who was eventually chosen by the task force turned out to be Mike Henningson Jr. The other viable candidate, who was a nonfamily manager, was promoted to executive vice president.

Common Mistakes of Succession Planning

More than half the family businesses in the United States don't have a succession plan in place. Why not? Most of these family businesses hope that their businesses will be successful enough to continue long into the future. Many have next-generation family members actively involved in the business in positions of upper management. But they often neglect the critical decision of who will head the company when the current leader retires.

Going It Alone

In most cases, the head of a family business should not choose her successor alone. This decision will profoundly affect the company, but the current leader will not be there to monitor it. The skills she brings to the family business are likely to be different from the skills the next leader will need to run the family business in the future, especially if the business has been successful and growth continues to take place.

If the leader does not involve others in the succession process, the likely candidates for succession will eventually wonder whether they are being considered for the job but will not have any information. If they aren't told that they are being considered, they might assume they are not and be resentful. Particularly when likely candidates are siblings or cousins, family dynamics will enter into the equation and create family stress.

I'll Think About That Tomorrow

It can be hard for the family business head to confront the issue of succession. After all, that's basically admitting you are mortal and you won't be around forever. A hard-driving, risk-taking entrepreneur might not want to think such thoughts.

The founder of a family business often identifies with that business. It's an extension of who the person is. His name might be the company's name. For someone who is so strongly tied to a business, admitting to the need to leave it and establishing a plan to do so might be more than that leader can stand to do.

Control Freak

Many family business leaders play the patriarch/matriarch role in the family. As such, being head of the family business gives them a unique position of power in the family.

Their decisions control the lives of other family members. Often, it is hard for these leaders to let go of the businesses they enjoy running because they think it means they will be giving up running the family as well. For those leaders who founded the family business, succession means letting go of their baby—the business they created with their own bare hands.

When the head of the family business makes a succession decision as a way to retain control over his children, the results can be disastrous for the business. A family member can be selected to run the business who is not interested in the position but feels responsible to take on the job. Such an unmotivated leader is not usually the best fit.

I Love All My Children!

Family relationships can be a hindrance to effective succession planning in another way. Some family business leaders are reluctant to choose among their children to elevate just one as head of the business. "I may have a daughter whose experience and education makes her the most likely successor, but wouldn't that hurt my two sons?"

Existing rivalries among siblings or cousins can be exacerbated by selecting one as successor. More than one potential candidate for succession might really want the job. When the successor is finally selected, those who lose out might decide to leave the family business. The best way to guard against this happening is to make the planning process open and transparent to all the parties involved. Face that issue before the decision is made: what happens to the candidates who aren't chosen? If the plan gives them a strong career path in the family business even though they haven't been tapped for the top job, they will be much more likely to remain with the company and enjoy the positions they hold in the future.

The Least You Need to Know

- ◆ Succession planning is probably the most critical task of a family business, and it might be the most overlooked.

- ◆ Many family businesses have no succession plan in place, which leaves them vulnerable if the family business leader is suddenly unable to continue in the position.

- ◆ Transferring ownership of the family business to the next generation is a complex process with many considerations: legal, financial, business, and family.

- ◆ A well-defined succession process involving key executives and outsiders will help make the transition to the next generation smooth.

18

Transition to the Next Generation

In This Chapter

- ◆ The founder's role in succession planning
- ◆ How to choose a successor(s)
- ◆ What potential successors can do
- ◆ The founder after retirement

The second generation of a family business is often called the sibling partnership. When the founder of the family business is ready to retire, he often looks to his children for company leadership. In the past, the eldest son was usually the heir apparent for the top job, but today it's not unusual to find the family business run by two or more siblings who have grown up in the business.

In this chapter, we talk about how the founder makes that transfer of power and ownership to the second generation. We also look at why family businesses have typically been slow to name a successor to the founder and what impact that reluctance can have on the business and the family. The things the founder and the potential successor can do to ease the transition are an important part of making the process work.

We also discuss what the founder can and should do following retirement from the family business. It's hard for any founders to leave the family business in the hands of anyone else, and planning for that eventuality will be a great help for all the parties involved.

First to Second Generation

A critical time in the lifecycle of a family business is when the founder of the business retires and a new CEO or president takes over the company leadership. This is called *founder succession*. When the new leader is a family member, as is often the case, the second generation of the family begins its tenure as business head.

def·i·ni·tion

Founder succession is the transfer of leadership in a family business from the original founder(s) to a new company head, often a family member from the next generation.

This transition can have powerful effects on the business. Sometimes, succession from the founder to the second generation rejuvenates and revitalizes the company. For other companies, the successor flounders and the business goes downhill or even fails.

In retrospect, the succession transition can be evaluated, and it can be obvious why a family business improved or worsened after the successor to the founder took the reins. But during the succession process, it isn't always easy to see how a candidate for the top job will fare down the road.

Following the process of succession planning as discussed in Chapter 17 can help make the transition to new leadership a successful one. But because this first turnover of company leadership is so key to the success or failure of a family business, it is important to understand the special issues involved in founder succession.

Founder's Vision Transferred

In Chapter 2, we talked about the founder of the family business as the person or persons who started a company with a strong idea about the product or service. The next leader of the company must understand that vision and be able to keep it vibrant when the founder is no longer part of the business.

The founder must sow the seeds for this transfer of her vision many years before succession is considered. Sometimes this is done gradually, as part of the family discussions around the kitchen table. The next generation is drawn into the business almost by osmosis, and some family members might learn to embrace the founder's vision for the business as they mature. But although the founder's vision for the business is always part of the company's values and mission, it will never be the same when interpreted by the next leader. The successor to the founder ideally shares the vision for the business but sees the differences in business climate that require a new way to translate that vision to the marketplace.

Founders are cautioned to look for a successor who is not too tradition bound. The next-generation leader of the company will surely face different business challenges than the founder has faced. Only someone who has the flexibility to adjust to future business conditions will be able to keep the business successful.

Family Stats

In most family-owned firms, 75 percent of strategic decisions are guided by a board of directors, an advisory board, or both. (Laird Norton Tyee Family Business Survey) A second-generation business has only a 53 percent chance of surviving 10 years. This means almost half of all family business don't continue within a decade of succession to the second generation.

Role of the Founder

In most family businesses, the founder is the ultimate decision-maker in the succession process. Although other people should be involved in the planning, and occasionally the founder prefers not to make the final choice, most of the time the founder selects his successor.

Leader of the Process

The founder of the family business is probably the most critical member in the process of succession planning. This person wields a great deal of authority within the organization—and likely outside the company as well. She knows intimately what it is like to manage the company. Unless forced out by illness, death, or stockholders, the founder is agreeing to hand over the reins of power voluntarily to the next generation.

Following the guidelines set out in Chapter 17, the founder should set up a succession planning process that will help her make the selection of successor. If a board of directors has not yet been established for the business, now is a good time to do so. If the company isn't ready for a full-fledged board, the founder can call on a few trusted advisors or colleagues outside the company to assist in the succession process. Although it can be hard, the process will work best if the outsiders are not all people who are in some way indebted to the founder—that is, the company attorney or company accountant. True outsiders who have no vested interest in the company are much more likely to give an unbiased viewpoint to the founder and anyone else brought into the succession planning process.

The founder might have a strong idea whom she would like to see as successor. Indeed, the founder might have been grooming a successor, particularly a child working in the business, for many years. That candidate should be brought into the process early and given opportunities to show her skills in work situations.

Told You So!

Founders need to remember that when they choose a child early on as potential successor or heir apparent, they are eliminating the possibility of considering all other qualified succession candidates. This drastically limits the pool of talent, which many experts point to as a reason so many family businesses fail following the retirement of the founder.

Why Some Founders Don't Plan for Succession

Many family business founders have tied their identities to the success of the business, with the company becoming another member of the family. Imagine this type of person stepping away from the company he created, nurtured, grew, and developed into the economic lifeblood of the family. It could be hard for a founder to let go.

There are countless stories of founders who refused to face the need for planning for a successor. Many of the tales are sad ones that end with the company in bankruptcy when the founder dies without clear instructions for a successor or even a way to find one.

Despite the numerous tragic stories, too many family business founders can give plenty of reasons not to plan for succession:

- They will have nothing to do if they retire.
- They think the business can't run without them.
- Leaving the business feels like losing their identity.
- They don't want to have to choose among their children for the next leader of the business.

- They worry that their income will drop if they aren't actively working in the business.

- Their ego won't allow them to consider that someone else could run the business as well—or maybe better—than they do.

- They won't be head of the family anymore.

Are these excuses legitimate? Yes and no. Of course, a strong entrepreneurial type of founder will often have trouble letting go of his creation. These kinds of issues will naturally run through any founder's head when contemplating turning over the business to the next generation. But for a successful family business, these fears and insecurities are unfounded. If the business has done well, the founder should be able to leave it on a strong footing. In fact, if a business can't survive the retirement of the founder, it's easy to argue that the business was operating on shaky grounds. A good business doesn't rise or fall with one single individual.

Most family business consultants say that their first relationship with a family business comes when the founder begins to consider if, when, and how to hand over the control of the business to the next generation. For many founders, it is the first time he has asked for outside help on a critical business decision. A consultant can help the founder move past his reluctance to name a successor.

Selecting the Successor

The eventual successor of a family business is likely to be very different from the original founder. As the business grows and changes, so, too, do the requirements of the company's leader.

A family business transitioning its leadership from the first to the second generation is often considered as going "from kingdoms to democracies." In many cases, the management style and strategy will be different in the second generation. What works for an entrepreneurial founder with a clearly defined vision will not work when the company matures and the successor is no longer the inventor, ideologue, or risk taker.

For many family business leaders, it can be hard to choose a successor when determined to select a family member. Parents can be blind to their children's failings, and when a founder refuses to look to any other candidates as eventual successor, the options are severely limited. Often, the founder is looking for someone just like herself, thinking that because she was able to start and run the company successfully, the same qualifications will be best for the next leader. But as we have discussed, those abilities that got the business started are not necessarily the same ones to bring the business into the future.

Succession from Parent to Child

The historical view of family business succession is of the male founder appointing his eldest son as the next head of the business. In some countries and ethnic groups, this practice is still widely followed today. But around the world, and certainly in the United States, that succession pattern has been broken. The second-generation successor is as likely to be a younger son, a daughter, or often a group of siblings who want to share management of the family business.

In fact, the highly respected consulting firm McKinsey & Co. studied family businesses in 2006 and determined that companies run by the eldest son underperformed the market by 10 percent. They caution that birthright isn't always the best way to choose a family business successor.

Sometimes, the founder is one dynamic person who has built the family business with her passion for a product and is known to be the personality of the firm. Henry Ford is one example of such a founder whose very name is synonymous with the company's products. He named his only child, Edsel, as his successor in 1919. Edsel, unlike his father, had grown up in the automotive business, and from his start with the company, was more interested in the business side. His expertise was more in sales, purchasing, advertising, and the numerous details of the daily routine. His leadership of the company left his father free to concentrate on engineering and manufacture. But Henry Ford famously undermined his son's authority at every juncture, retaining de facto leadership of the company throughout Edsel's reign as president. When Edsel died in 1943, Henry Ford resumed the presidency of the company, but his declining health forced him to pass the presidency to Edsel's son, Henry Ford II, in 1945.

Another kind of founder encourages the family to participate in the business and makes opportunities for everyone to learn about the business and develop skills. Although this type of founder is able to help her children become productive members of the business, such a founder can have real trouble choosing among the family members for a successor.

Sibling Partnership

Some founders choose to leave ownership equally to their children, creating a sibling partnership. This arrangement is not uncommon and creates issues among three siblings, especially if some of the owners don't work in the family business.

The relationships among the siblings from their youth naturally carry over into adulthood. Such rivalries might have seemed minor as young people, but when running the family business, the feelings among the siblings can easily hamper company activities.

In most successful sibling partnerships, one of the siblings takes the top job at the company, while the others either hold management positions or do not work for the family business at all. Unequal compensation issues among working siblings must be ironed out, and decisions made that everyone agrees are fair (refer to Chapter 7). Occasionally, siblings rotate in and out of the position as president, equally sharing management responsibility as well as ownership. The three Barebo siblings who run Otterbine Barebo, a manufacturer of water aeration systems, share equal ownership and management responsibilities for the company. It's an unusual arrangement that seems to work well for them.

> **Family Stats**
>
> Approximately 10 percent of family businesses in the United States have two people running them, mostly as sibling partnerships.

For a sibling partnership to work well, the siblings must share the same vision and commitment to the business. They must have an understanding that together they are able to do more for the business than if they worked separately.

Suggestion Box

Siblings who jointly own the family business must determine how responsibilities for the company will be divided. Even if the siblings plan to share responsibilities equally, they must delineate how the jobs will be divided and who will determine how well they are being done.

When the Founder Is More Than One Person

When a company has been founded by a family group, such as a group of siblings, the successor can be very different from the founders. Following group leadership, the next generation may require one single successor who can unify the company.

Succession dynamics can be particularly difficult in the case of partnerships. The second generation consists of children of each of the partners. Unless open and honest communication exists between the partners about the abilities and performance of their offspring, planning for one or more to succeed the original partners will be cumbersome and probably go nowhere. The story of a plumbing supply business in the Southeast demonstrates the tough issues partners can face when considering succession. In their case, two siblings founded the company and over many years hired members of their families into the business without consulting the other partner. When the performance of the one partner's son slipped, the two siblings had a quarrel that escalated into accusations about each of their children in the business. Needless to say, the firm eventually sold out, unable to make adequate succession plans to hand the business off to the next generation.

Selecting the Wrong Successor

Making the right choice of a new leader for the family business is one of the most critical decisions a founder will have to make. Many family businesses have failed after the second-generation leader turned out to be the wrong person for the job. Why does this happen?

The answer could be that the founder put off making the decision for too long. When she was finally forced to face the idea that a successor was needed, the choice might have been made hastily and without examining all the alternatives. And when the choices are limited to family members alone, a worthy successor can easily be overlooked.

Sometimes families want to protect an incompetent family member. Although it seems obvious that the strategy won't work, many families have promoted a member of the family to president because that person was deemed unable to make it outside the family business. The potential successor might not be ready for the job—too young or too inexperienced to handle the business.

> **Family Stats**
>
> The most frequent age cited for discussions to begin with the next generation about the business and their future involvement is between 18 and 25. (Laird Norton Tyee Family Business Survey)

Founders sometimes select their children as successors even when the children don't show real enthusiasm for the business. Thinking they'll learn to love it is a dangerous assumption for the business.

One famous example of an ill-suited successor is the choice of Fred Wang to succeed his father, An Wang, founder of Wang Laboratories. While there were numerous reasons for the company's demise, the insistence by An Wang to promote his son was looked on by most people inside and outside the company as a poor decision for the firm. Three years after becoming president, Fred Wang was fired by his own father. The company was never able to rebound from severe losses and filed for bankruptcy three years later.

When it is clear that the successor isn't the right person for the job, however, a family business must take steps to change the situation. If the founder is still around, she should assess her potential role in the failure of the successor. Perhaps the founder is still meddling in company business. Maybe the successor hasn't received enough coaching or mentoring in certain areas that could help turn around the situation. It must be determined whether the successor has the capacity to learn and change and remain in the job.

If not, the company will have to fire the successor and find a new leader. This is sure to create family strife, which should be anticipated and dealt with openly. As with a careful succession process, a well-thought-out plan to respectfully help the successor exit from the company and then find a new successor can be developed, but it requires good communication among family members and others in the business.

Obviously, a better succession process will need to be implemented in the company to select the new successor, to try to ensure that the same situation doesn't happen again. Choosing a successor who fails is hard on a family business from both a business and a family point of view. It is not a situation to be repeated.

Founder Support of Successor

When a successor is selected, the founder is the most important person in the organization to help the chosen successor gain acceptance throughout the organization. By showing others that he accepts the new leader's decisions, the founder can set the example for the whole company.

The founder must support the new leader publicly and express confidence in that person's abilities. If the founder doesn't show such support, the successor's authority is likely to be undermined, and others inside and outside the company will not accept his decisions.

How a Successor Can Help

It's not unusual for the successor generation to force the hand of the founder. In many family businesses, the child is ready to lead the company long before the founder wants to step down. Like Britain's Prince Charles, they might feel they have been groomed for a job that they will never have the opportunity to take.

But because a family business is not the same as the business of a royal family, a successor does have the possibility to assist with the transition from one generation to the next. We do not recommend a coup that involves a power play with the board of directors and stockholders to oust the founder. But the potential successor of a family business can take steps to help bring about a successful transition.

First, the potential successor must become truly knowledgeable about all facets of the company. This usually means learning the business from the ground up and moving through a number of line and management positions successfully. This process really has no shortcut. If the potential successor bypasses these steps and moves up without learning the business, everyone will know and she will not earn the authority needed for the top job.

A potential successor can be the one to broach the topic of succession planning with the founder. It might not be easy to talk with Mom and Dad about their eventual retirement, but if they have not brought up the subject, it can be appropriate for the potential successor to do so. If they are reluctant to discuss succession, they might have to be prodded, but continuing to keep the subject alive will help. The potential successor must be willing to hear that the founders haven't considered leaving the business to her and also be open-minded enough to participate in the process despite that fact. It's clearly a tricky subject, but one a potential successor can navigate if the lines of communication are open.

Suggestion Box _____

The successor must follow her own passions and interests in the business, rather than blindly follow the way the founder has always done business. The successor must trust her own instincts when in charge of the company, as the founder did. Use the knowledge you have gained inside and outside the business to enhance the success of the company, and don't be afraid to do things your way when you feel confident.

A potential successor can also become more knowledgeable about succession issues such as estate planning and ways to structure the business in the future. This will be useful when everyone is ready to seriously discuss succession planning.

A successful transition from the first to the second generation will occur when the successor is ready to take over the leadership. The successor will do best when the transition happens at the time she is truly ready, following sufficient education and experience, as well as trust from the senior generation.

The second-generation successor of the family business will often be seen as the new head of the family, as the founder probably held that position. This means the successor must be capable of handling the various family members who own shares in the business, as well as those family members who work in the business. Sometimes, the answer is to find two people for successor—one to succeed in leadership of the business and one to be in charge of the family. By the second generation, this can be a politic way to resolve the issue of two siblings who are in contention for the leadership of the family business. One might be better suited to the patriarchal role of head of the family, while the other might be the better business leader.

The Founder After Retirement

As we have mentioned, one of the main impediments to getting the succession planning process started is the founder's inability to see himself as retired. The founder needs to resolve several issues before he can be comfortable leaving the company in the hands of the next generation.

Financial Concerns

A financial plan for retirement should be established that ensures the financial security of the founder after he is no longer working in the business. This should be implemented many years before retirement to ensure sound planning for retirement income. If the founder remains working at the company into his golden years, it should be because he wants to be there and is making a contribution to the success of the firm, not because he still needs to bring home a salary.

Further, a financial plan for the ownership of the company needs to be established as well. If the second generation is to buy out the first generation's ownership interests, a plan for that gradual purchase of stock and how the successor(s) will obtain the money must be developed.

What Should the Founder Do Now?

Today's older generation is living far beyond the traditional retirement age of 65. For many executives, their mid-60s is an age when they can finally use the knowledge they have spent a lifetime learning. Many family business founders are nowhere near ready to give up their power at 65.

There are plenty of examples of family business leaders who remain in charge well into their eighth or ninth decades. Sumner Redstone, chairman of National Amusements (the conglomerate he has built from the business first founded by his father), was born in 1923. His daughter Shari might or might not be his successor, although her father has groomed her for the job for many years. Rupert Murdoch, born in 1931, is still going strong as chairman and CEO of the News Corporation that he founded. His children Lachlan, James, and Elisabeth have each been considered a potential successor to the business at different times. Robert Wegman was chairman of Wegman's Food Markets until his death in 2006 at age 87. He had run the company for over 55 years and had named his son Danny CEO only one year earlier.

Such long terms for family business leaders are not unusual. It is typical of family businesses to have leaders who remain in their positions much longer than leaders of nonfamily businesses. When a founder remains healthy and able to handle the demands of running the family business, there can be many benefits to the company. The maturity and experience of the senior generation gives a family business a long-term perspective. Several generations working alongside each other in a family business can be a great way for the family to stay together and involved.

But many issues are raised when the founder wants to retain her position well beyond the usual age of retirement.

Because the younger generation is probably anxious to start its leadership of the company, the founder should be honest with potential successors about when she plans to retire. Children might want to branch out beyond the family business if their parents plan to operate the company into their 80s.

Founders should have a few trusted advisors who are willing to tell them that it's time to let go when they think the company needs fresh leadership. It can be hard for a founder to see when the right time has arrived, and being open to hearing that message from a peer shows sound judgment for the future of the company.

For many founders, finding something interesting to do after formally retiring from the family business is the best alternative for everyone. The next generation gets to run the company before it is almost ready to retire, and the senior generation gets to reinvent itself. This can take the form of a new venture, perhaps funded by the family business. Another place for a senior executive to find meaningful work can be on corporate boards, in political office, in philanthropy, or perhaps in education. If the founder wants to maintain a connection to the family business, it can be done, sometimes as an ambassador from the business to the community, or as a mentor to young management.

Succession of Business Real Estate

A common succession problem for business founders is how to fairly divide the family wealth when only one member of the second generation will become the next business leader. What to do for the other child or children who won't be part of the business? Often, the solution to this problem is to give the business real estate to one child and the business to the other.

But many family business consultants caution that this is not a fair way to apportion business assets. This strategy can backfire for both the person who receives the real estate and for the child who becomes the new CEO.

The child who retains the real estate has the rental income from the family business to rely on only as long as the business remains in that location. If the decision is made to move the business elsewhere, the child with the real estate can be left with a property that no one else wants to rent or buy.

On the other hand, the family business CEO might want to negotiate a lower rent with his sibling who owns the real estate if conditions require it. The owner of the real estate is under no obligation to lower the rent, and in fact it could be financially difficult for the real estate owner.

The best solution is to keep the ownership of the real estate in the hands of the people who own and manage the business. Control of the physical assets of the company is critical to expansion, growth, and financial planning. Founders should find another way to give their children a share of the wealth in the family business.

The Least You Need to Know

- The founder is usually the key person in finding a successor.
- Although it happens far too often, it is very dangerous for the founder of a family business to have no plans for choosing his successor.

- ◆ Children who succeed their parents as head of the family business have to earn authority over time.

- ◆ Ownership and management of the family business by the next generation is a delicate balance.

- ◆ Founders who plan for retirement activities can move into new spheres after leaving the reins of the family business.

Chapter 19

Into the Third Generation— and Beyond

In This Chapter

- ◆ A team of cousins
- ◆ Changes to the business over time
- ◆ Family ownership, not necessarily family management
- ◆ How to maintain family business values

One of the oldest adages about family businesses goes like this: "From shirtsleeves to shirtsleeves in three generations." In Mandarin Chinese, the saying is "fu bu guo san dai," which translates to "wealth never survives three generations." In Italian, the phrase is, "Dalle stalle alle stelle alle stalle," or "from barn stalls to the stars to the barn stalls."

In any culture and any country, the history of family businesses has been the same. The founder starts the business. The second generation operates the business. The third generation destroys the business. But does this have to be the legacy of every family business? Of course not.

There are thousands of examples in the United States alone of family businesses that have thrived in the third generation of family ownership and beyond. Many of these businesses are among the largest and most successful in the country—The New York Times Company, S. C. Johnson, Cargill, and Nordstrom, to name but a few.

But the transition from second- to third-generation management and ownership is one of the most difficult challenges a family business will face. When the family business moves into the third generation of the founding family, the whole business often undergoes major changes that can transform the company. If handled well, the company will grow and succeed. If not, the response is often to sell the business and get out.

In this chapter, we talk about the transition into the third generation of family ownership and how the business might have to adapt to incorporate the parties involved. In this stage of the family business, how the company is governed becomes a critical influence on whether the company will succeed. The structures we have discussed in other chapters—such as the family council and the board of directors—are needed now more than ever before. We also talk about how the business itself must often change over the years in response to the times and how such adaptability helps a family business survive over the long haul.

Multiple Family Members Involved

The number of people who own a family business increases almost exponentially as the business survives over time. In the first generation, it's often only one owner. In the second generation, the children of the founder usually take over—two, three, or maybe four or five at most. But in the third generation, each of those siblings has children who might want to participate in the family business. The number of owners multiplies as the family business moves into and beyond the third generation.

"Cousin Collaboration"

The third or fourth generation of the family business is often referred to as the *cousin collaboration*.

Ownership in the hands of so many people in different branches of the family requires changes in the way the business has been run since Grandpa founded the company. In the owner-managed company, a single founder often is the sole decision-maker for the firm. In this first stage of the family business, the firm succeeds or fails largely through the efforts of that founder and the way he carries out the business vision.

During the next generation's leadership of the company, the founder's children are usually in charge. The sibling partnership we discussed in Chapter 18 is often the way second-generation family businesses are organized. Although this stage requires some adjustment to two or more people finding ways to share responsibilities for the firm, the parties involved know each other well. They have been raised in the same household and have learned about the essence of the company from Mom or Dad. If they are siblings who can work well together, in the family business's second stage, the siblings are able to continue the mission of the founder and add their own personal stamp to the business to help it grow.

def•i•ni•tion

Cousin collaboration is the generation of family business ownership (usually third or fourth) when cousins are the chief owners of the business. In this stage of the family business, ownership can be spread among many family members who might not necessarily know each other well or at all.

When the second generation is ready to retire or transition out of the business, the choices for company management often become less clear. Even knowing how to apportion the stock is complicated by issues of equity and fairness. In the second generation, the brothers and sisters might have held stock equally, but in the third generation, one sibling can have two children and the other four. Should each child receive one-sixth, or should the stock remain evenly distributed to the branches of the family?

Cousins aren't the same as siblings: they haven't necessarily grown up together and might not share the same values. Old family arguments might resurface in this generation, going back to how Grandma favored one of her daughters over another.

Voluntary Participation in the Business

When the family business reaches its third generation, many family members might work in the business. On the other hand, this might be a time when family members don't feel the tug of the family business as strongly. Whereas Mom or Dad might have felt compelled to enter the family business when they were young, members of the third generation often have fewer ties to the business. The family is more disparate, people have moved away from the town where the business is headquartered, and marriages have added even more people into the family mix.

At this stage, family members should be able to choose whether their interests coincide with the family business. Companies that have required young family members to work outside the family business first will have a more willing pool of family members ready to join the business. If cousins have dipped their toes into the pool of outside opportunities and have then decided they would like to join the family business, the commitment to the company will be real.

Both business management and ownership should be a voluntary choice for the cousin generation. With regard to stock ownership, family members who don't want to hold shares must have a way to sell them. Even if a company has the policy of maintaining ownership within the family, a system can be established that sets up a fair valuation of the shares and a way to redeem them. For larger companies, the option of going public also creates a market for shares, even if the family holds the majority of the stock.

Major Changes to the Business

Families that successfully weather the transition to the cousin collaboration do so in a variety of ways, but in almost every case, more formality and more structures are needed. The business must be run differently from how it was in the earlier stages because so many more family members are involved.

Critical for the family business in the third generation is the need for everyone to accept that the business won't be the same as it was in the past. Change is inevitable for a family business at this stage. If the business has survived to this point, it is probably larger and more family members are involved with it than in years gone by. Changes in materials, products, technologies, and more occur over time and change the nature of the business. A family business that wants to succeed across generations must be open to new ideas and new ways of operating. Doing things the way the founder did them simply will not work decades into the future.

But the essence of the business can and should survive—the philosophies and values of the company as created by the original founder. When a family business stays true to the spirit of the founder, the business can withstand any number of changes over time and retain its fundamental values.

The Marriott family businesses provide a good example of the kinds of changes a family business can undergo while still remaining true to its roots. Founded in 1927 as a nine-seat root beer stand, the company has moved from curbside food service to airline meal catering to institutional food service to hotels in the United States and all over the world. Although J. W. Marriott Jr., is still CEO (since 1972), the business is poised to move into its third generation as it continues to transform its business groups through senior living communities, timeshares, executive long-term housing, hotel franchises, and much more. Today, Marriott is a public company with some members of the Marriott family who remain in positions of senior management. But the company retains the essential mission of the original Marriott family founder—their commitment to "service to associates, customers and the community."

> **Family Stats**
>
> Studies show that 12 percent of family-owned businesses stay viable into the third generation. Three percent are alive at the fourth-generation level and beyond. (Family Firm Institute, Inc.)

Family Focus vs. Business Focus

In Chapter 4, we talked about the difference between having a family-focused business and having a business-focused business. This direction is usually set early by the business founder. Companies are either closely held and decisions made to benefit the family or are more open and the individual family members' needs are considered less important than the good of the business. When a family business reaches transition time to the third generation, the family-first or business-first orientation can play an important role in whether the business survives.

In a family business that prizes the family as paramount, troubles can arise in the third generation. At this point, the number of family members who are interested in management of the company might be bigger than the number of open spots. And if family is always to be accommodated first, the best recruits (that is, outsiders) for the jobs might go untapped. Problems with various family members become more obvious at this stage, with more family members involved in the business. The siblings who are partners in the second generation might not see eye-to-eye on the subject of whose children are best to succeed them.

When a family business operates under the family-first philosophy, the opportunities for dysfunctional family dynamics to enter into business decisions are greater. If the business expects family members to always take the reins, succession to the third generation can become a family dispute that results in the business falling apart.

A business-focused family business has a better chance of making it to and through the third generation transition. In a family business that puts the business first, hiring decisions are made based on finding the best person available—not necessarily a family member. People outside the family are brought in to help with decision-making, usually in the form of a board of directors or an advisory board. Compensation is based on the prevailing market rates for the jobs, and performance is measured periodically.

The business-focused family business tends to be more proactive about succession issues as well. Because it tries to keep family favoritism out of the business, it doesn't necessarily expect that a member of the next generation will become the successor to the CEO. So structures have usually been put in place before the transition to the cousin generation that provide for an organized way to select business leaders.

Suggestion Box _____

Sometime during the second generation of management, the family business should establish a board of directors that includes several nonfamily members. Bringing in an outsider's perspective at this time will ease the transition to the third generation, when even more family members become stockholders and might want to have a say in the management of the company.

The family issues that can arise for the business-focused family business are those of rejection and resentment. Children who might want to work in the business but are not offered jobs might be angry with family members who are part of the company. If family members own stock but have no management positions, they can feel cheated if the company doesn't pay out dividends. When promotion is based on merit, a younger family member might be senior to an older family member, which can be hard to handle. But by the third generation of family ownership, these issues have been dealt with if the business has always maintained its business focus.

In general, family businesses that put the business first as an operating philosophy are best suited to make the transition from second to third generation. The close family structure in the family-first companies might suit the founding and second generations. But when the cousins begin to spread the ownership around to a larger group of family members, it helps to adopt an attitude of business first.

Creating Opportunities Through Business Strategy

When multiple cousins work in the family business and several may be candidates for succession to the top spot, the family business might find itself with a difficult decision to make. How should a family firm choose among several cousins who have proven themselves competent in the business?

One way that has worked for some family businesses is to establish co-leadership roles in the third or fourth generation of management. When more than one strong potential successor exists, the best solution for some companies is to share the authority and power.

The cousins who own and run Graeter's Manufacturing Co. in Cincinnati, Ohio, are part of the fourth generation of the family that founded the ice cream business in 1870. As cousins, Chip, Bob, and Richard decided to each have a one-third ownership in the business because they share in the management of the company. Although by bloodlines Richard was entitled to a larger share of ownership than the other two cousins who are brothers, he understood that the individual family lines were no longer as important as seeing the family as a whole. He recognized that the spirit of working well together would stand the business in better stead for the future than a more selfish approach of holding more shares than either of his cousins.

The Ashforth Co., a real estate firm founded in 1896, is another family business now run by a cousin collaboration. Their parents owned the controlling stock of the firm, and one was the CEO. Now in its fourth generation, several of the siblings' children were likely candidates to run the company. It was decided that a co-managing partnership would be formed with two of the cousins, and several other cousins are part of senior management as well. As co-CEOs, the cousins have developed a relationship that works, with the help of many nonfamily senior executives. They keep ownership even between the two partners as well.

Another technique for creating opportunities within the family business for the third or fourth generation is to create new divisions of the company to be led by the up-and-coming cousins. In this stage, a number of well-qualified family members might be involved in the business but the senior generation might not be ready to retire yet. Finding leadership roles within the business by creating new business units or divisions can help to give the younger generation more responsibility and experience, while keeping them in the business. At Nordstrom, Inc., for example, several cousins are in charge of various divisions of the company—one as president and other cousins as president of stores, president of Nordstrom Direct, and president of merchandising. In this way, the publicly owned business maintains its family management control of the business.

Stock Transactions Within Family

In the third or fourth generation, many family members own shares of the business. Some might have senior management roles in the firm; others might be nonmanagement employees; and still others might not work in the family business. The question always exists in a family business as to whether uninvolved family members should be owners. At earlier stages of the business, having only the founder and then her children as owners while they work in the company and build the business can be easier.

But as the third and fourth generations grow and inherit stock, restricting ownership to working family members only is difficult. For many families with a successful family business, this is the primary asset that funds the entire family. And as we have discussed, forcing family members to work in the family business is not the best way to develop competent management.

Many family businesses prefer to keep ownership of the company in the hands of the family to maintain closeness and control. But if the company doesn't pay dividends regularly, the investment in the family business might not be best for some family members. It might be difficult for owners to sell their shares in the private market because they have a limited market of potential buyers (other family members).

It makes sense for a family business in this position to establish ways for family members to cash out their stock. A company can set an annual value of the stock and have a trust available to purchase shares if other family members are not interested. In this way, family members who don't want to retain ownership of the business don't have to feel obligated to the family business.

Family businesses at this stage usually do need some nonworking family members to hold onto stock, however. Too much liquidation might be impossible for the business to fund. The most successful family businesses at the third generation and beyond include at least some of the cousins in the ownership pool who remain owners of the company because they believe in what the business stands for.

Family Leadership

In this stage of the family business's lifespan, family leadership can be more important than ever. In the founding generation and the second generation, the family matriarch—Mom—is often the informal leader of the family. If Dad is the business founder, Mom is the glue that holds the family together through disputes and dramas.

But into the third generation and beyond, Mom is gone and a group of family elders will likely replace her in her role as family leader. At this point, it probably makes sense for the head of the family business not to take the role of family leader as well. The goals of the family and the goals of the business are two distinct things now, and separating their leadership helps to keep them distinct.

Family Council

In Chapter 8, we introduced the idea of the family council, a group organized to help the family make decisions that affect the business. At the cousin collaboration stage of the family business, the family council becomes an important structure to have in place. With more family members having an ownership stake in the company, the family needs a place where it can get information about the company and have input into business decisions that affect the family.

The family council can have a variety of functions at this stage. It can be the vehicle to plan family reunions and family meetings, research family history, and keep communication channels open among the family branches. More importantly for the business at this stage, the family council can organize ways to help family members learn about the family business, both for younger family members who might be interested in working with the business and to prepare more experienced family members for board of directors participation.

As the family grows and ownership of the family business becomes more dispersed, it is critical that family members have a good understanding of the family business, even if they are passive shareholders. Being more informed about the company's operations will help family shareholders understand company decisions and lessen resentment against family members who are part of company management.

The family council can also be the place to help family members branch out beyond the family business. Some cousins will probably have no interest in the family business, and some businesses will probably have no opportunities for all the cousins. The family council can make policies to help those family members with their own entrepreneurial ideas, using family business wealth to help family members create new businesses.

The family council can be the vehicle to start discussions about philanthropy. In family council meetings, the family can make decisions regarding the focus of charitable efforts, the specific groups to include, and how the philanthropic goals meet with the values of the business and the family.

Certainly, the family council deals with the issues of succession planning from the family's point of view. It sets a direction for the firm with regard to whether family business leaders will be family members, and it can recommend a procedure to choose successors. The family council is the group that maintains the spirit of the founding family in the business and ensures how the family identity is kept in the business.

Family Office

Whereas the family council is often where family decisions are made, the *family office* is usually the organization that carries out the council's decisions.

Many families develop a family office only when no members of the family are working in the family business, or when the family business has been sold and there is considerable wealth to manage.

The family that founded Pittsburgh Plate Glass (PPG), the Pitcairns, has a thriving investment family office that was established by the second-generation sons of the founder. The family office was originally set up to look after the family wealth from the business, which allowed the sons to pursue interests outside the family business but retain an ownership interest. By the fourth generation, there were 61 Pitcairns, and the family office needed to diversify its investments beyond PPG. In 1987, the Pitcairn Company divested all the PPG stock and the company turned to managing a portfolio of investments, and taking on other clients as well.

But the family office can be a useful organization even when the family is still active in the business. At this third- and fourth-generation stage, many family businesses establish a family office to help with the coordination of family interests.

The family office also is a useful structure to keep the family together without family becoming overly involved in the business management. For some families, the family business is the only thing that keeps them together, and family members might make decisions that affect the business as a way to maintain family closeness. The family office and family council help the family business make decisions based on what's right for the business, not what keeps the family together.

Keeping the Vision Alive

This gets back to the notion of the importance of maintaining the founder's vision for the company long after the business has grown into several family generations. For a family business to survive that long, there must be a reason for family members to want to be a part of the business—a reason that goes beyond merely making money or feeling like the family needs your help.

Sometimes family business succession is the way families try to hold the group together. Children and grandchildren are raised with the expectation that they will join the business when they are old enough. They work at the business on weekends and in the summer. When the time comes for the older generation to retire, it's a foregone conclusion that the next generation will take over. But what about the cousins who don't see the family business as their passion in life?

At every stage of the family business, but especially at the third- and fourth-generation stages, family members should be brought into the firm only if their interests and aptitudes match with the business needs. In fact, most family business experts agree that the family members who have opportunities outside the family business are the ones who should remain with the family business—they are the most capable and have the skills needed to help the family firm survive.

The core values of the family business are what propel it onward into the future and what keep family members interested and excited about the business. These values must be general concepts, though, not specific to a type of business, to continue throughout the change that can occur in the business. For example, if the business mission is "to provide the best plumbing services in the tri-state area," the business is limited to that line of work. Over the years, the firm might evolve into a general construction company or a plumbing materials supplier. In either case, the vision for the firm would no longer be appropriate. Such a business needs to revise its vision and think in more general terms.

Feld Entertainment is a privately held family business now moving into the third generation of family leadership. Founded by Irving Feld in 1967 when he acquired the Ringling Brothers and Barnum & Bailey circus company, the company is now led by his son, Richard Feld. Over the years, the business has remained in entertainment spectaculars but has branched out far beyond the circus tent to ice shows, Broadway productions, and even motor sports. Anything under the "entertainment" umbrella is fair game for the Felds. Third-generation Nicole Feld, Richard's daughter, joined the family business after growing up with the circus but making her professional mark in publishing. She made the decision to join the family business after the 9/11 tragedy, recognizing her need to carry on the legacy of her father and grandfather.

A family business needs to define itself as being "in the business of business" to have a truly long-range perspective that allows the business to change as it grows. When the third and fourth generations of family leadership are able to see the mission of the firm in the spirit of the founder, rather than a slavish devotion to the founder's specific goals, the business will be able to continue.

Family Stats
Family-owned businesses account for 60 percent of total U.S. employment, 78 percent of all new jobs, and 65 percent of all wages paid.

Lansky's, a clothing company in Memphis, Tennessee, made its mark as the "Clothier to the King"—that is, Elvis Presley. Founded 60 years ago by Bernard Lansky and now owned and run by his son Hal, the business has expanded beyond men's apparel in the Elvis style to gift items for the famous Peabody Hotel, children's toys, and upscale trendy clothing for men and women. Lansky 126 is operated by Julie Lansky, Hal's daughter, who has brought her unique style and innovation to the business. Hal Lansky credits Julie with a new perspective and youthful energy that the business needs to have to remain fresh.

Philanthropy

Family businesses at this stage have usually reached a level of financial success that makes charitable giving an important part of their financial planning. And philanthropic goals are another way to keep the spirit of the founder and the family alive through the years.

Many family businesses are generous to the communities in which they operate, as a way of thanking these communities for their support of the business. Family philanthropic foundations are started by successful family business, often by the second or third generation. Sometimes starting a foundation provides a new challenge for a family business leader who is ready for retirement, but not just the golf course. A family foundation can also be an outlet for a family member who wants to participate in the business but needs an alternative to the actual business.

S. C. Johnson Company, now in its fifth generation of family ownership and management, has a family foundation that is run by one of the cousins, Winnie Johnson-Marquart. The company chairman and CEO is H. Fisk Johnson, while divisions of the business are run by other cousins. Through the foundation, the company gives 5 percent of pretax profits to charity. The family's interests in the environment and education are the focus of the foundation's charitable giving.

Family businesses find a family foundation to be an important way for their families to give back and get positive publicity about the companies. Lyman Orton of the Vermont Country Store has established the Orton Family Foundation, whose goal is preserving small towns in America.

Creating the Culture for Success

For many family businesses that make it to the cousin generation, the family comes together in a way it never has before. Gone are the sibling rivalries that characterized the relationship between family members in the second generation. Cousins are often able to set aside old family jealousies and arguments because they didn't grow up in the same households with the family members with whom they now work.

It's a rare family business that makes it to the third and fourth generations, or beyond. Like most businesses that are begun by a single founder or partnership, the majority of family businesses aren't passed on to another family member. If the business lasts 25 or 30 years, many founders close up shop or sell to an outsider when they are ready to retire.

> **Family Stats**
>
> Four out of five firms have no procedure in place for dealing with disputes between family members. (PricewaterhouseCoopers 2007/2008 Study)

But for the families that keep the business going successfully through more than one generation, the rewards are many. Besides the obvious financial benefits, the family that works together often becomes close-knit. The pride associated with building and operating a successful business that carries the family name is a tribute to all the generations who have been involved, whether the conferences are around the kitchen table or in the penthouse suite.

Perdue Farms, founded in 1920, has weathered the storms of family ownership and today is led by third-generation chairman Jim Perdue. The Perdue website proudly announces "A Family Commitment to Quality Since 1920." Beginning with a chicken farm and moving through the years into every phase of chicken production, the company has retained its founder's values of "Quality, Integrity, Trust and Teamwork." The family name of Perdue was personified for many years by Frank Perdue in the company's advertising campaigns, and it continues today with Jim as the company spokesman. Perdue was the first company to make the family name the brand name of a commodity product.

Families that find ways to educate younger family members about the business, give opportunities to those who are genuinely interested and qualified to handle the responsibilities, and are comfortable with changes to the family business will succeed and even thrive for many generations.

Despite the discouraging statistics about how few family businesses make it into the third and fourth generations, there is good news for those businesses that do break through the second-generation barrier. If a family business survives the transition to the second generation, about 50 percent move on to the third generation. And 70 percent of those firms make it into the fourth generation. So the odds are strong for family firms that have found their formula for success beyond the founder.

The history of the Tuttle Farm in New Hampshire tells the story of a family that has literally nurtured its business, a family farm, since the 1630s. Today, the twelfth generation of Tuttles participates in selling the produce it grows. Their story has been told in a children's book, *Tuttle's Red Barn*, ending with young Grayson Tuttle, who is proud to remember his "great-great-great-great-great-great-great-great-great-grandfather."

Although not every family business will last as long as the Tuttle Farm in New Hampshire, every family business has its own unique history and lifeline. When the right combination of people, vision, and talents merges in one family, a family business can become a dynasty.

The Least You Need to Know

- ◆ At the third generation and beyond, ownership of the family business usually spreads out among many family members.

- ◆ Structures such as the family council and family office are important to maintain family communication at this stage.

- ◆ The specific business might change over time, but the family's core values persist through the generations.

- ◆ Flexibility is one of the keys to keeping a family business successful beyond the third and fourth generations.

Glossary

accounts receivable Money owed to you by your customers. If your customers owe you a lot of money, your business can suffer. Keep up with customer debt by sending monthly bills and following up with phone calls to late payers.

agency loss The loss a business suffers when owners are not also managers. Family businesses tend not to suffer as much agency loss as non-family businesses because family members often hold top management positions.

brand image What an average consumer thinks of your company. A brand image consists of the ideas and experiences associated with a product or business in the minds of consumers.

buy-sell agreement A document that sets the terms on how a business will continue when an owner wants to retire. A buy-sell agreement includes a mechanism to fix the value of the business.

capitalization The money required to start or grow a business—may be used for outfitting a store, purchasing inventory, paying initial salaries, purchasing goods and equipment, and paying other expenses associated with start-up or expansion.

collateral Security for a debt. If you default on your debt, the lender can sell or claim any property identified as collateral to pay the debt.

cousin collaboration   The generation of family business ownership (usually third or fourth) when cousins are the chief owners of the business. In this stage of the family business, ownership can be spread among many family members who might not necessarily know each other well or at all.

domain name   The name used by a business on the Internet. Usually, the best domain name for a family business is the name of the business. If that name is not available, try to relate the name to what your business does.

due diligence   A reasonable investigation of a proposed investment deal before the transaction is finalized. The investigation is usually done by the investor's attorney and accountant to check the investment's worthiness.

employee benefits   Compensation provided to employees in addition to their normal wages or salaries. Employee benefits can include but are not limited to: group insurance (health, dental, life, and so on), retirement funding plans, sick leave, vacation, Social Security, profit sharing, employer-provided or employer-paid housing, daycare, and tuition reimbursement.

employee stock ownership plan (ESOP)   An employee stock ownership plan involves the transfer of a business to its employees. For a family business, this transfer gives a stake in the company to outsiders as well as family members. Profits and productivity can increase for firms instituting an ESOP.

equity financing   Giving up some ownership in your business in return for cash. Equity financing is different from debt financing, which involves receiving money in the form of a loan.

familiness   The essence of any family business that helps to make the business successful based on the unique qualities of that family.

family business   A company with ties to a particular family in its ownership or management. Usually, there is the intent to involve more than one generation of the family in the business.

family ceiling   The limits of the upper level of management a nonfamily employee can move to in a family firm, where all the highest-level management jobs are reserved for family members.

family council   The family group that decides family policy in a family business. A family council is separate from the board of directors, which makes business decisions. A family council makes family decisions.

family dynamics   The patterns of relationships or interactions between family members. The dynamics of every family are unique, but similarities are seen in common situations.

family office   An organization that generally handles the wealth of a family who owns a family business. It can also have duties that range from providing capital for new family ventures to educating family members about the business to being the family's liaison to the business's board of directors.

feedback loop   The way in which information is fed back into a system to give new results. A strategic plan needs to be revised by new information about the family's goals and finances.

focus groups   Periodic gatherings of customers to ascertain their reaction to a family business. Focus groups should consist of 6 to 10 customers who are encouraged to criticize business practices they do not like and to provide suggestions on how the business could improve.

founder succession   The transfer of leadership in a family business from the founder(s) to a new company head, often a family member from the next generation.

governance   The method or system of sharing the rights and responsibilities of a family business with its various participants, including owners, management, and family.

graphic artist   A professional designer who assembles images and text to create commercial art.

intrapreneurship   Working within an existing company to develop innovative new business ventures, using the financial backing of the existing firm.

mediation   The process of solving serious family disputes that are in litigation or headed for the courts. An impartial third party helps the parties understand the dispute and helps the parties work through a settlement of family differences.

mergers and acquisitions   The buying, selling, and combining of companies that can finance or help a company grow rapidly without having to create another business entity. A merger is the combination of two companies to form a new company. An acquisition occurs when one company purchases another and becomes the new owner.

minority shareholder   An individual or a company that owns stock in a firm, but holds less than a controlling interest, that is, more than 50 percent.

mission statement   The main goals of the family business. The mission statement is communicated to employees, customers, shareholders, and investors.

nepotism   The practice of appointing relatives to positions in the family business.

organizational culture   The patterns of behavior used by people in a business to solve problems and deal with issues. These behaviors are based on assumptions the founder brings with him when the business begins.

perquisite   Compensation that is in addition to regular pay and usual employee benefits, resulting from one's position of employment. The term *perks* is often used colloquially to refer to special privileges that are more discretionary. Often, perks are given to employees who are doing notably well or have seniority. Common perks are company cars, hotel stays, free refreshments, leisure activities on work time (such as golf), stationery, and allowances for meals.

piercing the corporate veil   Courts will rule against family members when they find the corporation they have started is a sham. If family members fail to observe corporate rules and regulations, unduly enrich themselves, undercapitalize the corporation, fail to reveal the corporate structure, and generally disregard the corporation, those family members may be personally liable for debts.

primogeniture   The right of the eldest child, especially the eldest son, to inherit the entire estate of one or both parents.

return on investment (ROI)   How much money is made relative to the amount invested. This measurement helps a company measure how a project is doing compared to other possible investments. ROI is usually calculated on a yearly basis.

share group   A group of business owners from an industry that meets periodically to discuss common business problems and opportunities.

shareholder   An individual or a company that owns one or more shares of stock in a corporation.

sibling rivalry   Emotional competition among brothers and sisters, usually thought of as tying to win parents' approval, love, and attention away from the other siblings.

steward   A leader who is more concerned with making a contribution to the organization than with benefiting personally. Stewardship occurs when the goals of the family business align themselves with the goals of the CEO.

strategic plan   A document that outlines three- to five-year operational objectives for a family business. The strategic plan should be updated every year.

strategic planning   The process of putting together a game plan to guide future family business decisions. Most strategic planning documents last from three to five years and are reviewed on an annual basis.

succession   When the head of a family business steps down and hands over the leadership of the business, usually to another family member.

SWOT analysis   A tool for strategic planning that provides simple ways to examine factors both inside the firm (strengths and weaknesses) and from outside it (opportunities and threats).

venture capitalists   Investors, often in a group, who fund start-up businesses usually by taking an ownership share in the business.

Resource Guide

Here are a few organizations, books, and publications related to family business issues you might find interesting. Some are more scholarly; others are more practical. They all have good information for helping family businesses through the many issues they face every day.

Organizations

Family Firm Institute, Inc.
200 Lincoln Street, #201
Boston, MA 02111
www.ffi.org

USASBE (U.S. Association for Small Business and Entrepreneurship
c/o Florida Atlantic University, College of Business DeSantis Center
777 Glades Road, Building 87
Boca Raton, FL 33431-0992
www.usasbe.org

AFHE (Attorneys for Family-Held Enterprise)
11357 Nuckols Road, #115
Glen Allen, VA 23059
www.afhe.com

Periodicals and Websites

Entrepreneur Magazine
www.entrepreneur.com

Family Business Magazine
1845 Walnut Street, Suite 900
Philadelphia, PA 19103
www.familybusinessmagazine.com

Family Business Review
SAGE Publications Inc.
2455 Teller Road
Thousand Oaks, CA 91320
fbr.sagepub.com

Books

Beyond Survival, by Leon Danco. Prentice-Hall, 1975.
This is the granddad of family business books—interesting for an historical perspective.

Family Wars, by Grant Gordon and Nigel Nicholson. Kogan Page, 2008.
This book contains examples and case studies of family businesses and their struggles.

Keep the Family Baggage out of the Family Business, by Quentin J. Fleming. Simon & Schuster, 2000.
This entertaining book gives family members who are in business together advice on how to keep family relationships healthy at the family workplace.

Perpetuating the Family Business, by John L. Ward. Palgrave MacMillan, 2004.
Ward gives 50 lessons for business success at every stage of a family business's growth.

Strategic Planning for the Family Business, by Randel S. Carlock and John L. Ward. Palgrave, 2001.
This provides an overview of how a family business plans for its growth and success as a business, while maintaining the family values that shaped it.

Sustaining the Family Business, by Marshall B. Paisner, Perseus Books, 1999.
This gives you a broad overview of the issues affecting family businesses, with an emphasis on the author's personal experience in a family business.

Family Business Leadership Series (Volumes 1–22), by Craig Aronoff, John Ward, et. al. Family Enterprise Publishers, 1992–2008.

Family Business, by Joseph Astrachan, Torsten M. Pieper, and Peter Jaskiewicz, editors. Edward Elgar Publishing, 2008.

Family Business on the Couch: A Psychological Perspective, by Randel Carlock and Manfred Kets de Vries. Wiley, 2007.

Successful Habits of Family Business Successors, by Dean Fowler. Glengrove Publishing, 2004.

Generation to Generation: Life Cycles of the Family Business, by Kelin Gersick, John Davis, Marion McCollom Hampton, and Ivan Lansberg. Harvard Business School Press, 1997.

Intimate Leadership: The Power of Couples in Business Together, by Miriam Hawley, Jeffrey McIntyre. New Win Publishing, 2008.

Your Lawyer, An Owner's Manual: A Business Owner's Guide to Managing Your Lawyer, by Henry Krasnow. AgalePro, 2005.

Family Businesses: The Essentials, by Peter Leach. Profile Books, 2007.

Pass It On: The Entrepreneur's Succession Playbook, by Harry McCabe. Infinity Trust, 2007.

Centuries of Success: Lessons from the World's Most Enduring Family Businesses, by William O'Hara. Family Business Consulting Group, 2004.

Family Business Centers, Education Programs, and Forums

Alabama

Lowder Center for Family Business and Entrepreneurship
Auburn University
450 Lowder Business Building
415 West Magnolia Avenue
Auburn, AL 36849-5240
Telephone: 334-844-0454
Fax: 334-844-5159
ketchda@auburn.edu
www.business.auburn.edu

Arizona

The Global Family Enterprise Program
Thunderbird School of Global Management
Center for Global Entrepreneurship and Family Enterprise Institute
15249 North 59th Avenue
Glendale, AZ 85306-6001
Telephone: 602-978-7547
ernesto.poza@thunderbird.edu
www.thunderbird.edu/familybusiness

The Spirit of Enterprise Center
Arizona State University
W.P. Carey School of Business
PO Box 874406-4406
Tempe, AZ 85287
Telephone: 480-965-3962
Fax: 480-727-6185
marylou.bessette@asu.edu
wpcarey.asu.edu/seid/casb/family_business_forum.cfm

Arkansas

Small Business Advancement National Center
University of Central Arkansas
College of Business Administration
UCA Box 5018
201 Donaghey Avenue
Conway, AR 72035
Telephone: 501-450-5300
Fax: 504-450-5360
donb@uca.edu
www.sbaer.uca.edu

California

Carl and Celia Gellert Foundation
Family Business Center
University of San Francisco
School of Business and Management
2130 Fulton Street
San Francisco, CA 94117-1045
Telephone: 415-422-2514
Fax: 415-42r2-2502
muscat@usfca.edu
www.usfca.edu/fbc

EMC Business Forum
San Diego State University
5250 Campanile Drive
San Diego, CA 92182-1915
Telephone: 619-594-4949
Fax: 619-594-8879
cbianchi@projects.sdsu.edu
emc.sdsu.edu

Family Business Council
California State University, Fullerton
PO Box 6848
Fullerton, CA 92834-6848
Telephone: 714-278-4182
Fax: 714-278-3106
mtrueblood@fullerton.edu
www.csuffamilybusinesscouncil.com

Family Business Education and
Research Center
California State University, Northridge
College of Business and Economics
Juniper Hall, Room 3125
Northridge, CA 91330
Telephone: 818-677-2438
Fax: 818-677-6079
david.russell@csun.edu
www.csun.edu/fbc

Family Business Forum
University of San Diego
5998 Alcala Park
San Diego, CA 92110 2492
Telephone: 619-260-4231
Fax: 619-260-5988
jodiw@sandiego.edu
www.sandiego.edu/fbf

Family Business Institute
California State University, Bakersfield
Business & Public Administration
9001 Stockdale Highway
Bakersfield, CA 93311
Telephone: 661-664-2435
Fax: 661-664-2438
dropp@csub.cdu
www.csubbpa.com

Family Enterprise Center
San Francisco State University
835 Market Street, #592
San Francisco, CA 94103
Telephone: 415-338-7014
Fax: 415-358-4026
meeks@sfsu.edu
cob.sfsu.edu/fbc

Institute for Family Business
California State University, Fresno
5245 North Backer Avenue
Mail Stop PB5
Fresno, CA 93740-8001
Telephone: 559-278-5662
Fax: 559-278-6964
gvozikis@csufresno.edu
www.directory.csufresno.edu/details

Institute for Family Business
University of the Pacific
Eberhardt School of Business
3601 Pacific Avenue
Stockton, CA 95211
Telephone: 209-946-3912
Fax: 209-946-2586
peterjohnson@pacific.edu
www.pacific.edu/ifb

Leading Family Firms
Stanford Graduate School of Business
518 Memorial Way
Stanford, CA 94305-5015
Telephone: 650-725-2994
Fax: 650-725-2994
gray_stacey@gsb.stanford.edu
www.gsb.stanford.edu/exed/lff

Connecticut

Center for Family Business
University of New Haven
300 Boston Post Road
West Haven, CT 06516
Telephone: 203-932-7421
Fax: 203-931-6036
plsessions@aol.com
www.newhaven.edu/cfb

Family Business Program
University of Connecticut
2100 Hillside Road, Unit 1041
Storrs, CT 06269-1041
Telephone: 860-486-5628
Fax: 860-486-9116
pcale@business.uconn.edu
www.business.uconn.edu/familybusiness

District of Columbia

Center for Entrepreneurial Excellence (CFEE)
George Washington University
School of Business
2201 G Street—Funger 315
Washington, DC 20052
Telephone: 202-994-3760
gsolomon@gwu.edu
www.cfee.gwu.edu

Florida

Family Business Resource Center
Nova Southeastern University
Graduate School of Humanities and
Social Sciences
3301 College Avenue
Ft. Lauderdale, FL 33314
Telephone: 954-262-3022
Fax: 954-262-3968
pcole@nova.edu
shss.nova.edu

Family Enterprise Center
Stetson University
School of Business Administration
421 North Woodland Boulevard,
Unit 8398
DeLand, FL 32723
Telephone: 386-822-7565
Fax: 386-822-7426
mfidanzi@stetson.edu
www.stetson.edu/family

Florida Atlantic University, College of
Business
U.S. Association for Small Business and
Entrepreneurship (USASBE)
DeSantis Center
777 Glades Road, Building 87, Room 207
Boca Raton, FL 33431-0992
Telephone: 561-297-4060
Fax: 561-297-4009
usasbe@fau.edu
www.usasbe.org

Florida Entrepreneur and Family Business Center
The University of Tampa
The John H. Sykes College of Business
401 W. Kennedy Boulevard Box O
Tampa, FL 33606-1490
Telephone: 813-253-6221, ext. 1760
Fax: 813-258-7236
dwelsh@ut.edu
www.ut.edu/centers

Small Business Development Center
Florida Gulf Coast University
12751 Westlinks Drive
Building III, Unit 7
Fort Meyers, FL 33913
Telephone: 239-225-4220
Fax: 239-225-4221
dregelsk@fgcu.edu
cli.fgcu.edu/sbdc

The Eugenio Pino & Family Global
Entrepreneurship Center
Florida International University (FIU)
11200 SW 8th Street
VH 130
Miami, FL 33199
Telephone: 305-348-7156
Fax: 305-348-0011
entrepreneurship@fiu.edu
www.entrepreneurship.fiu.edu

The Jim Moran Institute for Global Entrepreneurship
Florida State University
223 Rovetta Business Building
Tallahassee, FL 32306-1110
Telephone: 850-644-7898
Fax: 850-644-5950
jostery@cob.fsu.edu
www.cob.fsu.edu/jmi

Georgia

Georgia State University
J. Mack Robinson College of Business
Suite 726
RCB Building
Atlanta, GA 30302-4014
Telephone: 404-413-7004
iduhaime@gsu.edu
www.gsu.edu

Cox Family Enterprise Center
Kennesaw State University
Coles College of Business
1000 Chastain Road, #0408
Kennesaw, GA 30144-5591
Telephone: 770-423-6045
Fax: 770-423-6721
joe_astrachan@coles2.kennesaw.edu
familybusiness.kennesaw.edu/fec

Hawaii

Family Business Center of Hawaii
University of Hawaii
Pacific Asian Center for Entrepreneurship
2404 Maile Way
Honolulu, HI 96822
Telephone: 808-956-5083
Fax: 808-956-5107
kmonaco@hawaii.edu
www.fbcofhawaii.org

Illinois

Center for Family Enterprises
Northwestern University
Kellogg School of Management
2001 Sheridan Road, Room 5228
Evanston, IL 60208-2001
Telephone: 847-467-7855
Fax: 847-491-5747
c-zsolnay@kellogg.northwestern.edu/
familyenterprises
www.kellogg.northwestern.edu/
familyenterprises

Entrepreneurship Program
DePaul University
1 East Jackson Boulevard
Chicago, IL 60604
Telephone: 312-362-8471
Fax: 312-362-6973
hwelsch@depaul.edu
www.depaul.edu

Indiana

Family Business Center
University of Saint Francis
2701 Spring Street
Fort Wayne, IN 46808
Telephone: 260-399-7700 x8300
Fax: 260-399-8174
slclark@sf.edu
www.sf.edu

Family Business Center
Loyola University Chicago
820 N. Michigan Avenue, Suite 314
Chicago, IL 60611
Telephone: 312-915-6490
Fax: 312-915-6495
akeyt@luc.edu
www.luc.edu/fbc

Family Business Council
University of Illinois at Chicago
815 West Van Buren Street, #321
Chicago, IL 60607
Telephone: 312-413-5433
Fax: 312-996-9988
barrens@uic.edu
www.uic.edu/cba/fbc

Family Business Program
Goshen College
1700 South Main Street
Goshen, IN 46526
Telephone: 574-535-7451
Fax: 574-535-7293
alanlw@goshen.edu
www.goshen.edu/familybusiness

Gigot Center for Entrepreneurial
Studies
University of Notre Dame
232 Mendoza College of Business
Notre Dame, IN 46556-5646
Telephone: 574-631-3385
Fax: 574-631-3979
hayes.37@nd.edu
www.nd.edu/~entrep

Iowa

Small Business Development Center
Iowa State University
2501 North Loop Drive, Suite 1615
Ames, IA 50010-8283
Telephone: 515-296-7828
Fax: 515-296-6714
mjupah@iastate.edu
www.bus.iastate.edu/Outreach/sbdc.asp

Kentucky

Kentucky Small Business Development
Center
University of Kentucky
225 Gatton College of Business &
Economics
Lexington, KY 40506
Telephone: 859-257-7668
Fax: 859-323-1907
lrnaug0@uky.edu
www.ksbdc.org

Kansas

Kansas Family Business Forum
Wichita State University
Center for Entrepreneurship
1845 Fairmont
Wichita, KS 67260-0147
Telephone: 316-978-3000
Fax: 316-978-3687
ron.christy@wichita.edu
www.wichita.edu

The Family Business Center
University of Louisville
College of Business
Louisville, KY 40292
Telephone: 502-637-7696
Fax: 502-637-7698
wc1503@insightbb.com
business.louisville.edu/content/
view/465/889/

Louisiana

Family Business Center
A.B. Freeman School of Business,
Tulane University
7 Macalister Drive
New Orleans, LA 70118-5645
Telephone: 504-862-8482
Fax: 504-862-8902
rosalind.butler@tulane.edu
www.freeman.tulane.edu/fbc/fbc.htm

Family Business Institute
University of Louisiana at Monroe
Entrepreneurship Studies Center
700 University Avenue
Monroe, LA 71209
Telephone: 318-342-1224
Fax: 318-342-3085
dunn@ulm.edu
www.ulm.org

The Stephenson Entrepreneurship
Institute
Louisiana State University
3307-A Patrick Taylor Hall
Baton Rouge, LA 70803
Telephone: 225-578-6411
Fax: 225-578-6983
cacarte@lsu.edu
www.lsu.edu

Maine

Institute for Family-Owned Business
University of Southern Maine
Abromson Center
88 Bedford Street
Portland, ME 04101
Telephone: 207-780-5935
Fax: 207-780 5954
tomj@usm.maine.edu
www.usm.maine.edu/ifob

Richard E. Dyke Center for Family
Business
Husson College
One College Circle
Bangor, ME 04401
Telephone: 207-973-1052
Fax: 207-973-1020
vasseyb@husson.edu
depts.husson.edu/cfb/

Maryland

Center for Closely-Held Firms
Loyola College in Maryland
4501 N. Charles Street, SH 419
Baltimore, MD 21210
Telephone: 410-617-2395
Fax: 410-617-2117
desai@loyola.edu
chf.loyola.edu

Massachusetts

Center for Family Business
Northeastern University
101 Hayden Hall
Boston, MA 02115
Telephone: 617-373-7031
Fax: 617-373-2056
ted.clark@neu.edu
www.fambiz.com

Families in Business: from Generation
to Generation Program
Harvard Graduate School of Business
McArthur Hall
Harvard University
Soldiers Field Road
Boston, MA 02163
Telephone: 617-495-6557
Fax: 617-496-9752
jbaugher@hbs.edu
www.exed.hbs.edu/programs/fib

Family Business Center
University of Massachusetts, Amherst
Family Business Center &
Continuing and Professional Education
100 Venture Way
Hadley, MA 01035
Telephone: 413-545-1537
Fax: 413-545-3351
bryck@contined.umass.edu
www.umass.edu/fambiz

Institute for Family Enterprising
Babson College
Arthur M. Blank Center for Entrepre-
neurship
231 Forest Street
Babson Park, MA 02457-0310
Telephone: 781-239-5651
Fax: 781-239-3927
charm@babson.edu
www.babson.edu/eship/ife

Institute for Technology Entrepreneurship and Commercialization
Boston University School of Management
595 Commonwealth Avenue
Boston, MA 02215
Telephone: 617-353-9391
Fax: 617-353-5003
itec@bu.edu
www.bu.edu/itec

Michigan

Family Business Center
Walsh College
Walsh Business Leadership Institute
PO Box 7006
Troy, MI 48007-7006
Telephone: 248-689-8282
Fax: 248-689-0920
jhubbard@walshcollege.edu
www.walshcollege.edu

Family Business Program
Saginaw Valley State University
College of Business and Management
7400 Bay Road
University Center, MI 48710
Telephone: 989-964-4035
rrheinri@svsu.edu
www.svsu.edu

Family-Owned Business Institute
Grand Valley State University
Seidman School of Business
401 West Fulton, Suite 386C
Grand Rapids, MI 49504
Telephone: 616-331-7377
Fax: 616-331-7583
schwarzt@gvsu.edu
gvsu.cdu/fobi

University of Michigan Flint
Michigan Family Business Center
303 East Kearsley Street
Flint, MI 48502-1950
Telephone: 810-762-3160
Fax: 810-762-3282
contactus@umflint.edu
www.umflint.edu

Minnesota

Center for Family Enterprise
University of St. Thomas
Opus College of Business
1000 LaSalle Avenue, SCH 437
Minneapolis, MN 55403-2005
Telephone: 651-962-4252
Fax: 651-962-4180
rlsorenson@stthomas.edu
www.stthomas.edu/execprofdev

Montana

Family Business Program
Montana State University
College of Business
PO Box 173040
Bozeman, MT 59717-3040
Telephone: 406-994-6796
Fax: 406-994-6206
ndodd@montana.edu
www.montana.edu/wwwdb/familybusiness/familybusiness.html

Missouri

Smurfit-Stone Center for Entrepreneurship
St. Louis University
John Cook School of Business
3674 Lindell Boulevard
St. Louis, MO 63108
Telephone: 314-977-3826
Fax: 314-977-3627
schultka@slu.edu
www.slu.edu/eweb.xml

Nebraska

Center for Family Business
Creighton University
2500 California Plaza
Omaha, NE 68178
Telephone: 402-280-2622
Fax: 402-280-2172
jeromesherman@creighton.edu
www2.creighton.edu/business/
familybusiness

Nebraska Center for Entrepreneurship
University of Nebraska
209 CBA
PO Box 880487
Lincoln, NE 68588-0487
Telephone: 402-472-3353
Fax: 402-472-5855
gfriendt2@unl.edu
www.entrepreneurship.unl.edu

New Hampshire

Center for Family Business
University of New Hampshire
Verrette House
6 Garrison Avenue
Durham, NH 03824
Telephone: 603-862-1107
Fax: 603-862-0100
barbara.draper@unh.edu
www.familybusiness.unh.edu

New York

Berkley Center for Entrepreneurial
Studies
New York University
Stern School of Business
44 W. 4th Street, Suite 7-150 KMC
New York, NY 10012
Telephone: 212-998-8943
Fax: 212-995-4211
william.baumol@nyu.edu
www.stern.nyu.edu/ei

Center for Entrepreneurial Leadership
The State University of New York at
Buffalo
School of Management
672 Delaware Avenue
Buffalo, NY 14209
Telephone: 716-885-5715
Fax: 716-885-5718
mgt-cel@buffalo.edu
mgt.buffalo.edu/cel

New Jersey

Family Business Forum
Fairleigh Dickinson University
The George Rothman Institute of
Entrepreneurial Studies
285 Madison Avenue
Madison, NJ 07940
Telephone: 973-443-8887
Fax: 973-443-8847
barrood@fdu.edu
view.fdu.edu/default.aspx?id=1218

Small Business Development Center
Pace University
163 William Street, 16th Floor
New York, NY 10038
Telephone: 212-618-6655
Fax: 212-618-6669
idavidson@pace.edu
manhattan.nyssbdc.org

Women's Business Center
Canisius College
Demerly Hall
2365 Main Street
Buffalo, NY 14214
Telephone: 716-888-6650
Fax: 716-888-8284
wbcinfo@canisius.edu
www.canisius.edu/wbc

North Carolina

The Family Business Forum
University of North Carolina at
Asheville
CPO # 1800, 308B Owen Hall
One University Heights
Asheville, NC 28804-8507
Telephone: 828-251-6797, ext. 8003
Fax: 828-251-6142
cclarke@unca.edu
www.unca.edu/fbf

Wake Forest MBA Family Business
Center
Wake Forest University
3455 University Parkway
Winston-Salem, NC 27106
Telephone: 336-757-1250
Fax: 336-757-1257
kathy.baker@mba.wfu.edu
www.mba.wfu.edu/fbc

Ohio

Center for Family Business
University of Toledo
College of Business
Mail Stop 103 Street #1044
2801 West Bancroft St.
Toledo, OH 43606
Telephone: 419-530-4058
Fax: 419-530-8497
dskutch@utnet.utoledo.edu
www.utfamilybusiness.org

Goering Center for Family & Private
Business
University of Cincinnati
College of Business
606D Carl H. Lindner Hall
2925 Campus Green Drive
PO Box 210228
Cincinnati, OH 45221-0228
Telephone: 513-556-7185
Fax: 513-556-7069
goering@uc.cdu
www.business.uc.edu/goering

Ohio Dominican University
Conway Family Business Center of
Central Ohio
1216 Sunbury Road
Columbus, OH 43219
Telephone: 614-253-4820
Fax: 614-761-9699
emens@familybusinesscenter.com
www.familybusinesscenter.com

Oklahoma

Entrepreneurship Center
University of Oklahoma
Price College of Business
307 West Brooks
Norman, OK 73019
Telephone: 405-325-7363
Fax: 405-325-2096
jwheeler@ou.edu
price.ou.edu/entrepreneurship/index.aspx

Family-Owned Business Institute
University of Tulsa
600 South College Avenue
Tulsa, OK 74104 3189
Telephone: 918-631-2684
Fax: 918-631-2083
claire-cornell@utulsa.edu
bus.cba.utulsa.edu/fobi/

Oregon

Austin Family Business Program
Oregon State University
College of Business
201 Bexell Hall
Corvallis, OR 97331-2603
Telephone: 541-737-6017
Fax: 541-737-5388
robin.klemm@bus.orcgonstate.edu
www.familybusinessonline.org

Pennsylvania

Delaware Valley Family Business
Center
340 North Main Street
Telford, PA 18969
Telephone: 215-723-8413, ext. 203
Fax: 215-723-8351
sally@dvfbc.com
www.dvfbc.com

E-Magnify, Women's Business Center
Seton Hill University
1 Seton Hill Drive
Greensburg, PA 15601
Telephone: 724-830-4625
Fax: 724-834-7171
info@e-magnify.com
www.e-magnify.com

Family Business Forum
The William G. McGowan School of
Business
King's College
Wilkes-Barre, PA 18711
Telephone: 570-208-5972
Fax: 570-208-5989
patricepersico@kings.edu
www.kings.edu/fbf

Institute for Entrepreneurial Excellence
Family Enterprise Center
Katz Graduate School of Business
University of Pittsburgh
1st Floor Posver Hall
Pittsburgh, PA 15260
Telephone: 412-648-1544
Fax: 412-648-1636
adugan@katz.pitt.edu
www.pittentrepreneur.com

Small Business Development Center
Temple University
1510 Cecil B. Moore Avenue
Philadelphia, PA 19121
Telephone: 215-204-7282
Fax: 215-204-4554
sbdc@temple.edu
www.temple.edu/sbdc

The S. Dale High Center for Family
Business
Elizabethtown College
One Alpha Dr.
Elizabethtown, PA 17022-2298
Telephone: 717-361-1275
Fax: 717-361-1226
fbc@etown.edu
www.etown.edu/family

Wharton Global Family Alliance
The Wharton School
The University of Pennsylvania
3733 Spruce Street, 4th Floor
Philadelphia, PA 19104-6374
Telephone: 215-898-4470
Fax: 215-898-1905
cieri@wharton.upenn.edu
www.wgfa.wharton.upenn.edu/
wgfa_about.html

Rhode Island

Institute for Family Enterprise
Bryant University
1150 Douglas Pike
Smithfield, RI 02917-1284
Telephone: 401-232-6477
Fax: 401-232-6416
wohara@bryant.edu
www.bryant.edu/wps/wcm/connect/Bryant/Community Outreach/
Institute for Family Enterprise

South Dakota

Prairie Family Business Association
University of South Dakota
School of Business
USDSU Campus
2205 North Career Avenue, Rm. 265
Sioux Falls, SD 57107
Telephone: 605-782-3225
Fax: 605-782-3226
badamson@usd.edu
www.usd.edu/fambus

Tennessee

Tennessee Family Business Center
2402 Belmont Boulevard
PO Box 121085
Nashville, TN 37212
Telephone: 615-460-0151
Fax: 615-460-0151
ltrella@tnfbc.org
www.tnfbc.org

Center for Entrepreneurship
Belmont University
Jack C. Massey Graduate School of
Business
1900 Belmont Boulevard
Nashville, TN 37212
Telephone: 615-460-6601
Fax: 615-460-6605
cornwallj@mail.belmont.edu
www.belmont.edu/ce

Family Business Program
Carson-Newman College
CNC Box 71887
Jefferson City, TN 37760
Telephone: 865-471-2048
Fax: 865-471-3599
hbeecher@cn.edu
www.cn.edu

Texas

Center for Entrepreneurship and Family
Business
Texas Tech University
Jerry Rawls College of Business
Box 42101
Lubbock, TX 79409-2101
Telephone: 806-742-2133
Fax: 806-742-2308
keith.brigham@ttu.edu
www.ttu.edu

Center for New Ventures and Entrepreneurship
Texas A&M University
4221 TAMU
College Station, TX 77843-4221
Telephone: 979-845-4882
Fax: 979-845-3420
lhuebner@mays.tamu.edu
cnve.org

The Institute for Family Business
John F. Baugh Center for Entrepreneurship
Hankamer School of Business
Baylor University
One Bear Place # 98011
Waco, TX 76798-8011
Telephone: 254-710-4159
Fax: 254-710-3724
mary_abrahams@baylor.edu
www.baylor.edu/business/entrepreneur

Vermont

Vermont Family Business Initiative
University of Vermont
319 Kalkin Hall
Burlington, VT 05405-0157
Telephone: 802-656-5897
Fax: 802-656-8279
vfbi@uvm.edu
uvm.edu/familybusiness

Virginia

Virginia Family & Private Business Forum
Virginia Commonwealth University
School of Business
301 West Main Street
Richmond, VA 23284
Telephone: 804-828-1745
Fax: 804-828-4011
cjgallag@vcu.edu
www.vcu.edu/busweb/vfbf

Washington

Family Enterprise Institute
Pacific Lutheran University
School of Business
Tacoma, WA 98447
Telephone: 253-535-7250
Fax: 253-535-8723
prattca@plu.edu
www.plu.edu/fament

Wisconsin

Family Business Center
University of Wisconsin-Madison
601 University Avenue, Suite 338
Madison, WI 53715
Telephone: 608-441-7338
Fax: 608-441-7337
fbc@exed.wisc.edu
exed.wisc.edu/fbc

Small Business Development Center
University of Wisconsin-Green Bay
Business Assistance Center
2701 Larsen Road, Suite A3
Green Bay, WI 54303
Telephone: 920-496-2115
Fax: 920-496-6009
tromblec@uwgb.edu
www.uwgb.edu/sbdc

Wisconsin Family Business Forum
University of Wisconsin-Oshkosh
College of Business Administration
800 Algoma Boulevard
Oshkosh, WI 54901-8678
Telephone: 920-424-2257
Fax: 920-424-7413
schierss@uwosh.edu
wfbf.uwosh.edu

Family Business Stories

This appendix contains stories that reinforce the topics and lessons covered in each chapter. Many of the stories were published by *Family Business Magazine*. We would like to acknowledge and thank them for their cooperation.

Chapter 1: Family Business Basics

Unique strengths of the family business ...

One example of a company that marshals the power of its unique family structure to enhance its business is Seven Sisters, Inc., an electrical contracting firm in Sedro-Wooley, Washington. Christine Thompson, one of the seven Snelson sisters who own the company, says that their tight-knit family has allowed them to work through some hard times that a nonfamily firm might not have been able to do.

Their father, William Snelson, owned a contracting firm, and the seven daughters feel they have grown up in the business. In 1980, they decided to band together and purchase an underutilized electrical division of their father's construction company that was being phased out. Each sister owns an equal share of the business and participates in its management, although only three actually work for the company.

Christine says that there are many advantages to working with someone you know as well as your sister. She and her sister Nancy, the president of the company, have always gotten along well, she says, and that compatibility continues into their professional relationship.

Nancy had worked for many years at her father's company, so she was immediately tapped to lead the sisters' new venture. But she was wearing too many hats to get all the jobs done well, and when Christine came on board, they quickly identified the accounting problems that were plaguing the company. The two sisters could rely on each other's expertise and focus on their jobs, which helped stabilize the company. As sisters, they are comfortable with each other's abilities and give each other independence to handle her own area of the company.

The name of the firm—Seven Sisters—helps them create a brand identity in their marketplace. "Are you really electrical contractors?" potential clients ask. "Are there really seven of you?" According to Christine, general contractors remember who they are by virtue of their unique company structure and family identity.

Entrepreneurial families ...

The Smith family of Kentucky seems to have the entrepreneurial spirit running throughout the family bloodlines. They are testament to the notion that entrepreneurial parents breed like-minded children.

Brothers Steve and Scott Smith started building new businesses as young men. Both started in the business of washing vehicles—cars or trucks—but built those companies and branched out from there. Scott Sr. started Medical Review Systems, a software company to review medical charges. His brother Steve invested in the company as it grew.

Steve's twin sons, Sean and Scott, started working in sales as soon as they graduated from college. Eventually, both were working as salesmen for their uncle's company. Scott Jr. says that he knew he and his twin brother would want to own their own business by age 30. Working with their uncle gave them access to the company's operations—something they would not have had with another firm. And being twins, Scott and Sean have a relationship that is closer than most siblings.

In 1995, the twins launched their own business, just as they had predicted. Coalition America, Inc., is a fast-growing company in the healthcare management field. In fact, they employ their uncle and former boss, Scott Sr., who joined them in 1998.

Experts agree that children in entrepreneurial families often become entrepreneurs themselves. Combine that with the tightly knit relationship of twin brothers, and it makes sense that the Smith family would be successful in any the business they create.

Carrying on the legacy of Grandma …

Brothers Adam and Jason Tenenbaum were both trained for professional careers: Adam as an attorney and Jason as a chemist. But they found their true calling in the business of baking cookies the way their Grandma used to do. For them, the business extends their family's tradition of baking and selling their grandmother Frieda's cookies to a new generation.

They founded Solomon's Gourmet Cookies in 2004, building on a smaller cookie business their mother and aunt had owned since 1992. Baking cookies according to Grandma Frieda's recipes and building a mail-order gift business around them is an extension of the way Frieda used to bake. Her cookies were always boxed and sent as gifts to special friends on a list. The company started by selling cookies retail to individual customers but now focuses on corporate gifts.

Chapter 2: Founding the Family Business

Clear responsibilities for couples …

Couples who start businesses together as "copreneurs" are a growing trend in family businesses. But husbands and wives working together can have pitfalls.

Pat and Tom Klein founded NorthWord Press in 1985. They learned that having clear job descriptions for each other's responsibilities helped them when tough decisions had to be made. Knowing who was in charge of what made it easier to reach a final decision when necessary.

The Kleins felt that in business, unlike in a marriage, someone needs to be ultimately in charge. If they disagreed on how to handle something, the person whose job it was to make that decision had the final word.

Unlike many small family businesses, the Kleins didn't hire friends and were insistent that employees not become friends. For the Kleins, this policy gave them some needed separation from the workplace after hours. They felt it helped them guard against uncomfortable personnel situations, particularly if an employee needed to be fired.

Working with your skills and talents …

Terry and Sanford Cohen found that their different talents made for a natural division of responsibilities when they founded a radio station together in Arizona in 1985. Terry handled accounting and sales, and Sanford was the public face and big-picture kind of guy. They agreed that their differences were obvious, so it was instantly clear who should take on specific responsibilities.

At work, their policy has been to treat each other as co-workers—not as husband and wife. For them, this helped remove emotion from business decisions.

Another key policy the Cohens maintained was to be open about everything in the business. They preferred to have no surprises, being sure to communicate before decisions were made. Now with four radio stations, the Cohens certainly have plenty to discuss, but their natural skills help them succeed in their business together.

Susan and Bill Kroyer are the co-founders of Kroyer Films, Inc., makers of animated films. They divide their responsibilities based on what each is best at. As equal partners in the business, they have different skills and talents, and their jobs are based on those specialties.

The couple admits they often disagree, but they resolve disputes easily by open communication and lots of discussion. Like the Cohens, they work hard to keep their personal relationship out of their business life.

Chapter 3: Family Business Structure

Divorcing ownership from management ...

Many family business owners believe that having the family as both owners and managers is the best way for a company to keep true to family values and traditions. When nonfamily members become managers, a divergence between what is good for the family and what the managers want to do with the business can develop.

However, the third-generation Muselman cousins who own DRG—a printer and publisher of magazines, books, and catalogs for needlecrafters and other hobbyists—see things differently. This Indiana company has put its faith in outsiders, both as company CEO and top management, and also as members of the company's board of directors.

Since the late 1990s, DRG has been managed entirely by nonfamily executives. According to board chairman Roger Muselman, that means the family owners can take the longer view and larger perspective. "We're flying at 40,000 feet instead of crop-dusting," Roger says.

In addition to having a family outsider as CEO of the company, the board of the company consists of two cousin owners, the CEO, and four outside board members. The outsider board consists of executives with extensive experience in publishing and catalogs. The board meets in person quarterly, confers by telephone in other months, and also works on other projects on an as-needed basis. The board doesn't handle family concerns. It's just focused on dollars-and-cents issues.

Although the cousins have an active role in the business because of their board participation, they have sensibly decided that their talents and interests are not suited to the day-to-day operation of the company. They have managed to keep the business humming by finding executives who have the skill set and the interest to keep the company on a profitable path.

Keeping shareholders happy and profitable ...

As the family business grows and passes from generation to generation, the growth of the business might not occur quickly enough to serve the needs of all the cousins who are now becoming old enough to work in the business. Here are some different ways family businesses have chosen to handle the diverse needs of subsequent generations:

New England Coffee Company's third-generation owners have a policy of refusing to have inactive shareholders. Anyone who owns a stake in the company has to work in the company. That way, the company has avoided the issue of someone not on the payroll insisting on a big dividend. The five cousins who own the business decided to buy the company from the second generation rather than wait to inherit it, and they have done so without having to use outside sources of capital.

Another way to deal with previous-generation stakeholders in a company is to continue keeping them on the payroll. That is how Maine Plastics, Inc., of Zion, Illinois, keeps the second-generation minority shareholders from selling their interests in the company to outsiders. Under a buy-sell agreement, if the minority second-generation shareholders want to sell out, the third-generation owners have the opportunity to match the offer. The third-generation owners have decided to compensate the semi-retired second generation to give them some cash flow so they won't actively look to sell their interests in the company.

Sometimes a company reaches a point when it is time to sell out. The Bancroft family owned *The Wall Street Journal* for many years and successfully resisted many offers from other media companies to buy the company. Although the Bancroft family was not active in managing the company on a day-to-day basis, it was very concerned that any new owner retain the *Journal*'s high publication standards. Many outsiders were surprised that the company was sold to Rupert Murdoch, the media mogul who had been pursuing the company for years. But because of Murdoch's huge offer and the wish of many family members to cash out, Murdoch's pursuit eventually was successful. When there are a lot of family shareholders because the business has been in the same family for many generations, the interests of the shareholders and the business can diverge so much that a sale becomes almost a necessity.

Chapter 4: Family Dynamics

Parent-child issues ...

Brothers Bobby and Burt Patton founded Patton Electronics in 1984 while still in college. The company manufactured and sold data communications equipment. Their father, Bob, who had loaned them the start-up money for the venture, was supportive but not involved. But within two years, the company was doing well and needed an infusion of capital and talent. Bobby and Burt chose to go to their father for help with both needs.

It's an unusual move to hire your father to run your company. More often, the issue in family businesses is how to hand over the reins of power from the older to the younger generation. But the Pattons needed the management expertise, and their father seemed just the right man for the job.

Everyone was a little reluctant to take the plunge. Bob provided them with both capital and management skill, although at first they all were working for no salary. In fact, it took Bob's wife Barbara to convince him that working with his sons was a risk worth taking. Bob admitted it was something he had always wanted to do, and Dad was hired.

Today, Bob has recently moved to serve as chairman of the board, and Bobby has taken over as CEO. Besides brother Burt, other Patton brothers Bruce and Ben are involved with the company, and brother Barry owns a distributorship that handles Patton Electronics products. The company is flourishing with strong growth. The Patton family has found a way to work together without the struggles one might expect when the tables are turned and sons hire Dad.

When parents don't want the child to take over ...

Twin brothers Bill and Terry Vose, the fifth generation of their family business, Vose Galleries of Boston, were discouraged by their father Robert from joining the firm. He told them it was a very hard way to make a living, based on his experience of having had to leave college during the Depression to help his father keep the business afloat. Years ago, Robert and his brother S. Morton Vose agreed that the business would be dissolved rather than expect the boys to succeed them.

It took a family tragedy to change his mind. Bill was in a near-fatal boating accident, and during his long recuperation, he found himself helping around the gallery. When he realized he enjoyed working there, he encouraged his brother Terry to join him and learn the ropes. Since 1970, both brothers have worked at the gallery, and they spent many years becoming experts before the older generation retired in 1985. Terry views that time as an "apprenticeship" and thinks it was a requirement for becoming truly knowledgeable.

Although he was initially reluctant to bring his sons into the business, Robert ultimately admitted he was pleased that they joined and succeeded him. Today, the brothers are co-presidents of the firm, Bill's wife Marcia is company treasurer, and daughters Elizabeth and Carey are now assistant directors at the gallery. They stand ready as the sixth generation of the Vose family in the business, following their extended "apprenticeship," of course.

Sibling rivalry ...

The unique relationship between brothers Walt and Roy Disney was fraught with sibling rivalry, but it helped to create the dynasty we all know as the Disney empire. Walt was, as everyone knows, the creative genius behind the company. But equally important to the business was his older brother Roy.

In 1923, they founded Disney Brothers Studio, with Roy raising the money for the venture and Walt creating animated short films. Each brother's talents were utilized according to his abilities, and each played a critical role in the development of the company. But their sibling rivalry was well known. They often clashed on business decisions, with Walt being a freewheeling spender who ignored cost overruns when creating a new project. Roy was clearly the financial and management thinker who instituted such critical business concepts as a film distribution company and licensing opportunities for Disney characters.

Their rivalry extended to the people who worked with them, with employees in the company divided into "Walt's boys" or "Roy's boys." They disputed bitterly over the creation of Disneyland as well, with Roy the naysayer and Walt forging ahead. Eventually, Roy relented and structured a partnership with ABC to create the park and bring Disney into the television age as well. Although this battle raged between the brothers and almost drove them apart, they eventually came together based on their mutual respect. After that, the two brothers seemed to work better together and at Walt's death in 1966, were planning Walt Disney World in Florida. It was opened in 1971, months before Roy, too, died.

Chapter 5: Strategic Planning

Even if you're over 100, you must change with the times ...

The saying "You can't teach an old dog new tricks" might be true for dogs, and even for humans, but it doesn't apply to business.

Ironrock, Inc., a ceramic tile manufacturer in Canton, Ohio, has survived as a family business for five generations. However, it must constantly reinvent itself to ensure it doesn't just fade away.

Ironrock started as a manufacturer of paving brick and became so successful that it was the largest manufacturer of paving brick in the world. But the market for paving brick declined, and by the early 1960s the company had to completely change the nature of its business. The company sold off its old brick plants and concentrated on the tile market. The company became smaller, but the business was on the right track.

The company had other strategic challenges in the 1990s, as the market for imported tile grew and "big box" stores created intense price competition.

Amelia Renkert-Thomas, who for a time was CEO of Ironrock (and also the first and only president of the Tile Council of America), said that there were several rules her family business followed to stay healthy over generations of business. One was that the business ownership would be concentrated in the present generation of management. This enabled the managers to reinvest profits in the business rather than have to pay it out to shareholders.

Ms. Renkert-Thomas also said that the family should treat the business as a challenging opportunity rather than a guaranteed paycheck. Ironrock made a point of holding family members to a very high standard of performance. She recommended that a family business closely watch its debt levels and never pledge assets the business cannot lose.

Monday morning quarterbacking ...

Sometimes the best-laid plans come from just talking to each other.

Take Garvey's Office Products, Inc., located in Niles, Illinois. The five siblings who run the $25 million office supply business meet every Monday morning at 7 A.M. just to ... talk.

"Through conversations and analysis we tend to reach a lot of unanimous decisions," says Bernie Garvey, president of the company. "No one is digging their heels in so hard."

It was at one of those Monday morning meetings a few years ago that sales manager Kevin Garvey came up with the concept of enhancing the company's website by letting customers see product prices without registering on the website. Despite vigorous debate among the five sibling owners, the idea was approved. Today, any visitor to www.shopgarveys.com can see prices and actually buy products online. The site gives the family history. Its home page has special product offers to entice customers to use the site.

A little Monday morning quarterbacking (and strategic planning) can help a company grow. By sharing ideas in a nonconfrontational manner, business owners can regularly assess where they are and where they should be going and growing.

Chapter 6: Day-to-Day Management

Sibling partners ...

Classic organization theory argues against siblings sharing management responsibility. Without one firm steward of the business, the traditionalists would argue, the business will be rudderless and unable to move forward.

Yet some sibling partnerships do well with a shared responsibility. For some families, shared leadership is the only sensible solution when there are a number of strong, competent leaders in the second generation and beyond. Here are two examples:

The Barebo siblings Charlie, Chris, and Carla run Otterbine-Barebo, Inc., a water-quality management company that their parents bought in 1980. When their parents retired in 1993, the siblings, then in their thirties, were put in charge of the company. Their parents had established three councils of key executives—one for manufacturing, another for sales and marketing, and a third for research and development—to help steer the company. The parents had also hired a family business consultant to give advice.

Since then, the siblings have devised a compensation plan that flattens out pay differences between them and have divided the responsibilities of running the company. Important decisions must be made by consensus. If a true disagreement occurs that cannot be resolved by discussion, the sibling in charge of that area has final say.

Because the siblings meet for breakfast and lunch every day, they have the constant communication necessary to run a business by committee.

Another company with siblings running the business together is the Allen Lumber Company of Vermont. A family-owned business for over 120 years, the five Allen brothers are the fourth generation to run the business.

All five brothers have an active role in today's Allen Lumber. Gary Allen serves as president, Burnie is the treasurer, Paul and Tom are vice-presidents, and Steven is the company's secretary. In addition to being officers of the company, each brother handles a different segment of the company's day-to-day operation.

Even though the five brothers maintain a strong family control of the company's fortunes, they are willing to let other long-time employees have a significant role in the company's operations. When they started a new kitchen and bath division, the company turned to Dave MacAskill, their purchasing manager, to head up the new division.

The Allen brothers are a close-knit family, with frequent meetings to discuss important family issues. All the brothers are willing to take active roles and make important company decisions. Because each brother has a clearly defined area of expertise, the brothers often defer to the managerial decisions of the brother who has the most experience in a particular area.

An investment in education …

Gilbane Building Company, founded in 1873 by William and Thomas Gilbane, is one of the nation's oldest builders. Listed as one of Fortune's 100 Best Companies to Work For in 2009, Gilbane also has been ranked as one of the country's top training organizations. In 2005, the company invested $5.8 million in what it calls Gilbane University, which teaches 1,200 courses on a range of topics, including steel erection, project management, client satisfaction, and ethics. The investment of Gilbane in employee education is far above the industry average. The chairman of Gilbane Building Company, Thomas Gilbane Jr., says, "We view learning as one of our main long-term investment strategies."

The investment in targeted education has paid off for Gilbane, which constantly monitors client concerns and incorporates client issues in its educational curriculum. According to CEO Thomas Gilbane Jr., "We continue to measure the improving scores from our client feedback, and the responses are now consistently achieving a 96 percent satisfaction level." According to Gilbane, the improvement in client satisfaction scores can be directly linked to the courses provided at Gilbane University.

Chapter 7: Personnel Issues for Family Members

Erecting employment barriers ...

There is no one "right" way to hire family members into a family business. Some families feel that only family members are qualified to carry on the traditions and quality of the family business. Other family businesses prefer to treat family members and outsiders equally, hiring strictly on the merits. And some families put up more difficult barriers to their own family members than outsiders.

Connecticut clothing retailers Jack and Bill Mitchell decided that none of their seven sons could come into the business until they had worked at least five years for another company. They could join the company only when there was an open position for which one of the children was qualified to fill.

The brothers' employment decisions stunned their father, Ed Mitchell, the founder of the business. All four of his sons had entered the business, and he saw tremendous talent emerging in the next generation. He thought the company would "lose" the grandchildren because of the stringent employment barriers his sons had erected.

But the brothers persisted with their employment policy. They believed their children would receive a realistic assessment of their talents only if they worked in a nonfamily business. The brothers said it was crucial that they think of their business as a business first, and a family business second.

The third generation did drift away from the business for a while and found success in other fields. But the policy proved effective in the long run. Before he died in 2005, founder Ed Mitchell saw all seven of his grandsons eventually back in the family business, and today, two grandsons are co-presidents of the company.

Cross-training ...

Many people practice cross-training at the gym. One day you exercise your arms. The next day it's your legs. The third day you use the treadmill for a cardiovascular workout.

Family businesses need cross-training as well. Larrie Laird, CEO of Laird & Company, says that if he were suddenly incapacitated, his daughter and nephew could take over the company without skipping a beat. The $48 million company that makes brandy and whiskeys has a policy of training top executives in all aspects of the company.

Laird & Company spreads out its inventory in two locations and insures the beverages at market value instead of cost. All these policies, plus the cross-training of executives, are part of the company's plan to spread risk.

The company has established its policies of preparing for disaster because it has survived difficult times in the past. During Prohibition, Laird stopped making alcohol products (except for licensed medicines) and switched to making applesauce and cider. During World War II, Laird became even more innovative and used the pectin from the residue produced by making cider as a preservative for canned foods. It even started doing some tomato canning.

These experiences made Laird & Company aware that a business should be prepared for any emergency. And those preparations bore fruit when Larrie Laird was sidelined for more than a month with a hip replacement. Other well-trained executives were able to step right in and keep the family business on an even keel during Laird's recuperation.

Chapter 8: Communication

Telling the world about your problems …

How should a family business handle a disaster? The first necessity is to deal with the crisis. But after you have the crisis under control, it is important to deal with the media. The media will want to cover a breaking story, and it is important to put the family's view of the situation out front.

When Joe Fasula received a predawn call that one of his family's Gerrity's Supermarkets was on fire, he rushed to the scene. Once there, he had to assess the damage, but he was also surrounded by newspaper reporters and television crews who wanted an immediate reaction. After talking to firemen and surveying the store, Fasula gave the reporters the story they wanted. He told them the fire had started in the electrical system, and he didn't know how bad the damage was.

The store ended up closing for a month and a half, and Fasula estimates the store lost about $2 million in revenue. But partially due to publicity about the fire and the store's reopening, business at the store has increased about 10 percent since the fire.

"My advice is to be as open and frank as possible," Fasula says about talking to the media. "Certainly you can't give out information that's proprietary, or information that's libelous," he says, "but anything you can tell them, tell them."

The importance of a family council …

A family council is a way for the family members of a business to have their voices heard and their needs met. A family council can interact with the board of directors to make sure they address business concerns of the family. The council can also communicate family and business decisions to family members not working in the business or on the family council. A family council usually is not necessary during the business start-up stage and might not be appropriate in the second generation of a family business if most family members communicate frequently. But a family council becomes increasingly important in subsequent generations of a family business, when the number of family business owners can multiply and include many family members who do not work day-to-day in the family business.

It took the Eddy Family Council, consisting of members of the family that owns Port Blakely Companies, two years to become fully organized. It took the family council almost four more years to complete work on the Eddy Family Constitution.

The Eddy Family Constitution comprises the governance documents of the Eddy Family Council. It also includes a vision and values statement and a setup for the family assembly and family council. Governance documents include a redemption policy to help family members liquidate their ownership in the company, if necessary. Other governance documents include a family employment policy and a family director policy, which encourage the family to include daughters as well as sons on the board of directors.

Another task of the Eddy Family Council is educating family members on topics such as financial planning and estate planning. Youth education focuses on the family businesses, including hands-on activities for very young family members.

The Eddy Family Council also has an annual meeting that focuses on business updates as well as family-centered activities. One of the important byproducts of creating the family council has been the establishment and deepening of friendships of the many branches of this fifth-generation family business.

Chapter 9: Marketing the Family Business

What's in a name …

One of the most valuable assets of a family business is its name. Attaching the family name to the business is often a great branding idea. If the family wants to instill its values and traditions into a business, using the family name makes perfect sense.

Having an unusual name helps. How about Zagat? If you live in New York City or many other metropolitan areas, one concept comes quickly to mind: food surveys.

Tim and Nina Zagat established the Zagat survey in 1979 as a small hobby—a way to compare the values of different New York City restaurants. In their first guide, the

Zagats enlisted their friends to rate different restaurants. Out of that humble beginning, Zagat surveys have grown tremendously, now reviewing restaurants in 70 cities with input from more than 250,000 individuals. The Zagat guides rate restaurants on food, decor, service, and cost on a 30-point scale.

The name Zagat now creates instant identification for millions of people. Because the Zagat name has become almost a synonym for food surveying, it is a valuable commodity.

Birthday celebrations: yours and your customers ...

What's everyone's favorite holiday? You guessed it: their birthday. Lots of presents, parties, and phone calls from friends and families.

If you're running a business, have a birthday party and celebrate with some special guests—your customers. Whether you've been in business 1, 10, 25, or 100 years or more, have an anniversary celebration every year.

Gordon's Youth Shop in New Jersey used a great advertising headline for an anniversary celebration: "It's our birthday, but the presents are yours!" The store used giveaways and special promotions to lure customers into the store. A business anniversary is an excuse to have a sale, but the celebration aspect adds lots of good feelings.

Copps' Supermarkets in Wisconsin had a "100th year in business" birthday celebration that lasted the whole year. Its marketing team came up with 100 ideas for celebrating the special anniversary, which ranged from giant parties to coloring books about the history of the company for children. The promotion reminded customers about the family nature of the business and the fact that it had been part of the community for a long time.

When should you have your business's anniversary celebration? Many companies try to figure out exactly when the business started and have it on that day. When the starting date of the business is not so precise, many companies celebrate their anniversary in August. Why? Because August is the only month without any regularly scheduled holidays!

Chapter 10: Balancing Home and Business

A business that grew from the dining room table ...

Sometimes a family business can literally grow out of the home. Robin Vecchio started her business tutoring students learning to be court reporters right in her family dining room. Balancing her role as a mother to five children with her desire to stay in business, Vecchio grew her dining room tutoring of a half-dozen students to a court reporting and legal training school with more than 300 students and 33 employees.

Along the way, Vecchio's family became part of the business. Nine family members participate in the business, and now Vecchio is both mother and boss. She says those two hats necessitate a delicate balance between love and supervision.

Vecchio tries to keep the business and family life separate to ensure that family problems don't interrupt business routines. But she likes the sense of informality in the business that comes from having so many family members in the company.

Her children have had various roles at the schools. Many worked as custodians while in high school, but after college they have become recruiters, an admissions director, and a business manager. One of her sons says that every day is like a family reunion.

Vecchio's husband James, who is a lawyer, is now the CEO of the firm. They try to leave personal discussions at home and business discussions at the office. To discourage rivalries, Vecchio encourages her children to take the job that suits each one best. She is trying to delegate more and more responsibilities to her children so she can pursue other activities.

Reversal of roles ...

Jack Misset was a well-known television reporter in Chicago in the 1960s. He was often recognized when his family went out to dinner. People would come up and ask him, "Aren't you Jack Misset from TV?"

Jack says he had his fame and never really enjoyed it. So when Jack's wife Judi wanted to move to California to start an aerobics program, Jack didn't object. He agreed to stay home with his daughter Shanna because he enjoyed cooking and taking care of the house.

Judi's aerobics business blossomed into Jazzercise, Inc., an international empire of franchised exercise classes, instructor training, and video exercise programs. As the business grew, Jack was pulled in because of his video training. He agreed to make video training tapes of Judi's choreography. During the weekend, Judi would be on stage, Jack behind the camera, and little Shanna handing out fliers announcing demo classes.

Today Shanna is the company's vice-president of international operations, and the company has franchises in 32 countries. Jack deliberately has limited his involvement to video productions plus some special events and publicity planning. He says, "I'm not running the show. From the start I made the decision with Judi that it was her company to run." But Jack provided the critical home support that made it possible for Jazzercise to become a worldwide success.

Chapter 11: Expansion of the Family Business

Growing through diversification ...

Some family businesses find a profitable niche and keep everyone in the business focused on a reliable source of income. But other family businesses have found that diversification can be a reliable way to avoid the perils of putting all your eggs in one basket.

Consider S&S Leather, a producer of small leather goods founded in 1906 by brothers Aaron and Abraham Schwartz on New York City's Lower East Side. For years, the company prospered using Eastern European immigrants to make items such as purses, key cases, and suspender trimmings. In the 1920s, leather hair curlers became the company's signature item.

During the Depression, though, sales of finished leather goods dropped, and Aaron's son Hyman refocused the company's sales efforts into handicraft leather kits. The company focused on the vocational rehabilitation market, transforming partially finished leather products such as comb cases and small purses into handicraft kits. The company developed relationships with organizations such as the Lighthouse for the Blind and the Leathercraft Guild of America. It expanded its craft kits for uses at camps, municipal parks, and recreational programs across the company. Since then, it has expanded to sell physical education products and started selling products to daycare centers such as KinderCare. Today, S&S Worldwide has annual sales of $60 million and houses much of its merchandise in a 250,000-square-foot warehouse.

S&S has followed a successful path to increase its business through diversification. It has followed some important family business principles for successful growth:

- Grow if possible in fields where your expertise is useful.

- Develop relationships with other businesses and expand your product line to satisfy your customers' needs.

- Never bet the ranch on a new line of business. If you can fund expansion internally, you'll be better prepared to sustain the ups and downs of new product lines.

Expanding even while competition is fierce ...

Walgreens is a large family business that has more than 1,500 drugstores in America and is the fastest-growing company in the drugstore industry. Walgreens adds 425 drugstores each year and plans to have 7,000 locations worldwide by 2010. But competition for consumers has also increased while Walgreens has expanded. Deep discounters have put up no-frills stores that offer very low prices on basic goods such as toothpaste and shampoo.

At the same time, supermarket chains are marketing health and beauty products because of the high margins generated by those sales. Today, more shampoo is sold in supermarkets than in drug stores, which marks a significant departure from past consumer buying patterns.

Walgreens' answer? An emphasis on prescription drugs and convenience. Walgreens places special importance on selecting sites in high-traffic areas and sets up its stores to serve consumers promptly with the items they want. Walgreens wants to be in the right location for a busy executive who is on a 30-minute lunch break. The average customer spends less than 10 minutes in the store. Scanners have replaced many cash registers to speed up the checkout lines.

Walgreens' emphasis on prescriptions has paid handsome dividends. Drug sales at Walgreens have grown by an average of 25 percent in the past decade. Its investment in cutting-edge technology allows the company to maintain an extensive customer database. All Walgreens stores are linked into one network, which gives the company access to customer prescription records wherever customers shop, including at the Walgreens website. In fact, Walgreens is the largest private user of satellite technology, second only to the U.S. government.

Walgreens has decided to fight its competition with expansion, up-to-date technology, and profitable site locations, and by providing customers with the products they want when they want them. So far, the strategy is paying off.

Chapter 12: Outsiders in the Family Business

Even if you specialize in the old, you can try something new ...

Samuel T. Freeman & Co. of Philadelphia is America's oldest auction house and has a long history of selling old items at a profit. Yet this company specializing in the "old" needed some new ideas, according to sixth-generation owner Samuel M. Freeman. Freeman said that the auction house had been just a processor of goods for close to 70 years. "We weren't going anywhere," says Freeman.

He brought in an outsider, Paul Roberts, who was president of Phillips North America to bring some fresh ideas to the old company. Roberts's biggest initiative was to emphasize margin over volume. In 1999—the year Roberts came to Freeman—the company achieved gross revenues of $6 million on 60,000 lots sold. In five years, Roberts transformed the company's performance and brought in $15.5 million on just 11,000 lots. The following year he set an all-time high of $21.25 million in the company's 200th anniversary year.

As part of his plan to increase gross revenues, Roberts helped the company toot its own horn. The company was well known in Philadelphia, but Roberts launched marketing initiatives to increase the company's reputation. Roberts didn't achieve growth by adding personnel. He was able to actually cut staff from 33 to 25 and at the same time replaced some previous staff with outside experts.

The seventh generation of the Freeman family supports the profound changes in the family's business. Jonathan Freeman says, "I considered it almost a new business venture, a brand-new business starting out."

The Freeman story shows that even if a business has been successful for many years and is profitable, stagnation can set in. Often, talented outsiders can provide the ideas and dynamics to turn the company in a new, more profitable direction.

Knowing when it's time to quit …

Sometimes, even when a family member has been groomed to carry on the family business, the transition is just so difficult that calling on an outsider to take over is the best solution for the company and the family heir.

That is what happened to William Lauder, the grandson of Estee Lauder, who founded her famous cosmetics company in 1946. Even though he became CEO in 2004 at age 44, William had to cope with two constituencies. His 74-year-old father Leonard didn't fully turn over the company to William. He remained chairman of the board, in an office larger than his son's. He questioned William's decisions with handwritten memos. William also had to mediate disputes with other family members.

Also, Estee Lauder had gone public in 1995. So in addition to dealing with family politics, William had to satisfy corporate shareholders focused on quarterly profits.

William told *The Wall Street Journal* that it wasn't easy having to answer to board members "who remember you as a child and feel free to call you at home any time." He continued, "Leading a public company is a sentence. But leading a publicly held, family-controlled business is a life sentence."

William decided to turn the helm of the company over to a nonfamily outsider, Procter and Gamble executive Fabrizio Freda. Because an outsider is not bound by family emotional ties, an outsider can have more freedom to guide a family business without second-guessing. Sometimes the weight of a family business can be too oppressive for the next generation and an outsider is the best solution for the family as well as the business.

Chapter 13: Financial Decisions

Don't give away the store …

One of the most important decisions a family business has to face is whether and how to pass the business to the next generation. The founder of the business has many options. The owner can sell to an outside company. The owner can sell to his children. The owner can even give the business to his children.

Often, the best solution is to sell the business to the next generation. That way, the owner can secure retirement while still keeping the business in the family. That was the path taken by Luca Sena, the second-generation owner of Ristorante Panorama and the Penn's View Hotel in Philadelphia.

When Luca's father Carlo was ready to turn the business over to Luca, the son paid the father 10 percent over the appraised value of the business. He paid a premium price because he didn't want his five brothers and sisters, who didn't work in the business, to feel that he had cheated them out of an inheritance. Luca had to take a second mortgage on his house to complete the purchase.

The transaction worked out well for Luca. He plans to follow the same procedure when his son, also named Carlo, is ready to take over. The younger Carlo says, "I have been working in the business since I was five. But I won't feel that I own it until I buy it outright."

When a family member in the second or third generation buys a business, he feels like a true owner and doesn't feel like decisions have to be made with the blessings of the previous owner. When there is a gift, emotional strings are often attached. Also, the new owner can feel the resentment of other family members. When the business is sold at close to fair value, nobody feels cheated.

A small business with big dreams ...

What do you do if you have a small business with great ideas but not enough money to achieve your dreams? One path is to set your sights lower and gradually build your business. But that hasn't been the route taken by brothers Brad and Eric Blumberg, building their company Smarter Agent.

Brad and Eric worked for years developing a product with patented GPS technology that allows consumers to shop for homes using their mobile phones. They won several technology awards for their application. They could have devised a solution that focused on just one brand of cell phone or just worked with one carrier. Instead, they were convinced that their idea should work on all cell phones and all telecommunication companies.

After borrowing and working with family money for a number of years, Brad and Eric eventually convinced a venture capital fund to invest $6 million into Smarter Agent. With this capital, Brad and Eric were able to make their technology work with most mobile phones. They were also able to partner with major telecommunication companies and brokerage firms to give their product the widest possible distribution.

Despite developing a product during down years in the real estate business, Brad and Eric are optimistic about the future of their company. The venture capital they were able to raise has given them the opportunity to build a company as big as their dreams.

A family business should look at a funding source that matches the needs of the business they are trying to develop. Although many businesses can grow slowly and organically, a technology company might have to go to outside sources of capital to stay competitive in a rapidly changing technological environment.

Chapter 14: Protecting the Family Business

Again, what's in a name ...

One of the most valuable assets a family has is its name. That is why a family should make sure in internal family disputes and in a sale or partnership with another company that it retains control of the use of its name.

Manny Randazzo is a baker of "king cakes—a tricolored confection that is a must-have during Carnival season—in New Orleans. He ignored this basic rule in a divorce proceeding with his wife and lived to regret his oversight. As part of a divorce settlement, Dianne Randazzo received $882,000 as settlement for her stake of the Randazzo family business. Manny Randazzo was allowed to keep the business.

However, Manny neglected to have Dianne sign a noncompete agreement as part of the divorce proceeding. He said, "The whole point of it was that (the payment money) should have been sufficient."

But it wasn't. Dianne subsequently decided she wanted to open her own king cake business. And she wanted to use her name on her business. Manny sued, claiming that if Dianne used her married name it would draw customers to her business.

But in the absence of a noncompete agreement, Dianne was entitled to start her own business and use her own name. To avoid confusion, the judge ruled that Dianne would have to use both her first and last name in the business and couldn't use phrases like "Randazzo Family Recipe" or "Randazzo Family" in her advertising.

The ruling was probably a fair resolution of the dispute, given that there was no legal impediment to Dianne starting her own business. But in the divorce settlement, Manny could have made sure his business/family name was protected by having a noncompete clause as part of that agreement.

Even in sales of a business or licensing part of a business to a third party, family businesses should ensure that their names are not being used in a way they would be uncomfortable with. A lawyer can help a family business owner maintain some control over the way her family name is being used.

Where there's a will, is there a way ...

Sometimes, too much legal complexity can be a bad thing. Jack Kent Cooke amassed a $1.3 billion empire of media companies, real estate, and sports teams (including the jewel of the crown, the Washington Redskins football franchise).

To protect his empire, he wrote a convoluted will, which he amended eight times, and appointed seven executors to administer his wishes. But the plan backfired, and the result was seven years and $64 million in professional fees to figure out how to do what Jack Kent Cooke wanted. The legal proceedings resulted in the forced sale of the Redskins.

In his will, Cooke decided that one of his holdings, the Chrysler Building, would be sold to pay his federal estate taxes. But the building was not worth enough when he died to accomplish this task, so the executors decided to sell the Redskins instead. The only executor who objected was Jack's son John, who subsequently put together a group to bid on the Redskins.

The group couldn't match an $800 million bid from Washington businessman Daniel Snyder. Although John's share of the estate was increased because of the high sale price of the Redskins, he was tremendously disappointed that the family could not keep control of the successful football franchise.

John's disappointment, and the staggering legal fees, could probably have been avoided if Jack Kent Cooke had fashioned his will in another way. By trying to do too much in his will, Cooke created a nightmare for his family business.

Chapter 15: Consultants and Mediators

Grab the life preserver ...

Sometimes consultants can bring family business problems to the surface, and sometimes consultants can save a family business. In the case of Graeter's Manufacturing Co. in Cincinnati, consultants did a little bit of both.

Graeter's Manufacturing Co. wrestled from 1990 to 2004 with transferring the business to three cousins from three third-generation families. If the shares were transferred according to bloodlines, one of the cousins would own one half of the business (an only son) and the other two cousins (brothers) would own one quarter each. The remaining shares were in another branch of the family and would have to be redeemed.

Both of the brothers with sons interested in running the business hired their own consultants. One hired a management consultant; one hired an attorney. An accountant and insurance agent were also brought in, but to no avail. No solution seemed fair to all the parties involved.

Finally, another consultant, a psychologist, was brought in to help resolve the dispute. The psychologist helped the cousins meet to determine a plan. The trio began to see "how important it was to put the interests of the business first and have complete faith in our partners," recalled the cousin who was entitled to the bigger share if the business were divided along family lines. That cousin eventually decided that all three cousins should have equal shares in the business, which was accomplished through share gifting, redemptions, and some financial sacrifice by the cousin entitled to the largest share.

The moral of the story: consultants work only when there is buy-in from all parties. When different family members bring in consultants who represent only some family members, achieving a result satisfactory to all family members can be difficult.

Getting help on board ...

It can be a big mistake for a family business to exclude outside directors from its board of directors. Only about 25 percent of family businesses have outsiders on the board. The family's desire for privacy is understandable, but by excluding outside directors, the family business is missing out on some potentially helpful advice. As consultant Jeff Hester says, "There's a Chinese proverb that says: If you're not in the game, you can easily see the next move."

Hester, who now is president of Collaborative Resources, a consulting and investing firm, serves on two family business boards. Hester has firsthand experience with family businesses, having served as president of Pierce Foods before that family business sold out to ConAgra Foods in 1997.

Hester says he doesn't play favorites. "I concentrate on what's best for the company. I may side with one person on one issue and another person on another issue." That independence of thought sometimes is difficult to achieve among family members who either have hardened positions or are too intimidated to rock the boat.

Many times the best outsiders to serve on family business boards are retired executives. These older executives are battle-tested and have the time to assess a family's business needs.

After serving as an outside director himself, Don Rauch, the president and CEO of M&C Specialties (a third-generation family business), decided to hire an outsider for his own board of directors. It took him several years to find the right person, but later, one of the outside board members was appointed chairman of the board.

Rauch believes in having outsiders on a family business's board of directors, even as chairman of the board. He says, "When they're in charge you get real accountability from the CEO, and board meetings are about more than just management issues."

Chapter 16: Sale of the Family Business

The best time to sell ...

It seems paradoxical, but the best time to sell a family business is when the business is doing well. When you are making lots of money and the future is rosy, other companies will see your situation optimistically. When the bills are stacked high and the competition is grabbing your best customers, you might want to sell, but you might not be able to find a buyer.

John Ratliff started Diplomatic Language Services after a 28-year career in the federal government. The business expanded rapidly, and in 12 years annual revenues grew to $6 million.

John made a dispassionate analysis of his business. He considered the competitive environment, the market potential, his own and his family's entrepreneurial experience, the safety of a sale for retirement, the resources necessary to grow the company, and its current versus future value. All these factors argued in favor of the sale of his business. The only factor arguing against that was the fact that his wife, son, and daughter-in-law all worked in the company and that a sale could jeopardize their long-term employment prospects in the company.

John and his family decided after their analysis that a sale made sense. They found a certified business intermediary and within six months had sold the business. One of the key lessons of the process? "Don't wait until you suffer business reversals or employee morale problems that can hurt the potential sale price." John also advises not to wait until you are 65 to sell. In other words, try to sell at the high, not the low.

There's life after a sale …

After a CEO has sold the family business, she can take one of many routes, including:

- Sticking with the business for a time (or for many years) as an employee and/or advisor

- Retiring and perhaps spending some time advising or serving on the boards of other companies

- Starting a new career

The third option was the path chosen by Don Silver, CEO of Penn Ventilator Company, an $80 million business. Despite being CEO, Don was a minority shareholder in the company and often clashed with members of the previous generation of owners—including his father—over management issues.

In the fall of 1997, after several difficult years of operation, the once cash cow of a company had its credit line called by its bank. In his personal life, Don and his wife separated. He was in crisis mode, and he managed to find a strategic buyer for the business that paid more for the company's assets than what was owed.

Don decided to do something different. He enrolled in a part-time Master's degree program in creative writing. He also became director of Temple University's Family Business Alliance and started coaching CEOs of family businesses.

Eventually, Don found a literary agent and his novel *Backward-Facing Man* was sold to the Ecco division of HarperCollins. The novel received many complimentary reviews and completed Don's transition from businessman to novelist. The sale of his family business was a springboard to a whole new career.

Chapter 17: Succession Planning

Planting the idea of succession planning ...

The Kellogg family—not the cereal folks, but another branch of that same family—has built its garden products business over three generations with careful thought about succession. Kellogg Garden Products of California is a $55 million business, helping develop outdoor landscapes for such locations as Disneyland, Dodger Stadium, Hearst Castle, and many more. The company was founded in 1925 by H. Clay Kellogg, and a clear line of succession was established for the business. H. Clay Kellogg Jr. inherited the business, while his sisters inherited other properties. In the next generation, H. Clay Kellogg III was groomed for the top job by his father.

The current generation of Kelloggs sees the wisdom in such planning. Kathy Kellogg Johnson, H. Clay III's sister and corporate secretary, thinks it made great sense to leave the management of the corporation in the hands of only one of the offspring in each generation and to provide equal assets outside the corporation to the others.

Both grandfather and father spoke openly about succession of the family business while in charge of the company. H. Clay Jr. knew of his own heart condition and prepared for his eventual demise by grooming his wife Janice to handle the company for several years until H. Clay III was ready. She recognized how her role as interim company head during the period right after her husband's death kept the company strong by providing a seamless transition.

Many family business leaders operate as if they will be immortal and make few plans for future generations of leadership. The Kelloggs have understood through the years that careful succession planning helps to strengthen the company by providing a framework of management that everyone understands.

Succession planning for a two-family business ...

The story of Easy Day Manufacturing in Massachusetts is an interesting one on the subject of succession planning. The two owners of the company were not related to each other, but their sons joined the business and became an integral part of top management. This structure raised a number of succession issues that the company dealt with for many years.

As is often the case, the younger generation provided the stimulus for starting a succession planning process. Knowing that the lack of family ties between them gave them less incentive to work together, Harris Footer and Rob Michelson recognized the need to formalize transfer of ownership and management—even while their fathers resisted such planning.

They found that by working on strategic planning for the company's future, they could approach their fathers with some succession issues. As they worked through a process of planning for the company's future growth, they were able to begin a conversation about how to structure handing the business to the next generation. They found it was easier to talk privately about succession when the direction for the company was settled with family and nonfamily employees.

Both Rob and Harris developed a strong sense of shared values and goals through the strategic planning process, which helps to make them more of a team for future succession. They understand that the strategic direction of the company must be firm before succession decisions can be made.

Chapter 18: Transitioning to the Next Generation

Sibling partnership …

Sometimes the transition from the first to second generation in a family business goes directly to one child. But in many cases, several siblings are interested and involved in the family business. In that case, a sibling partnership can run the company—if the siblings work together as a team.

One such sibling partnership that makes teamwork seem easy is the threesome that runs Sullivan and Cogliano, a computer consulting firm in Massachusetts. The three Cogliano brothers, Jay, Herb, and Jim, work as a team to build their business.

When their father John Cogliano, who had founded the firm in 1966 and ran it himself since 1984 was ready to step down, he consulted with family firm advisors who all recommended he choose one son as his successor. He sons began to compete with each other for the top job. John felt the atmosphere was harmful to the company, so he asked them to start working as a team again, which they were happy to do. When he handed over the management of the company in 1998, he did so to all three sons together. As a group, they decided who would have the specific title of CEO, president, and COO. However, they worked together as a team to make decisions and grow the company.

Their executive teamwork made business sense because their clients required overlap among the several divisions of the firm. Managing as a team has trickled down into other levels of management in the company, which has been beneficial for attracting new clients.

They divided stock equally, too: father and mother retained one fifth each, and each of the brothers received one fifth. The brothers decided to receive equal pay, as well. Such monetary teamwork helps them remember that each member of the team is equally important, no matter what title he holds.

As children, the Cogliano brothers were encouraged to work together. As adults, they have taken those lessons to heart and used them to build their family business around teamwork.

Chapter 19: Into the Third Generation—and Beyond

Maintaining the business focus ...

The Coors Brewing Co. provides a good example of how a family business can successfully bring family members into the company. Pete Coors, now chairman of MolsonCoors, is a member of the Coors family's fourth generation. When he was president of Coors Brewing Co., he attributed the family's ability to transfer the business through the generations to a professional attitude that required family members to be even more qualified than nonfamily members to get ahead.

Family members interested in growing with the company were encouraged to get the academic credentials for the job—Pete Coors, for example, holds an engineering degree as well as an MBA. Other family members who expressed interest in management positions had to do the same.

But as the company grew, the opportunities for family management have become fewer. Now that Coors has merged with Molson and has an alliance with Miller, the company has a nonfamily president. Coors family members still hold most of the voting stock along with Molson family members, though, so family control is maintained.

Keeping the vision alive ...

Maintaining a family business through several generations can require changing the underlying line of work while retaining the company vision. Berman Leather was founded in 1905 by Meyer Berman. At that time, the company was in business manufacturing leather shoe soles. Meyer's grandson Ira, who led the business at 30 years old, saw more opportunity in providing leather for the top side of shoes (the uppers). His business was as a leather middleman and warehouser.

The business continued to evolve as needs for leather changed. A market for leather-crafting materials developed in the 1970s, and a catalogue was started. The company tested the market for finished leather goods, and today those products comprise the bulk of the Berman Leather business.

As the fourth generation of the Berman family to run the company, Robert Berman recognizes how important it is to change with the times but stay true to the family's commitments and business vision. Throughout the years, although the specific product mix has changed, the company has maintained its strong relationship with its customers. Customer demand prompted the many product changes in the leather business for Berman leather, and the company is proud of its high standard of customer care and service.

Cousin collaboration ...

The five Vellano cousins who now own Vellano Bros., their family's water pipe supply business, tell the story of the 12 years it took to buy out their fathers. As the third generation of the family business, the Vellanos are the textbook example of the cousin collaboration.

All five cousins own the business. One of the difficulties of buying out their fathers was to avoid one of the families having sole control. For them, the solution was to split the stock 50-50 between the families. The two brothers on one side divided their half, and the three brothers on the other side divided theirs. In this way, the fathers were finally content to sell their stock, knowing that neither branch of the family owned more than the other.

The five cousins have a successful working relationship, dividing responsibilities for their three subsidiaries according to the individual talents of each person. Over the years, they have expanded their on-the-job knowledge base with academic programs to give them even more professionalism. They currently have 16 branch locations in the Northeast and Southeast and continue to expand their technical knowledge in their field.

Joe Vellano chalks up their success as a family business to simple factors: all the stock-holders work in the business and everyone does his job well. Because all the cousins are relatively close in age, they have been in tune with each other's goals for the business at each stage of the company's growth. They recognize that the family business provides all the cousins with a good living, and they know it is in everyone's interests to protect that.

Index

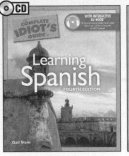

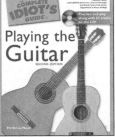

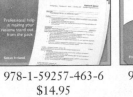